For Carolyn, so that your pastoring will be possible

BOB SITZE

Not Trying Too Hard

New Basics for Sustainable Congregations

Foreword by Janet O. Hagberg

An Alban Institute Publication

Library of Congress Card Number 2001094870

ISBN 1-56699-255-9

08   07   06   05   04   WP   2   3   4   5   6   7   8   9   10   11

CONTENTS

ix   Foreword, *by Janet O. Hagberg*

xiii   Preface

xvii   Acknowledgments

1   PART 1. WHAT'S GOING ON?

3   Chapter 1. Starting the Work
      3   What's ahead for your eyes and ears
      4   Where this book originates
      5   Current currents
     12   Some other basic matters

19   Chapter 2. Trying Too Hard
     19   Sustaining a manageable institution
     22   You've heard this somewhere else
     25   What does it mean to "try too hard"?
     28   How you can know when it's happening to you
     35   What "trying too hard" is not about
     39   What happens in your congregation
     43   Why this behavior continues
     44   How to start "trying less hard"

55   Chapter 3. Seeing Too Little
     56   What's real about reality?
     56   A real congregation
     57   How congregations can ignore reality
     63   The reality of evil
     66   The reality of emotions and feelings
     73   How your congregation can "get real"

80   Sisyphus redux
82   Using "The Reality Check"

87 **Chapter 4. Knowing Too Much**
88   What it means to "know too much"
93   How knowing too much is trying too hard
94   Where the "information culture" might lead
97   "Information toxicity" in congregations
100   Assessing information overload
107   Reducing the glut of information
112   Your yearnings match your capabilities

115 PART 2. WHAT'S AT THE HEART?

117 **Chapter 5. Finding What's Good**

118   "Sacred" and "secular"
120   How the church understood the problem
121   The problem with this "problem"
131   Where is the "good" in God's "good world"?
151   A final note on this matter

157 **Chapter 6. Equipping Who's Here**

157   Clericalism and anticlericalism
158   A little deeper look
159   A short history
160   What causes clericalism and anticlericalism
165   How is this behavior "trying too hard"?
167   How to spot clericalism
171   Redeeming the role of the pastor
182   Equipping who's here
186   Starting at the beginning

189 **Chapter 7. Leaving a Legacy**

189   Things can't keep going like this
193   Looking at the horizon
203   Back to your spirit
204   The shape of your legacy
208   What might shortchange your legacy
213   Thinking and acting to ensure a legacy

221 Part 3. WHAT'S POSSIBLE?

223 Chapter 8. Playing With Substance

    224   How most folk think of "change"
    225   Why that view doesn't work any more
    229   How change has changed
    232   How change occurs
    233   "Leading" change
    235   How change theory affects congregations
    239   How to plan for change
    241   The alternative: asset-based planning
    243   Case Study: The Surprising Stewardship Program
    247   The entrepreneurial spirit
    249   Playing it out

251 Chapter 9. Getting to Start

    252   Getting to start
    252   How thoughts spread
    259   How "tipping points" occur
    261   "Tipping points" in your congregation
    263   Practicing the small-steps approach
    268   What's basic?
    277   Last things

281 Appendix
    281   Workshop: (Not) Trying Too Hard

305 Bibliography

FOREWORD

Soul. There's a lot of talk these days, outside of the religious world, about soul. Many have come to believe that restoring the soul of organizations is necessary if we are to have a vital work force and a healthy economy. The cataclysmic events of September 11, 2001, have called into question the very soul of nations and underscored the essential concept of soul leadership.

More than ever before, I hear talk about purpose, meaning, and spirituality. This conversation seems to encompass a variety of topics: working with integrity; finding meaning in the tasks we do; behaving ethically in the workplace; working on greater good in the world; healing self and others; living out the tenets of faith; supporting a collegial team model; feeling free to be creative; living out one's deepest heart's desire.

There are workshops, task forces, and classes on spirituality in professional organizations, corporations, nonprofit organizations, medical schools, and universities. Articles appear with some regularity in business magazines, talking about God and about spirituality at work.

Several years ago, I was preparing to present a brown bag lunch series called "Spirituality in the Workplace" at a Fortune 500 company. I expected 25 people to show up for a nice discussion. To my complete amazement, two hundred people attended each session. Clearly, there is a hunger for depth, for meaning and purpose in our work and personal lives, for connection with something intangible and not easily named.

Today, opportunities to address soul in the workplace abound. And a telling component of this movement is illustrated by a question that always surfaces when I speak in corporate America: "When you speak of spirituality and soul, are you really talking about religion?" The discussion that follows invariably reveals that the questioner is put off by the structure, the perceived rigidity, the ironclad belief systems and patriarchy of traditional, organized religion. So, while there is a great deal of interest in restoring soul, many people no longer consider organized religion a viable option in their searching.

Some of these disenchanted people flock to new, nondenominational churches with modern music and baggage-free language or to New Age gatherings. But most seek to discover or rediscover their souls in recovery groups, professional self-help groups with like-minded people, therapy, nature, or books.

Perhaps it is time to restore the soul of the church.

The Christian church in America is doing its best to be relevant. Its leaders are trying harder, working longer hours, offering more programs, and trying to solve more problems. Not coincidentally, more clergy than ever before are burning out or "browning out," losing their edge, becoming lethargic. Perhaps the modern church is experiencing its dark night, the time in which it is possible for God to break through and bring new life into being.

How do we move beyond this sense of despair and hopelessness? What does it mean to restore the soul of the church? How can it become more relevant unto itself and to people like those with whom I talk in the workplace—those who eagerly seek meaning?

In *Not Trying Too Hard*, Bob Sitze has taken the bold first step on this journey of restoring the soul of the church. He suggests that clergy and staff who identify with some of these characteristics are ready for this book:

- Dread is taking up permanent residence in you.
- Scrambling skills (patching and fixing) are becoming second nature.
- Shaming and blaming are entering your bloodstream.
- You develop a searching eye (darting, refocusing, quick to adopt new techniques or quick fixes), a wandering heart (canned sermons, programs that require little personal investment), and a bad case of the meeting blues.

In a skillful blending of left brain/right brain, concrete and abstract, Bob points to the latest in change theory, social science, business management theory, brain research, and asset-based community development to substantiate his ideas.

He offers vital alternatives for building a more relevant church. He shows how the most credible learnings from outside the church can be used creatively to restore the souls of both clergy and lay people. And he does all of this with gentle humor, allowing readers to lighten up just a little.

Bob goes directly to the heart of the matter. He presents suggestions for ways to return to our core, to our individual, intimate relationship with God. This is where we discover what it means to be relevant to God and where we open to God's deep relevance to us.

Clergy and laity already have what it takes to be God's partners in something truly exciting and essential. Bob stresses that we have great capacity for change. We are ready to be surprised by God's spirit because inside each of us is a passion for ministry seeking expression. We can accept our personal power, which is truly a gift of God's spirit.

Rooted in the concept of significance, Bob provides practical, inviting suggestions for exciting and relevant ministries. But there is a twist here that laity and clergy will find astounding and revitalizing. I won't be specific because I don't want to spoil the surprise. It is enough for now to say that I am drawn strongly to the idea of a church based on the concepts that Bob sets forth in this inspiring book.

What is the nature of a soul-restored church? It will have vitality that is palpable. People will be excited to be part of it, because it will empower them to do their finest work in the world while restoring lost intimacy with God. Everyone will be more authentic, within the church, in their personal lives, and in the world of work. Church will be a place where fear, anger, anxiety, resentment, and intolerance are not present. People will reach out to each other freely, experiencing unconditional love. These things will happen.

Bob Sitze's book has helped to restore my soul.

JANET O. HAGBERG

These pages began to take shape because of a few quiet conversations about one question: Why is it so hard to keep a congregation from falling apart? In the minds of the pastors and congregational leaders who told me of their frustrations, there weren't many good answers. I started to notice that these faithful servants of God were out of ideas, energy, and humor.

The more I read books about "the decline of denominations," the fewer solutions I found. Each analysis of the problem seemed to suggest the same way out of the morass: work harder. This seemed an ironic answer for folk already smushed between the walls of their expectations and their outcomes, out of balance with too much work and too much information about the problems they faced.

Inside a few leaders and congregations, though, I sensed hope and lively engagement with the question. I wasn't sure what characterized these folk, but I was sure that, if not marching to a different drummer, they were at least *not* listening to the beat of ecclesiastical success-oil salesmen or grim Jeremiahs.

I also started to find more shreds of hope outside the church. In the worlds of theoretical physics, applied brain science, social science, and business management theory I could see God's own hand making sense of social systems.

What characterized all these hopeful signs in congregations and outside the church were a few simple precepts that could be distilled into this basic idea: We may be trying too hard to "do church."

The skeleton of a book began to take shape—a jotted note here, a "think piece" there; ideas tried out in various workshops, formal documents, and vision statements; incisive and critical conversations with loved colleagues. Little by little, the hesitant questions yielded tentative axioms. The metaphors of change theory combined with the tested wisdom of asset-based community development. Thought-contagion science and neurotheology unexpectedly splashed new water in my face.

The book didn't start to breathe, though, until a compelling reason presented itself, in the person of an old friend and continuing seminarian whose lifelong call—as yet unanswered—has been to become a pastor. What a sad irony it would be if this devoted servant of God entered a vocation whose predictable end was the same burnout, cynicism, and ineffectiveness faced by continuing generations of pastors and leaders! This outcome was something I might prevent, perhaps in a book written for people like my friend.

What about you?

I think of you as one of the people I have met over the 30-plus years of my career as one of God's worker bees. I imagine that glimmers and flashes of energy, hope, and mission still burn inside you, that you are willing to try counterintuitive thought. I think of you as someone who doesn't always follow the crowd, run with the pack, hitch to the same star, or use tired metaphors like these.

As I have shoveled these words into this book, I've thought of how your curiosity about church systems is still bubbling. I've carried a mental image of you refusing to let go of your yearning for sustainable ministry. I've thought of the steely resolve in your eyes—eyes that say you know down deep that you still have what it takes to be one of God's partners in a venture truly exciting and necessary.

If you're a pastor, rabbi, or priest who has "tried everything" and found that most of it didn't work unless you manipulated some system precisely, with great loyalty and ardor for its precepts—we've been down the same slippery slope. If you've had more than a passing thought that "this congregation's problems probably continue because of me," or if you've noticed that your brain seems to be both "stressed and stupid"—we've faced the same devilishly mistaken notion.

Mostly, I've held you in my mind as someone with whom I could talk honestly about these things we speak of, someone who could agree or disagree with my ideas but who would always be willing to keep talking.

What this book will do for you

I hope this conversation is interesting, important, and useful. For some of you, "interesting" will be enough, as you tussle with new ideas that challenge your way of working and thinking. Others will notice how the material in the book coincides with other resources you've read recently. If this book reinforces what you've found interesting, you will see this book as "important." Still others may want more than "interesting" and "important," and are ready for tools and ideas.

To get at "interesting," "important," or "useful," I've formatted the content of each chapter in this way:

❏ I present a usual way of looking at a subject or ideal.

❏ I help you come to terms with possible difficulties of that usual approach.

❏ I trundle out some new ways to think and act, and offer some tools for those new behaviors.

"Interesting," "important," and "useful" indicate several stages of meaningfulness. "Interesting" is what you say when I attract your attention. "Important" happens when you and I stack several "interestings" next to each other. ("Interesting" and "important" say "Hey, look at us!") And "useful?" It's "important" after we put on our work gloves. ("Useful" says, "Hey, look at you!")

How to read this book

How should you read this book? Any way that pleases you! The content is both sequential and looping, allowing you to start anywhere, move in any direction, and finish where you'd like. This book is a place for you to play with newer ideas about the church, to frisk around them like a puppy off its leash. The margins are a good place to record your reactions to what you read, including the "what-ifs" that might expand the book's usefulness in the future.

Play with whatever you find worthwhile here, as a preschool child combines different pieces of modeling clay to make a wonderful sculpture. If the whimsy and sneaky humor of this book tempt you to chuckle your way into your own joyful ways of approaching your ministry, good! Laugh out loud with your God. If you want to consider these ideas with others, use the suggestions at the end of each chapter to act on what you've just read.

As you begin reading, I want you to know my prayer for you, that this book may rekindle in you what you most value in yourself: a readiness to be surprised by God's own Spirit.

Throughout the book you'll find side notes like this, and other sidebar material—stories, parables, readings, surveys, checklists, attributable quotes, tongue-in-cheek quotes—that I hope will add to your knowledge of the subject. Think of them as side trips for your eye, little rest stops that get you ready for the rest of the narrative, or information that can tickle your inquisitive brain.

ACKNOWLEDGMENTS

This book involved the work of more than one person, and so these first pages necessarily include my thanks to the collection of brains whose excellent thoughts have made this book possible.

First I acknowledge God's blessings. I am graced every day by God's forgiveness, by Christ's example, and by grace that will never quit. Because of God's own witness, amazing people have accompanied me along the herky-jerky journey of writing this book. And so I thank:

My parents, Vera and Estel, whose lives of stewardship have always been my example.

Chris—wife, friend, and illustrator—without whose critique most of what I have done would be ordinary, stupid, or ordinarily stupid, and without whose drawings this book would have been much too serious!

Beth Gaede—editor, collaborator, friend, and not-so-secret visionary in her own right—whose wise and insistent presence added the precision required of all good communication.

Carol MacKenzie, design wizard at Alban, for the deft touch that made pixels and scribbles into delightful places for eyes and minds to wander and play.

Jean Caffey Lyles, whose sharp eye and pen added the fine edges and smoothed the rough ones.

Janet Hagberg, for the gift of a soul-probing foreword, and for her comforting descriptions of power that helped me find my voice and authority at a difficult time in my career.

Colleagues in the enterprise of renewing the part of Christ's church called the Evangelical Lutheran Church in America: Nancy Snell, Michael Meyer, Laurel Hensel, Marcie Rogers, Tammy Tyson, Jeri Elliott, Kathy Hetland, Phil Reitz, Lita Brusick Johnson, John Golv, Ted Schroeder, Liz Hunter, Evelyn Soto Straw, Tim Frakes, and Marilyn Shomler.

I would also like to acknowledge the considerable influence of Dr. Billy ("William") Poobah, whose fictitious essence has allowed me the pleasure of having a make-believe friend well into my maturity, and from whose wisdom I have distilled the godly nectar of complete and utter foolishness.

Jay Beech, composer/musician and wry seer, for his encouragement and example in using humor to say what is true.

Kind and generous thought-providers: Professors Kurt Hendel and Vitor Westhelle (Lutheran School of Theology at Chicago), Dr. Jody Kretzmann (Asset-Based Community Development Institute), Dr. Bob Sylwester (University of Oregon), and business consultants Deb Hornell and Amy Hohulin.

Fellow members, conspirators, and entrepreneurs at Faith Lutheran Church in Glen Ellyn, Illinois, whose lives of excellent ministry in the world inspire me again and again.

And finally, friend and eminent vision spinner, Sally Simmel, whose pioneer spirit has sustained the "ministry in daily life" movement through these several decades. Without her encouragement, these words would still have been vapor.

Part 1
WHAT'S GOING ON?

A good place to start our conversation is the question "What's going on here?" This first section of the book shuffles several answers in front of your eyes. We'll think together about:

- The essential premises of this book (chapter 1, "Starting the Work").

- What "trying too hard" and "sustainability" mean (chapter 2, "Trying Too Hard").

- How limited knowledge of the world diminishes vision and increases work (chapter 3, "Seeing Too Little").

- How information-overloaded minds and lives weigh down spirits and effectiveness (chapter 4, "Knowing Too Much").

What's going on? God graces our conversation with insistent questions. God has been here before us. We'll talk and think together in safety and assurance about God's hopeful answers.

1
STARTING THE WORK

S hortly you'll decide whether to read the rest of this book. Since you want your precious reading time to be delightful work, you will make up your mind fairly quickly. To help you with that decision, I've used this first chapter to set the stage for the rest of the book. Here's what I've included:

◆

A good beginning makes a good end.

English proverb

❑ What's ahead for your eyes and ears, a quick summary of the book's contents.

❑ Where this book originates, the premises that guided its writing.

❑ Current currents, an introduction to each of the main areas of contemporary thought that inform the propositions in this book.

❑ Other matters, some of the quick-change realities of contemporary Christianity.

What's ahead for your eyes and ears

In this first chapter you'll see and hear the following subjects and how they connect to your congregation's life. These ideas are organized into three parts:

Part 1. What's Going On?

What are the essential elements of this book's content? (chapter 1, Starting the Work)

What does it mean to "try too hard," and how can you

learn to change that behavior so your congregation can sustain itself? (chapter 2, "Trying Too Hard")

When you look at God's world, what is it that you might be missing? What would you like to see? (chapter 3, "Seeing Too Little")

What can you do with too much information, too much knowledge? (chapter 4, "Knowing Too Much")

◆

It is a test of a good religion whether you can joke about it.

C. K. Chesterton

Part 2. What's at the Heart?

❑   What can you learn from what God is doing in the world? (chapter 5, "Finding What's Good")

❑   How can pastors and leaders find significance in their roles? (chapter 6, "Equipping Who's Here")

❑   Where can you find a sense of perspective about yourself and your congregation? (chapter 7, "Leaving a Legacy")

Part 3. What's Possible?

❑   What does it mean "to change?" (chapter 8, "Playing With Substance")

❑   How might you start making changes? (chapter 9, "Getting to Start")

The book ends with a weekend retreat design that incorporates some of the elements of the book into a series of workshops.

Where this book originates

The ideas in *Not Trying too Hard* have been collected from a variety of streams of enterprising thought in contemporary Western culture. As you flip back and forth through the chapters of this book—always a good way to read!—you will correctly note that most of these sources do not originate within the church-as-institution. And you will also be correct if you surmise that I have purposely featured nonchurch sources in this book.

One premise that guides this book is that *there is much of God's wisdom in the "worldly realm."* The wisdom-legacy of the church notwithstanding, we who are partners in God's fullest enterprise (for example, creating, redeeming and sanctifying, bringing order, rubbing out evil) can benefit from attending to what God may be saying in the fascinating worlds outside God's church.

Another axiom draws together the presuppositions of this book: "When you change the questions, you get different answers." It may be true that, in the recent decades of "church renewal" thinking, we who are thoroughly bound up in finger-gazing or pointed-finger-following have been watching the same hand, asking the same questions over and over. Our vocabulary may not have changed substantially over a generation—20 to 25 years in most of our lives, five to ten years in "new congregations." That's why we may circle around the same questions, puzzling among ourselves why each "new answer" seems to be a variant of previous answers, why each new "sure-fire" system" and each mysterious "magic bullet" feels vaguely familiar.

"What would happen," we might ask, "if we took advantage of some of God's other wisdom, posed other questions, and paid attention to what happened next?" That question sums up the matter of this book's investment in sources outside the institutional church.

Current currents

Several streams of contemporary thought are resources for the ideas in this book. These areas of knowledge are instructive about the nature of the church, and form the basis of the theses you will meet in these pages. Each has some connection to the topics of "trying too hard" and "sustainable congregations." Let's briefly preview each of them.

Brain theory/science

Individually and collectively, human behavior is rooted in the workings of the human brain. If you want to understand how and why futile overexertion continues in your life, you might begin asking questions about how your brain works. That's why we'll spend time looking at brain science.

Contemporary brain theory/science began in earnest because of deep interest in and distress over two important lifestyle elements in the 1970s:

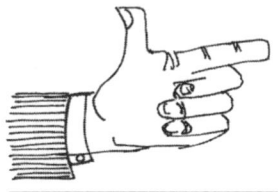

DOG DILEMMA

For untrained pets and truly divergent thinkers, the pointing finger creates an engrossing dilemma: What do I look at? If I look where you are pointing, I will see only what you see or want me to see. If I continue to look at your hand, I will see only you. The dilemma continues when I consider my next action: If I look at where you're pointing, I will likely take actions similar to those you would take or would want me to take. If I continue to gaze at your finger, I will gather more accurate information about your hand and its deeper qualities. As a metaphor, this canine conundrum symbolizes:

❏ The matter of whom you trust (or distrust).
❏ Your willingness to follow (or learn from) another's experience or attention.
❏ How easily message and messenger can be confused.
❏ How triviality and importance come together.

In pointing-finger situations, you might ask, "Am I supposed to be a disciple here or a steward?" (A "disciple" might follow the presumed line-of-sight; a "steward" might want to know about the pointer's intent.)

❑ Stress-related illnesses.

❑ The addiction of some Vietnam War veterans to opium-derived substances.

Using powerful new research technologies, brain theorists came to verifiable conclusions about each of these matters—stress influences a wide band of behaviors, and opiates mimic the brain's own feel-good chemicals. Brain theory eventually broadened its scope and matured into a full-fledged science. Variously dubbed "neuroscience," "neurobiology" or "cognitive neuroscience," this growing collection of empirical data and practical applications now informs fields as diverse as education, parenting, criminology, psychology, epidemiology, advertising, and theology. With the advent of more sophisticated brain-imaging technology, what we can expect to discover about the human brain will quickly dwarf what we already know. Because of the growing success of pharmacology in ameliorating or healing brain conditions, our ability to care for our brains will increase as well.

Because it is now possible to understand with some general assurance how the brain works, it makes good sense always to ask the question, "What's most likely going on in people's brains?" whenever we plan or undertake a task in the church. It makes even more sense to wrestle with the implications of these answers for our ways of working together as congregations.

A variety of examples of applied brain theory are included in this book, not so much as ultimate proof—"The buck stops at the brain"—but as illustrations of how answers to "the working brain question" can help you know what's happening as you try to understand how you can sustain your congregation without trying too hard.

◆

A great deal of intelligence can be invested in ignorance when the need for illusion is deep.

Saul Bellow

Organizational development

This field of human energy has continued its spread from the world of economic theory into a broader application: explaining how *any group organized for a common purpose* behaves or could be constructed for optimal effectiveness. In the past few years, there has been a flowering of thinking about organizations—and business enterprise as well—that can legitimately be called "spiritual."

The quality of thought in business-management literature is to be judged positively not only because of its newly expressible piety, however. Some business leaders and prophets have also grappled with the questions of overexertion and sustainability. Because contemporary organizational development writers are concerned about "bottom lines"—some now defined as "the worth of workers" or "the sustainability of the organization over time"—we can learn from their rugged pragmatism how to evaluate our thinking about congregations.

The insights of organizational development theory may be important to the church for two reasons:

❑ Lay church leaders who are also business leaders understand and practice these matters five (or more) days a week. They could teach you something about leadership.

❑ Not-for-profit enterprises are also being shaped by the work of organizational-development thinkers.

In the chapters of this book, you'll find references to current organizational-development writing, some of it just new and edgy enough to feel counterintuitive to what you have learned about congregational structures or behaviors. Have fun with the mental tussles these new ideas provoke.

I've found the best thinking about "the spirituality of work" among Roman Catholic writers, who have been encouraging parishioners to value their work for generations. The number of journals, events, and books devoted to this general subject has increased dramatically. My recent reading includes *Spirituality@work* by publisher and community organizer Gregory Pierce. Pierce collects and comments on "ordinary people" who talk about their sense of God-graced work.

Chaos/complexity theory

One reason you may be trying too hard is that you overvalue "order." Understanding and accepting the value of chaos might be one way for you to calm your soul and find a new way of sustaining your congregation.

In this book I use "chaos/complexity theory" to characterize a variety of interrelated fields of endeavor, loosely grouped by their supposed capacity to describe the physical/biological world and the "laws" by which its changing realities are understood. (You may know these areas of knowledge as "theoretical physics" or "complexity/simplicity theory," or by other terms.) In the past five years, chaos/complexity theory has become a useful way to describe more organic (and human) systems. So applications of chaos/complexity theory have found their way into business management and organizational development, and are now thought to be more fully descriptive of the processes of change than the previous simple notions of "cause and effect."

Another recent migration of chaos/complexity theory is toward metaphysics and theology. For some philosophers and theologians, the nature of God, the relationship between science and religion, and matters of ecclesiology can all be understood through the lens of chaos/complexity theory.

In this book, only a few of the basic suppositions of this growing body of theoretical and practical knowledge will be used. They include the following:

◆

Chaos is a name for any order that produces confusion in our minds.

George Santayana

❑ All ordered systems are poised on the edge of disorder; all disordered systems are poised at the edge of order.

❑ Therefore, "chaos" and "order" are neither good nor bad; neither is a permanent state of any organism or system.

❑ Small changes—the "tipping points" and "small-step approaches" discussed in chapter 9—always have the potential to effect great change. (The well-described Amazonian butterfly can beat its wings and be the "cause" of a typhoon off the coast of China.)

❑ At the same time, "cause" and "effect" may not always be useful terms, because they can oversimplify causalities whose nature is only partially known. Therefore, the concept of "change agent"—an instrumental leader by whom desired change can be effected—may be too simplistic to be useful or realistic.

❑ Within seemingly chaotic systems exist "strange attractors" (or "emergent simplicities")—factors, elements, formulas, or metaphors that, when applied to seemingly disconnected events, suddenly reveal the order that was already there.

❑ In the face of undesired chaos, participants in systems can simply wait for a small change to tip the system back to order, or take advantage of an emergent simplicity when it occurs.

In the following chapters, the basic presumptions of chaos/complexity theory will find their way into questions about simplified congregational systems.

Asset-based planning

In an interesting twist of social history, "asset-based planning" is something we learned from so-called Third World countries. Asset-based community development began in the 1970s with the rural development efforts of nongovernmental agencies, working in impoverished countries to develop more sustainable and manageable means by which indigenous people could improve their lives. (The "teach a man to fish" mantra of that era comes to mind most readily.)

In the 1980s and 1990s, a variety of community development organizations, most notably the Asset-Based Community Development group at Northwestern University, Evanston, Illinois, and the rural "capacity analysis" programs of Western Illinois University, in Macomb, and the Rodale Institute in Emmaus, Pennsylvania, incorporated the precepts of established overseas programs into the life of rural and urban North American communities. Today, asset-based thinking and planning have virtually supplanted "needs-based planning" in social-service work, business, government, and nonprofit agencies. The institutional church is just beginning to pay attention to this field of endeavor.

The principles of asset-based thinking and planning can be summed up in several key metaphors and axioms:

❑ The glass is half-full, not half-empty.

❑ Planning that begins with needs is difficult to complete successfully; planning that begins with capacities (assets) has a high probability of long-term success.

❑ "Assets" are more than "gifts." A gift is known by its being given or received; an "asset" is known by its utility. Except for people who think they are their own gods, all assets are gifts. Not all gifts are assets for an individual or a group, unless they are put to good use.

❑ Assets are more than what some church leaders have traditionally named as "spiritual gifts."

❑ Assets include money, property, tools, desirable character traits (hope, kindness), social capital (who trusts and is connected to whom), and skills (painting, computing, selling, managing).

❑ Every community has within its asset-base the capacity to do much of what it wants to do.

"Spiritual gifts inventories" have encouraged a positive orientation to congregational ministries. But in some list "gifts" are limited to those named in Scripture, and are connected only to a congregation's need for volunteers. In these cases, "gifts ministries" can limit an understanding of God's enormous and continuing creative power. My favorite example of parochialized "gifts ministry" is the gifts inventory that values "singing in the church choir" but not "singing in the community choir." As to the claim that "asset" is a hard, "secular" word that does not belong in the church, I can only respond with a sigh and a smile.

❏ The first step in asset-based planning is to name the assets of a group so that they can be mapped and organized into categories that suggest immediate action.

❏ "Planning" is a matter of taking small steps naturally derived from the assets map, actions that draw people together in cooperative work that combines thought and action.

❏ "Long-term planning" may be difficult or ineffective because of the changing nature of a community's asset-base.

You may want to put a bookmark at this page for your reference in chapter 8, where this "strange attractor"—and isn't that a strange term?—will be described in detail.

In this book, asset-based thinking or planning is presumed to be a primary "emergent simplicity" that brings order to congregational planning, and to the self-image that all congregations need to develop to become sustainable and manageable institutions.

Change theory

It's possible that you may be trying too hard because you think that your basic role as a leader is to change people or systems. I hope this book will relieve you of that unnecessary burden.

As a direct result of the application of chaos/complexity physics to social systems and a growing weariness about the general pace of life, thinking about "change" is itself now undergoing some change. Understanding the changes in change theory is complicated because the switch from older, cause-and-effect models to newer, complexity-based theoretical models is just now taking place.

If this book had been written two years earlier, you would not be reading any of this material. At that time, "change" was still being driven by the growth of technologies (mostly communication and entertainment technologies), and "the new economy" was flying high and wild in the minds of all except a few grumpy economists. At the time of this book's writing, that "economy" is still settling back into financial mud, and some serious writers are talking about "change toxicity." (See chapter 8 for further treatment of the subject.)

I do not necessarily assume that the pace of change will continue to accelerate, nor am I certain that "change" should be considered an automatic and desirable attribute of social systems. And to further rile your spirit, I hope to question gently the proposition that your job as a leader is to be a "change agent."

Information-overload science

You may be trying too hard to sustain your congregation by providing too much or the wrong kinds of information to members.

For about 10 years now, social critics have been noting the growing quantity of information that sweeps through the skies and lights on our ears and eyes. In their view, at some point—perhaps we've already reached it—"information" is no longer useful to the brain or the human spirit. These front-edge thinkers argue that real power comes not to information holders but rather to those who are able to organize and simplify the increasing amounts of information.

The elements of information-overload science that are important to congregations include these:

❑ The brain has a built-in capacity to shut out "noise"—information that cannot be readily or willingly processed into a meaningful construct—and readily uses that capacity. (There are more so-called "inhibitor cells" in our neuronal system than there are cells that initiate actions or reactions.) To put it another way, the innate "fight-or-flight" mechanism of the human brain probably also applies to information!

❑ The direct result of providing more information may be a corresponding lack of attention to it.

❑ In the near future, delimiting (or simplifying) information will be a highly valued skill in such organizations as churches. In businesses it already is!

If you want to get both a dismaying and a hopeful look at this subject, read architect Saul Wurman's *Information Anxiety 2*, his second look at the problems of this pervasive reality we seem to gather around ourselves. He's hopeful enough to suggest some specific ways to cut back on information overload. And because he practices what he preaches, his book is a delightful example of what he proposes!

THE OLDEN DAYS OF THE INFORMATION AGE

Because of its importance in the life of congregations moving through generational or developmental changes—seeking to appeal to "millennials," "new Christians," "seekers," "postmoderns," and other labeled ones—the subject of information overload will constitute the entire content of chapter 4.

Thought-contagion theory

This branch of social theory emerged from social biology and, more directly, from the concept of "memes." (You will recall from your study of memetics, of course, that "memes" are nonquantifiable-but-real units of hardwired human memory; they supposedly determine the nature and scope of specific traits or behaviors. Thus there could be a "meme" for kindness *and* a "meme" for mean-spiritedness.)

In thought-contagion theory—its practitioners now claim "science" describes their work—the spread of ideas within human communities occurs according to the same biological rules that describe the spread of epidemics. "Infectious agents," "viruses," and "mutations" are used to describe ideas. The growth of ideas replicates the manner in which viral or bacterial agents propagate. "Hosts" and "carriers" can be identified. Idea-epidemics eventually play themselves out (or even defeat themselves). Evolutionary theory also contributes to the concepts of thought-contagion—for example, "survival of the fittest" may also apply to the generation, survivability, and growth of ideas.

In chapter 9 you'll see how this theory might explain the processes by which ideas, excitement, energy, the elusive "vision thing," trust, and attraction grow and spread in a congregation. You may also begin to realize how naturally those processes can occur.

For a bit of Web-based fun, type "thought contagion" into your browser's topic bar. Note the number of entries. Every week for the next six weeks, try it again and see how quickly—or slowly—the number of entries has grown. Try the same exercise on other idea-families, including those in this chapter. Or try the exercise on ideas that the church has honored over decades, like "Sunday school" or "church growth." Which ideas seem to continue being contagious, and which have stopped growing, at least electronically?

Some other basic matters

Finally, here are several fundamental presuppositions about the church that guide my ministry. Each of the following connects to one or more of the theses of this book.

The "needy church" is all but gone

For at least a decade, loving and critical church leaders have pointed out that the "presumption of neediness" that has guided several generations of pastors and thousands of mission statements is essentially flawed. These criticisms seem to group themselves around these premises:

❏ "Needs-based thinking" is basically negative, and because brains do best what brains do most, continuing attention to neediness "trains" congregations and their leaders to be essentially negative-thinking people.

❏ "Solving problems" as a fundamental, continuing reason for existence is hardly a joyful and forward-looking way to live, personally or institutionally.

❏ Most people don't think of themselves most of the time as "primarily needy." When nudged in that direction, however, they will accept the ministrations of need-filling pastors and lay leaders. (This observation raises the question of whose needs are being filled.)

❏ "Neediness," whether as a direct corollary or a direct effect of sinfulness, doesn't just go away when one piece of it is resolved. Like "the elephant in the living room," presumed neediness tends to stay in congregations and to occupy more space than it deserves.

❏ Presumed neediness seems, at first, to benefit pastors and caring professionals. (When they are able to "meet needs," their personal significance is immediate and obvious.) But over time, the sheer scope and depth of "neediness"—when it is universalized to describe most members—overwhelms and eventually burns out pastors and other caring leaders.

❏ There are more helpful and hopeful ways of thinking about pastors and other caring leaders than as "wounded healers."

❏ The Vietnam War era is over; so are the 1980s and 1990s. New realities have emerged.

The proposition "Let's move beyond needs-based assumptions about the nature or purpose of the church" is strengthened by the experience, energy, and erudition of some of the church's current prophets. Jodie Kretzmann, Loren Mead, Peter Steinke, Celia Hahn, Erwin Friedman, Martha Ellen Stortz, Gregory Pierce, and Russell Shaw come immediately to mind. For a good example of early comments on the subject, see Mead's *The Once and Future Church* and any of its progeny.

You may find general assent that "needs-based thinking" is not good for congregations or their leaders. You may also know that most congregations—and most pastors and other leaders—still behave and structure themselves as needs-filling institutions. Cognitive dissonance rises, suspicions of hypocrisy propagate, and congregations—and their leaders—start to feel trapped between ineffective practices and old ways of thinking. (We'll visit this subject again in chapter 8.)

What about the metachurch?

For the past few years I have watched with dismay as the casualties of the metachurch movement have piled up quietly on the sidelines. "Trying too hard" seems to characterize the majority of leaders who have been only partially effective in applying "church-growth principles" to the dynamics of their situations. My experiences with these leaders have led me to the assumption that the metachurch will not, in its present form, sustain itself into the next generation.

The good that these congregations have accomplished in God's kingdom is undeniable. Much of the present vitality of the Christian church can be attributed to the theorists and practitioners of metachurch formulas and programs.

I believe that this "movement" in the church's life is likely to be replaced by other, yet-to-be-seen models or metaphors of "church." The reasons for this natural transition:

❑ The metachurch movement has been described as another kind of Enlightenment. In the history of U.S. Christianity, these renewing movements seem to last about one generation. In a few years, the metachurch phenomenon will be approaching its generational birthday.

❑ The supply of metachurches may soon exceed the size of their market. Regardless of the claims of universal appeal that form the rationale for metachurch expansion, marketplace logic would suggest that this niche of the market will eventually be tapped out.

❑ Some recent "trend scholarship" suggests that a strong yearning among so-called postmoderns is for spirituality that values ritual, quiet, perhaps even mystical experience. Some of the elements of metachurch practice may work against these trends.

❑ To reach sustainable sizes, metachurches have to move large numbers of "seekers" into the presumably more mature state of "disciple." Seekers do not yet, by definition,

"Metachurch" refers to congregations of any size that are begun and maintained according to fairly stringent systems, models, or plans. These congregations can be described by their systematic approach to growth and development of ministries, or their working of a particular model based on "proven examples." In this book, "meta" includes but is not limited to "mega."

contribute substantially to the funding and membership of metachurches. Therefore a process of maturation in the faith is absolutely necessary for these churches to maintain themselves as viable institutions. That process takes time, effort, and money, which can be in short supply in undercapitalized enterprises.

❑ Many elements of metachurches, especially worship, are based on the benefits of continuing high emotion. This is a difficult state to sustain because the brain cannot support high emotion for a protracted period. Just as "praise services" may gradually require more and more effort for worshipers to reach a desired emotional state, so congregations based on emotional response may have to continue to work harder to find and maintain heightened states of emotion.

❑ Some elements of the metachurch have already begun to resemble denominations, a worrisome development for some of their leaders. As they evolve through fairly predictable sociological processes, metachurches can expect to encounter the difficult decisions faced by earlier Christian movements that eventually became denominations.

❑ Growing numbers of pastors and congregational leaders have tried metachurch programming, philosophies, or structures, and have "failed," at least by the standards they have adopted. Many of them, unfortunately, blame their own imagined inadequacies. Others have tried repeatedly to find just the right combination of techniques or programs that will somehow redeem their previous attempts. Eventually these leaders and their collective anguish will raise a large question mark about metachurch processes.

Trend scholars make sense of current events, market analysis, cultural artifacts, and vaguely authoritative syntheses of data. These modern prophets are able to see patterns where the rest of us see only confusion, and can be helpful as early adapters or early warning systems about cultural phenomena of which we are not yet aware. For example, in the matter of "postmoderns," a good work to study is Tom Beaudoin's *Virtual Faith*. Beaudoin analyzes his generation's spiritual qualities from the perspective of an inside prophet.

While it is not my purpose to dissect or otherwise damage any form of congregational vitality, I am certain that just over the horizon we may see the slow change of metachurches into another manifestation of "congregation." A "second wave theory" of social change (see following section) suggests that self-renewing organizations begin their next transformation while they are still experiencing relative success. Some metachurches are doing that right now.

Over-the-horizon thinking

Much of what is written here may seem counterintuitive because you have not yet seen cause for concern in your own context. From your perspective, the needed changes are already in place, or your congregation has adopted the principles and practices of a good system that seems to be working just fine, thank you. You may be right—and so you may not be ready for the propositions of this book right now.

But there may be reason for you to consider revamping your assumptions about "doing church," to start thinking now about how you'll face what's coming over the next hill. Whether you take a cyclical view of history or a linear view of God's action over time, you probably accept the historical axiom that all kingdoms wax and wane, except God's own, of course. The "kingdom" of the institutional church is therefore subject to the same life cycles as other human endeavors. So, whatever you do and for however long you do it, your congregation will eventually reach a point in its life cycle when death or decay becomes apparent.

"Second wave" theory is a way of explaining necessary organizational change, given the inevitability of the life cycles of every human organization. The key to the launching of a successful second effort, "reinvention" or "repurposing" of an organization: timing. Start too soon, and the "second wave"—a powerful motivating force like the surge of a high-tide breaker—robs the "first wave" of its vitality. Start too late, when the organization is working with stress-induced fear and anger, and the second wave is deprived of its emotional resources. Wait until the organization is thrashing about in its death throes, and efforts at renewal may be futile.

"Second wave theory" suggests that the best time to renew your congregation is precisely when "it ain't broke." In this book you will find repeated encouragement to build on what is already good in your congregation to create an enterprise that can renew itself for yet another life cycle before the first wave has run its course.

Generational theorists and historians William Strauss and Neil Howe (*Fourth Turning: An American Prophecy*) have suggested that western history can be divided into 80-to-100-year cycles which are themselves partitioned into four 20-to-25-year generational "turnings." These turnings are cyclical and predictable. Generations are affected by—and themselves affect—the generations before and after them. Economic behaviors are strong predictors of "what's coming next." What is the "fourth turning"? A time of extreme difficulty, catastrophe, and disorder. Its onset? As early as 2004 or 2005. What's after that? A predictably better time. The book is unnerving and comforting at the same time.

Sustainability and manageability

One intent of this book is to help you find new and less difficult ways to achieve sustainability and manageability. Let's start the conversation here:

READER: So just what does it mean "to be sustainable and manageable"?

AUTHOR: In plain terms, "sustainable" is about your congregation being able to last for a long time, and "manageable" means being able to do that with the resources you have around you.

READER: It's that simple?

AUTHOR: Well, the *idea* is that simple, but we're having this conversation because *doing the idea* isn't all that simple.

READER: Can you say more?

AUTHOR: *(cleverly)* If you read the rest of the book, I'll say more. But if we could talk only right now, I'd say this much: Too many of us are ignoring the long haul, and an equal number of us are trying to do more than our present abilities allow.

READER: So you're concerned about *not* deferring facility maintenance and about asking more people to volunteer?

AUTHOR: *(inching toward next chapter)* Well [*pause*] that's a part of the "sustainability/manageability vector," but there's more to it than just—

READER: *(unaware of next chapter, living in the moment, starting to get interested and vexed at the same time)* "Sustainability/manageability vector"? They overlap, do they?

AUTHOR: *(now tempted by the reader's interest to stay in this chapter forever)* Yes they do, because if you don't have the long view, you won't care about managing well now. And if you don't manage well now—Poof! There goes your sustainability!

READER: *(really starting to understand)* And "sustainability" is probably about "collegial cogeneration of vitality without organizational codependencies" and "manageability" could equal the coefficient of effort plus assets?

AUTHOR: *(beginning to respect the reader greatly)* Why, yes, that's a good way to state the matter.

READER: So I should go on to the next chapter?

AUTHOR: *(relieved)* Yes, but only if you let me ask the questions next time.

◆

Anyone who starts plowing and keeps looking back isn't worth a thing.

Jesus

PARSING THE CHAPTER

You can make good use of this chapter's contents by continuing a discussion about any of the following matters:

1. With which of the areas of human enterprise in this chapter were you already familiar? Which were new to you? Which seemed especially applicable to congregational life? How do you think they might apply?

2. As you examine the development of other areas of thought in the worlds in which you live, which hold great promise for the church? (A possible example: How does the development of genetics shed light on the way people behave in groups?)

3. Collect a group of "worldly-wise members," asking them to tell you what's especially important or relevant in their field of work or knowledge. Ask them how the church is especially important or relevant to their work or knowledge, too.

4. Which premises in this chapter still give you pause, especially as they promise to have something to say about the way your congregation behaves?

5. In the margins of this chapter, cite references to brand-new developments in any of the fields of thought that are covered here. In that way, the information in this chapter can stay fresh and lively.

2
TRYING TOO HARD

The alert reader in chapter 1 was right: congregational leaders want sustainable and manageable churches. You'll get to play around with those two ideas at the beginning of this chapter. With those two matters firmly in mind, let's consider this book's basic premise, that most of us are "trying too hard" to manage and sustain our congregations. In the remainder of the chapter you'll think about:

❑ Where else you've heard about this idea.

❑ What "trying too hard" means (and doesn't mean).

❑ How you can know when it's happening to you.

❑ What happens when institutionalized overexertion continues for a while.

❑ Why you may keep behaving this way, even though you know it isn't good for you.

❑ How to begin diminishing the ecclesiastical exertion that is troubling you and your congregation.

◆

Stop the habit of wishful thinking and start the habit of thoughtful wishes.

Mary Martin

Sustaining a manageable institution

"Let's keep this church alive." That's probably one reason why you're now one of this book's "alert readers," isn't it? Even if, in your earlier years, you toyed with the notion of deinstitutionalized churches, you may have come to dread the prospect that your personal legacy would be somehow marked by a congregation lying like a wrecked car in a fogbound chain-reaction accident. You don't want to waste

One of the most incisive applications of biologically based organizational development is the work of Christian A. Schwarz et al., whose "Natural Church Development" resources present theoretical and practical implications of "biologically based congregations." Schwarz describes a large research project from which he factored out eight characteristics that correlate with congregational health and growth. His critique of some metachurch systems: that they may be inadvertently positioned against biologically fundamental realities that determine and guide our lives together as God's creatures. (You can visit www.churchsmart.com to get the details.)

your life or the precious legacy you received: an institution that meant and did wonderful things for the world in God's name.

And so you desire sustainability in your congregation just as you desire it in yourself. Social biologists suggest that you're hardwired for self-preservation and self-propagation into coming generations. Social biology extends personal sustainability into institutions such as congregations. According to that way of thinking, churches could become self-perpetuating enterprises whose inner workings allow for an organic, renewing source of energy and order.

However your congregation's sustainability is assured, though, it is dependent somewhat on "manageability," the relative ease by which you know and engage the intricate factors or elements of your church. Whether you "control" or "direct," or even "just manage to stay ahead," you work toward outcomes that are hopeful and helpful.

Of what does "manageability" consist? An enterprise like a congregation is manageable when:

❑ Its goals can be met without a level of exertion that exceeds the capacities of "managers" or other leaders.

❑ Its outcomes match its general expectations.

❑ Human interactions—i.e., one person to another—are the primary arena for important activities and decision-making.

❑ It can readily slough off or discard nonproductive programs or goals.

❑ New capacity is generated as a result of most activities; capacity-building is a process embedded in every program.

Management consultant and philosopher Peter Block bases his understanding of organizational development on an inverted pyramid: The job of the manager is to add value to the core workers for customers' benefit. In its application to congregational systems, the concept could be rephrased, "The job of the pastor and congregational leaders is to add value to the members' lives for the benefit of God (and God's world)." Block's further wisdom on this matter is embedded in his book *Stewardship: Choosing Service Over Self-Interest.*

One caution: manageability can also be misunderstood as the inherent bent of an individual or system to be managed, moved, changed, or otherwise manipulated. In that way of thinking, congregation members are most "manageable" when they are willing to be acted upon, docile, submissive, or at least easily persuaded by superior logic, doctrine, or charisma. In that misguided pyramid of power:

❑ Pastors and leaders act, and members react.

❏ If you are a leader, you might see yourself as "shepherd" and your members as "sheep."

❏ You can start down the slippery slope of "members-as-pastor's-helpers."

Because it demeans and dismisses abilities, this view of manageability is at the center of the problems faced by many leaders, perhaps a natural partner to the overexertion that this book calls "trying too hard."

THE RULE OF 150

The place where "manageability" starts is in the human brain and its limited capacities to receive, interpret, and act on sensory input. Science writer and columnist Malcolm Gladwell (*The Tipping Point: How Little Things Can Make a Big Difference*) gives an example of this kind of manageability in what is called "The Rule of 150." This rule is a "strange attractor" that seems to occur in a variety of places in human society. It may describe the optimum—perhaps maximum?—number of individuals with which a single human brain can mindfully interact.

The rule is based on the work of R. I. M. Dunbar, ("Neocortex size as a constraint on group size in primates," *Journal of Human Evolution* [1992], vol. 20, pp. 469-493), whose examination of the brains of humans and other primates yielded a ratio between the size of the neocortex and the size of the entire brain. This ratio seemed to correlate with the maximum size of the group in which primate groups had pleasant, nonviolent relationships.

In Dunbar's analysis, the ratio for humans came to 147.8, which yields the assumption that the maximum size of pleasantly relating groups for humans would be about 150. Dunbar's anthropological research revealed various interesting examples for this "rule of 150," among them:

● The average number of villagers in 21 hunter-gatherer societies around the world is about 150 members.

● Military planners have consistently limited to under 200 the number of soldiers in an effective fighting unit.

● Over their long history, Hutterite communities have kept the number of individuals in a single community to 150, using that number as the decision point for starting new communities.

● Gore Associates, manufacturers of Gore-Tex fabric and Glide dental floss, have built their organizational philosophy around this rule, delimiting the size of manufacturing plants to 150 employees.

For fun, you might speculate on how this rule could apply to your congregation, and on the effort it takes to manage groups of over 150 members. You'll have a further occasion to examine Gladwell's *The Tipping Point* in Chapter 9.

You've heard this somewhere else

You don't have to look far to find evidence of this "trying too hard" phenomenon in the worlds around you. Think about the people around you. You probably know more than one person or family who have recently expressed more than normal distress with their fast-paced lifestyles. Poke around a little in those conversations and you uncover the hot coals that keep those fires burning: In blurred-speed occupations, in overactive parenting, in minimalist personal relationships, many people are working too hard, but gaining too little satisfaction or too limited results.

In other words, it's harder and harder to find a place in life where the energy output (work) approximates the energy input (results). Aside from mythical "dot.com millionaires"—whose 24/7/365 lifestyles constitute a variety of "trying too hard" that defies description—most folk live with the dull sense that some parts of their lives could be seen as "futile" or "lacking reward."

You have probably seen this scurrying in your own life, or at least in the lives of those close to you. You may have missed other evidences of the problem and its emerging solutions. Some examples might help:

❏ Developments in neuropharmacology suggest the possibility that therapists and their patients have been working hard to ameliorate conditions that are now more simply addressed by slight changes in the levels of brain chemicals. (John J. Ratey's *A User's Guide to the Brain: Perception, Attention, and the Four Theaters of the Brain* frames the question well.)

❏ One way to understand Jesus' regular deflating of the supposed "righteousness" of the Pharisees: He was criticizing these religious leaders for trying too hard to find and practice "purity." The Purity Codes' sheer complexity kept all except the professionally religious from any realistic expectation of "obeying the Law." Jesus' sharp criticisms of the Pharisees included the explicit warning that they were ignoring the simpler—and just—ways of understanding God's will for the people and the world. (See William Herzog's deft and definitive exegesis of Jesus' understanding and teaching of the Torah in *Parables as Subversive Speech: Jesus as Pedagogue of the Oppressed.*)

❏ "Change fatigue" has now entered the vocabulary of management theorists. Change fatigue is described as a slow draining of energy in businesses that are changing too rapidly and too frequently. (See *The End of Change: How Your Company Can Sustain Growth and Innovation While Avoiding Change Fatigue*, by Peter Scott-Morgan and others.)

❏ "Social capital"—the binding and bonding power of institutions—has been declining since the mid-1960s. In reaction, institutions have increased both their hand-wringing and hard work to counter individualism. (Robert Putnam's *Bowling Alone: The Collapse and Revival of American Community* exquisitely details these pervasive and continuing trends.)

❏ At first glance, the journal *Fast Company* seems to be an audacious glorification of "the new economy." Its popularity may come instead from its thoughtful and practical commentary about essential and continuing values that enrich the human spirit, such as living a balanced, contented lifestyle.

❏ "Feminized" workplace philosophies have increased the value of collegiality and cooperation. These ways of thinking have also resulted in increasing trends toward part-time workers, home-based enterprises, and workers unwilling to give their entire selves to their occupations. (Margaret Wheatley's *Leadership and the New Science* embodies some of this hopeful ethic.)

❏ The simple-living phenomenon continues to attract adherents. Practitioners, theorists, organizations, events, journals, and new vocabularies proliferate. (Try a Web-search exercise with the words "simple living" or "downshifting" and see how many sites invite your visit.)

The matter of trying too hard and getting too-limited results is best remembered in the story of King Sisyphus, punished by Greek gods for his impertinence.

In the myths, Sisyphus is king of Corinth and either a truth-teller or a death-defying trickster. The gods decide to punish him with subtle torture: Sisyphus is condemned eternally to meaningless and futile work. His never-ending and always-incomplete task: to roll a large rock to the top of a high hill, whereupon the rock quickly descends, in obedience to the law of gravity!

In some versions of the myth, Sisyphus garners the gods' ire because he has dared to notice Zeus' theft of a maiden and has told her father. In other versions, his punishment is meted out because he has outwitted (or avoided) Death. So he is punished either for truth-telling or for following his biological urge for self-preservation. Neither, it seems, is especially pleasing to those mythical deities, perhaps because of Sisyphus' underlying scorn of them and their ordering of the universe.

Sisyphus' unmanageable lifework includes these elements:

❏ Because the labor needed to move the large rock is nearly Herculean, Sisyphus is not engaged in pleasant gamesmanship with a manageable-yet-unfulfilling task. Instead, he is doomed to continuing overexertion, and no matter how hard he works, he will still never be "successful."

❏ Sisyphus must keep laboring uphill because, absent his effort, the large rock would crush him on its descent. Whether or not he works, Sisyphus risks defeat.

❏ Part of the curse of this work is that Sisyphus engages in it by himself, with no others present either to notice his hard work or to help him with it.

❏ The only way to think of Sisyphus' life as worthwhile is by engaging in a mind-bending approach, such as "If he sees the task itself as rewarding, he won't be frustrated by a lack of results." Thus overexertion with no reward becomes a virtue.

Sisyphus' lifelong task might be emblematic of the lifework of church leaders who are "trying too hard." (See accompanying illustration.) The story reveals what many pastors and church leaders feel: "No matter what I do, and no matter how hard I work, it seems as though I am doomed to having little success at best. At worst, if I stop pushing this congregation uphill, it will roll back down to crush me."

What does it mean to "try too hard"?

The simple answer to the question might be, "Well, you'll know it when you feel it." That reply would resemble a way of thinking/knowing that philosophers call *qualia* and what neuroscience might call "the biology of consciousness." If you've worked with children, you've encountered this phenomenon more than once, in the face of puzzling questions such as, "What makes red red?" or "How do we see?" The word *qualia* (plural for *quale*) describes a state of awareness that can be described in no other way than by its own essence. So "red" cannot be reduced to a wavelength on the spectrum, nor can "see" be reduced to light waves hitting rods and cones at the back of the eye. In a sense, *qualia* are irreducible awarenesses of various elements of life, and we "just know them."

"Trying too hard" ultimately describes a condition inside the brain and its inner workings, where various modules—think "columns of interworking neuronal bundles"—work together to motivate the rest of the mind to engage the rest of the body in work that does not seem to be rewarding. Because it is beyond the pale of this book to describe this condition in terms of brain science, let's agree that "trying too hard" is a matter of what's going on in your mind, your consciousness, and your self-awareness. Hold the thought that "trying too hard" is biological in its first and final description.

You could also describe this condition in your life with metaphors or comparisons. In that vein, "trying too hard" is like:

❑ Archetypal lemmings—they are the example for everything, aren't they?—whose large group food-searches get easily confused with mass lemmicide. "We just wanted to go out for a bite to eat" results in unintended mass annihilation.

❑ Lifting weights that are too heavy, and doubly injuring yourself by lifting the wrong way.

❑ Pushing hard to open a door that is clearly marked "Pull."

❑ With one foot, standing on the hem of a garment you're trying to step into with the other foot.

For neurobiologists and other curious investigators of the human state, *qualia* present intriguing penultimate questions. One good example is Francis Crick's *The Astonishing Hypothesis: The Scientific Search for the Soul*. Crick reduces "seeing" down to its mystically beautiful molecular level. On their own terrain, brain scientists are closing in on the quale of "self-awareness" and beginning their neurotheological work on "praying." Is it possible that we may soon "know" what now "we just know?"

❑ Using a pipe wrench to hammer tacks into a wall.

❑ Asking another motorist, one with out-of-state license plates, for accurate directions.

❑ Wearing clothes that don't fit, but which you hope will hide or shape your body nonetheless.

❑ Deciding to play chess without the queen.

❑ Trying to use logic with a crying two-year-old.

❑ Running a brand-new program with minimum RAM (random access memory) on your hard drive.

Let me be a little more specific by noting some places where I've seen "trying too hard" in congregations I've been part of. You may recognize similar feelings and actions in your own congregation.

Hoping for different results/answers. When you expect different outcomes from the same action or the same question, you may be working too hard. Stephen Covey and others have alluded to this as a simple way to define "insanity."

"Selling" ideas. If you're "selling" or "push marketing" supposedly new or better ideas or programs, you're probably trying too hard because you make yourself the "cause" or "motivation" for their generation or success.

Allowing function creep. In this well-meaning and supposedly efficient way of thinking, a planned activity or program gets overloaded with expectations, goals, or tasks. The added functions diminish flexibility, ease of work, and eventual success.

Depending on professional staff. Someone will always be trying too hard if your congregation depends on staff alone to carry the burden of programs, activities, vision, or attitudes. One result: clericalism and its twin, anticlericalism.

Building long-range plans. Because most conditions change even while the plans are being made, this way of thinking may perhaps be described as "imagination turned into work." The saddest examples: elongated processes for forming "vision statements" or "mission statements."

Working a "sure-fire system." Perhaps the most pernicious version of overexertion among newer congregations and newer pastors, this phenomenon is also called "seeking the magic bullet." It fits in the "trying too hard" family because no strategy is universally applicable, and because most systems best fit their original audience and situation.

Operating with bad data. Lacking accurate data, you can make decisions that require you to work too hard. In the next chapter you'll learn how "seeing too little" is also a way of describing a kind of unnecessary blindness to the movement of God's hand in the world today.

Losing long-term energy. When you try too hard, you expend enormous energy. Over time it becomes more difficult to renew the available energy, and not enough energy is available to begin or maintain even the simplest action.

Operating with singularity. "Determined effort" is an admired trait among leaders. But sometimes it turns into a "tunnel-vision" leadership style that doesn't readily allow for diversions, flexible approaches, restful side trips, or sudden creative flashes. Plow horses usually get the furrows straight, but rarely work out of their field.

Cooperating in codependencies. Leaders who try too hard may find themselves locked into subtle codependencies with judicatory officials, key members, or large contributors. Mutual neediness is reinforced especially when those relationships are based on the imagined significance of "helping out a colleague [or pastor] in distress."

Focusing on the institution. In this overreaching of purpose, pastors and leaders see the institution as an ultimate manifestation of God's work anywhere, and so move "congregation as institution" from instrumental means to ultimate goal and proof of labor.

Overfocusing on techniques. Techniques—or tactics—are always based on deeper realities and fundamental conditions. Overemphasis on techniques without giving strong attention to the underlying conditions yields ultimately to an institutional "eating of seed corn."

In his counterintuitive and insightfully curmudgeonly work, *After Progress: Finding the Old Way Forward*, British philosopher Anthony O'Hear describes what philosophers call "pessimistic meta-induction." Careful students and admirers of previous generations note that "the best theory of every age proves eventually to be misconceived, very far from an accurate picture of the universe." This is why I encourage the alert readers of this and other chapters to approach even the theses of this book with their own meta-inductions!

Trusting "inevitable progress." The western Zeitgeist imagines that "progress" is inevitable, and that its highest manifestations are evident here and now. Each generation presumes itself to be "just a little bit superior" to the preceding cohort, and therefore too readily discards or disregards the wisdom of previous generations. Here pastors and leaders can "try too hard" to find effective ways of working, and overlook those that have already been discovered and proven.

How you can know when it's happening to you

Let's be honest with each other: We all try too hard at one time or another. So finding yourself as a congregational leader or pastor in the preceding descriptions should have been as easy for you as it was for me to find "the overearnest author" in my own descriptions. It would be useful for us to notice this kind of behavior before it becomes a habit.

The following tests or indicators of behavior and thought may indicate whether you're "trying too hard" in your congregation. Try a few to see how overexertion may be sneaking up on you.

The "dread factor"

You know you're trying too hard if dread or foreboding take up permanent residence in the pit of your stomach or the back of your brain:

❑ Before a meeting begins.

❑ At the start of the program year.

❑ When you consider your day's calendar.

❑ When the phone rings.

❑ Any time a governing board member approaches you.

❑ When other people get excited about a "new idea."

Scrambling skill

If you're trying too hard, you might find yourself constantly scrambling, busily patching and fixing what you believe might otherwise fall apart. So you are constantly alert to these stimuli that you believe require your quick reactions:

❑ Dissatisfied or burned-out leaders.

❑ Unfilled positions in the congregation's structure.

❑ Committees or working groups that don't meet often.

❑ Strong, principled disagreements between participants in meetings.

❑ Visitors who appear to be the kind of "new members" you'd love to have in your congregation.

❑ Slight downturns in contributions.

The shaming/blaming rule

You can start to suspect that you're overexerting if you find shame and guilt feelings entering your bloodstream any time that:

❑ You hear a question that just might be construed as critical of your work.

❑ You read in your denomination's publications about the "successes" of other congregations or leaders.

❑ You inadvertently get caught in a "braggers' group session" at a denominational gathering.

❑ You write a report, complete a survey, or compile statistics about your congregation.

❑ You are asked to "invite a friend" to attend worship or participate in a congregational program.

◆

Out of intense complexities intense simplicities emerge.

Winston Churchill

From the brain's point of view, a habit is a pathway of electrochemical reactions, most notably seen at the synapses, or points of connection between brain cells. Just as muscle groups benefit from exercise—"use it or lose it"—so the brain's pathways benefit from repeated use. In unfamiliar situations, the brain first chooses the familiar pathways to determine reactions or make patterns. These neuronal connections—now more like superhighways—help the brain to be quicker and more assured in its actions. Habits are the brain's most efficient pathways.

The searching eyes

Your always-darting eyes might be a sign of trying too hard if you find yourself consistently looking for:

❑ Quick-fix methods or techniques, usually described in glossy paper brochures.

❑ Sure-fire systems of "success" or "health" or "growth," sometimes presented by individuals who seem just a tad over-active themselves.

❑ "Model" or "best-practice" congregations whose efforts led them away from the state you think you're in right now.

❑ Anything that has the word "new" attached to it.

❑ Anything endorsed by your denomination's guru-of-the-month.

❑ Any catchy title or easily remembered formula.

Wandering heart

This sign that you may be trying too hard requires you to examine the "loves of your life," the places where emotion and fervor attach. You find your heart moving quickly—perhaps too quickly?—toward (or away from):

❑ Anything that attracted your searching eye (above).

❑ People who "really need" your services as counselor, healer, friend, listening ear, advice-giver, or comforter.

❑ Programs or activities that promise little or no preparation, cost, or energy investment. (Remember, it's the too-hard work of "wandering" that can tire you out, not the eventual program you might choose.)

❑ Canned sermons, prepackaged services, one-stop shopping. (Again, it's your constant seeking that's wearing you down here, not the things themselves.)

❑ Any program, event, or activity instituted by your predecessor or a colleague whom you admire.

◆

What will you gain, if you own the whole world but destroy yourself? What would you give to get back your soul?

Jesus

Singing the nomination blues

You might be an effort-bound leader if, at the time of "empty leadership positions," you feel like singing the blues when you:

❑ Check your church's constitution or bylaws for the minimum number of people you'll have to ask.

❑ Enter into a formal procedure that requires several meetings whose result will be the same small selection of "willing names."

❑ Include only the same small selection of names on the list of people you're actually willing to ask.

❑ Try to fill every position.

❑ Come up short when you try to think how to be persuasive and yet friendly with possible nominees.

❑ Find yourself wondering when your term will be completed, so you don't have to ask for any more volunteers.

Slotted people test

In this "Nomination Blues" adaptation, you might be trying too hard if you find yourself:

❑ Avoiding all that "gifts-based ministry" stuff because it takes too long.

❑ Wishing there were a better way than "time and talents" systems to fit people into "just the right position."

❑ Negotiating with everyone who doesn't say no right away, so that they'll say yes to something, anything even vaguely resembling the original task or job.

❑ Remaining more concerned about filling the slot than fulfilling the volunteer.

Measured meetings

You can measure "trying too hard" at meetings, if you:

❑ Overformalize and overtrust procedures like agendas, minutes, decision-making processes.

❑ Hold all your meetings in the same three rooms at church, and at about the same times each month.

❑ Allow, in the interest of "democratic decision-making," off-task mental meandering, storytelling-as-proof, and personal venting.

❑ Don't notice that most "group discussion before making a decision" is really a clever way to postpone a decision that might require meeting participants to add work to their already busy lives.

No "flow"

You might be prone to overexertion if you rarely have "flow" experiences. You may be trying too hard if you seldom feel:

❑ The rush of nearly tearful joy at the sheer pleasure and privilege of certain moments in your ministry.

❑ "Puppy delight" at the prospect of being with the unique people who make up your congregation.

❑ A tingling in your senses as you anticipate the start of a new day.

❑ Joyful sadness and fulfillment at weddings, funerals, departures, graduations, or other significant life events.

❑ An almost visceral certainty that your life is complete at this moment, in this place, among this group of people.

If you recognized yourself in more than five of these behaviors, you may be trying too hard already, and prone to continue to think and act in that way.

"Flow" is most completely described by social scientist Mihalyi Csikszentmihalyi in his book, *Flow: The Psychology of Optimal Experience*, as an emotional/logical feeling of complete absorption in an activity, a state of well-being in which you are so immersed in the pleasure of the action that you lose track of what else is happening around you. Musicians call this state of being a "groove," long-distance runners "the runner's high," fishing enthusiasts "a grand day on a trout stream," and miscellaneous others "the zone." One other thing: If you can say "MEE-high Chick-SENT-mee-high," you'll honor this man's legacy of wisdom with the sound of his name!

YOUR BRAIN GOES TO A MEETING

To understand how meetings might be "trying too hard places," imagine what might be happening in your brain as you engage in a more-or-less typical meeting.

You enter the room at the end of a long day, your mind still filled with memories of the day's activities. If you're wise, you've had time to reset your mind with a meal, rest, or conversation, and are now ready for the meeting. If you're running late, you bring all the stress with you.

If the meal was especially filling or composed of just the right amounts of carbohydrates, proteins, and other chemicals, your brain might find itself in a familiar tussle with your digestive tract, which requires a significant increase in blood supply to do its work. "Attention" and "creative thinking" may be in short supply, at least for a while.

You're in the same room as always, with the same people. The same smells, lighting, and sounds tell your brain to find in its many files the familiar modules that describe "meeting." Within seconds the modules are connected, and your brain signals itself to expect the familiar. "Nothing new" is what your brain has sensed from the surroundings and setting.

Because the group is sitting at tables, your eyes can't accurately read all the body language that communicates feelings. The faint smells of the evening meal, cigarette smoke, the custodian's cleaning chemicals, and coffee keep your most-trusted olfactory sense from accurately describing what's happening. The leader's behavior is matter-of-fact, the tone of voice calm but tinged with some edginess about "needing to make a decision together tonight." Your brain senses weariness in the leader's eyes, and you file away the possibility that this person is physically overextended.

Little or no physical movement occurs in the meeting, and so your eyes go on automatic pilot; you read the words that have been written on newsprint and catch the facial expressions of the other participants. But with little or no movement, no really extraordinary sounds—you don't hear even the sound of your first name—nothing to touch except your pen, and few critical internal decisions to make, your brain has excess capacity to use in other venues. So you daydream, reviewing the day's emotions and relationships, assuring yourself of the wisdom of this past day's decisions, and replaying short tapes of the most pleasurable interchanges you had with other people.

And then, suddenly, out of nowhere danger erupts. One group member is angry at something and begins blaming you, of all people! Immediately your brain shifts into its protective stance. An immediate response is necessary, so the amygdala quickly takes over decision-making. The hippocampus—with all its reflective capabilities—can wait. Cortisol secreted by the adrenal cortex fuels a full-blown stress-response. Your own anger—and even a little fear—comes to the front of your consciousness. You are ready to fight back, or at least to defend yourself. You call up quick verbal defenses and put them to use instantly. No logic needed here; this person's words are a threat to your well-being, and your brain knows what to do in response to something that requires immediate action: fight back!

Your words come out, strongly phrased and directed at the source of the danger. You notice that anger has now started to infect other participants, whose brains now engage as yours did. The leader works hard to patch around the sudden emotional flare-up, to get the flow of discussion back on track. After a few moments, your hypothalamus signals the rest of your brain to kick into its logical mode. You suddenly realize that your words have been too quick, too direct and "not helpful." A small regret begins to form.

(continued)

Now you are confronted with difficult choices about what to do and say. Was the danger real? How can you put back together what seems to be falling apart? Have you misjudged the situation? Outwardly you seem to be participating in the continuing conversation, but a good share of your brain is now trying to integrate your action with your self-worth. Unanswered questions are demanding wise replies. Nearly automatic shame and feelings of guilt replace the anger and fear you felt earlier.

Even though you aren't completely focused on the meeting's smaller details, you notice that the discussion is circling around possible action. The leader is starting to get just a little more insistent and even animated as the group's shared words collect like water behind a dam. Something must be done, something decided. And when the decisions are made, some among you will have new responsibilities added to their lives. "More work" is the name of the module that your brain now connects together. A quick check verifies what your quicker emotions have told you: "More work" is not a pleasurable prospect. Once again, you sense a minor danger—if only the addition of work to your already stressed life—and your brain sets into motion all the resources required to mount an avoidance response. The whole brain agrees: You will not take on more work tonight!

You stay quiet for the rest of the meeting, to allow your brain to sort out the meaning of the quick-anger incident and as a good strategy for not taking on more work. You are understandably less-than-helpful at the point where the group leader asks for "any creative suggestions" and "any more questions." Even though you notice that the leader is subtly trying to re-engage you regarding the substance and direction of the meeting, your brain has more important things to do: to protect itself and make sense of this situation.

When the meeting is over, you drag unspoken apologies, regrets, and weariness home, matters your brain will work through for the rest of your waking hours this evening. Except for the written notes your logical-rational neocortex suggested you take, the meeting will fade from memory quickly. Tomorrow will be another day.

What "trying too hard" is not about

By now you may be wondering if "trying too hard" describes every dysfunctional behavior in a congregation. Of course not, even if dysfunctions seem to find each other and form large herds that romp through your congregation's psyche like a good halfback through a sloppy defense. It may be helpful for you to consider what "trying too hard" is not.

Working hard

"Trying too hard" is not the same as working hard or long. There are few things in life that can be achieved easily, and therefore hard work is an expected cost of being a leader. What distinguishes an overexerted leader is the quality, direction, and wisdom of the effort. Working hard at the wrong things is "trying too hard." Working hard at the right things is rewarding.

The difference? Perhaps the direction the rock is to be rolled. If you're taking advantage of the metaphorical rock's general tendencies or qualities—its obeying the laws of gravity—you're working hard. But if you're always pushing uphill against what seems to be natural or real, you're most likely trying too hard.

You can easily distinguish "trying too hard" from "working hard" by looking at the kind and amount of stress you feel. Both "eustress" (good stress) and "distress" (bad stress) can be a result of your work. Both kinds of stress call forth the adrenaline-based physiological changes that make your body better able to do the work—narrowed blood vessels, increased heart rate, etc. But it's distress that especially triggers your brain's entire "fight or flight" mechanism; it's in distressing situations that anger and fear operate most readily. One way to distinguish between simple hard work and "trying too hard" is to assess inside your soul the level of anger or fear you feel, and how strongly you want to defend, attack, or run away from the situation.

The opposite of "trying too hard" is not avoiding any work, minimizing responsibilities, or banking the fires of high expectation. Why? The avoidance itself—because of fight or flight mechanisms in the brain—is a sign that you're still trying too hard, under any seemingly calm exterior.

◆

I put my shoulder to the wheel, my ear to the ground, my nose to the grindstone, and my eye on the future. I wonder how long I can keep on like this.

Anonymous congregational leader

Having a sense of mission

You are not "trying too hard" if you are passionate about your life of service in God's realm. Passion drives both feckless and effective people. In the first case, their work has little power or effect; in the second case, there is some end, some goal to their work, and that goal draws closer to fulfillment with their effort.

"Vision" or "mission" statements are not always good evidence of a congregation's purpose. How can you tell? Some possible tests:

❑ The longer the mission/vision statement, the less likely it represents the congregation's true sense of purpose.

❑ You can tell how difficult it was to discover (or instill?) a sense of mission among congregation members by the length and complexity of the process by which the written statements were formed.

❑ The heavy presence of "code language" may indicate platitude assembly or negotiated correctness. The less code language is evident, the more likely the statement can be understood and practiced.

One measure of a congregation's mission is the degree to which members feel free to start programs or activities, and to enlist others to work with them. This "entrepreneurial spirit" shows a congregation's sense of its purpose. In most places that spirit reveals more about mission-mindedness than the imagined quality or universal appeal of purpose statements. (See chapter 8 for further discussion of this subject.)

Changing the status quo

"Trying too hard" has an interesting relationship to change (a subject treated at length in chapter 8). You can be trying too hard if you hold a false expectation that you are a "change leader" who moves others beyond the status quo. Laboring under this premise, you can invest heavily in what you perceive to be desirable changes, and you can be emotionally crushed when circumstances beyond your imagination or control keep you from instituting or enabling those desired changes.

You could also be trying too hard, on the other hand, if you tried to hold together the present state of affairs, working hard to avoid or resist all the changes swirling around you.

The middle ground? It might be wise to maintain a surface calm and continuing status quo, where small changes can occur naturally.

Simplicity

"Trying too hard" is an activity that overvalues complexity, or overestimates your capacity to understand or control complexities. Trying to "understand" or "know" all the facts and their complex relationships before making a decision is itself a sign of trying too hard. Without getting stuck in an eternal analysis of complexities, your goal is to try to find a simplicity that distills and takes into account most, but not all, of the complexities.

Giving up, dropping out, shutting down

One way to avoid "trying too hard" is to give up, not to try at all. But premature acceptance of "the eventual futility of all effort" actually requires more work than first apparent, and can become a form of "trying too hard."

Because individuals and institutions have an almost-biological urge to stay alive, shutting down life-seeking systems creates an opposite reaction, the violent thrashing of still-operating and still-active social organisms. There is great power in congregations' will to live, and fighting against it may result in overexertion, trying too hard.

One of God's gifts is that you, like God, do not let your existential clocks wind down, and thus you work against entropy. When you drop out, shut down, or give up, you deny part of your best self, or even your well-being.

You can see entropy working in pastors or leaders who never associate with their peers, whose congregations exist as diminishing islands of light, and whose isolation marks their personal and institutional identity. These leaders look and act tired because they may be trying too hard to squelch the Spirit's voice in their hearts. They may be purposely diminishing their response to God's generosity. They may be quieting the call that first compelled them to seek this ministry, this leadership. Fighting God-given instincts is always too-hard work.

More than a generation ago, futurist Buckminster Fuller suggested that humans were antientropic. His observation coincides with what brain scientists now know about the human brain: It always seeks and makes meaning from its sensory input. Except during times of deep sleep, the brain is awash in electrochemical energy, instantly responding to what it perceives, checking familiar patterns against incoming information, and creating new maps by which to process data. Brain-imaging techniques—among them magnetic resonance imaging (MRI) and positron emission tomography (PET)—reveal a brain constantly "lighting up" as blood and chemical receptors and low-level electrical energy course through the hundreds of billions of cells and their nearly infinite possible connections with each other.

THE VISION AND MISSION TEAM THAT DIDN'T KNOW ENOUGH

What happens in your congregation

"Trying too hard" can be a debilitating condition for you as an individual leader. It can also diminish the effectiveness of your congregation and set up a whirlpool of negative activity, nonactivity, and self-doubt. Some of the possible effects of whole-congregation overexertion might include the following.

Forest-fire burnout

If it continues long enough, widespread overexertion "burns out" the brains of pastors and other leaders, overtaxing attitudinal capacities past their biological limits. In a kind of neuronal meltdown, brains protect themselves by shutting down or shutting off sensory stimuli that might be dangerous or otherwise harmful in the long term.

◆

Martyrdom is the only way in which we can become famous without ability.

George Bernard Shaw

Beginning with a pastor—the individual most likely to be affected by "trying too hard"—burnout can spread like a wind-driven forest fire. The continuing dysfunction of one leader quickly infects others. (See chapter 9 for a description of "thought contagion," how ideas and their emotional fuel spread like plagues.)

The subject of "clergy burnout" is a continuing concern for clergy and the people who love them. Some resources that help ameliorate these torchings-of-self include:

❑ Roy Oswald's *Clergy Self-Care: Finding a Balance for Effective Ministry*. This book is chock-full of tools and strategies for finding and making habitual a balanced approach to pastoral ministry.

❑ *The Equipping Pastor: A Systems Approach to Congregational Leadership*, by R. Paul Stevens and Phil Collins. This well-reasoned leadership model gives hope to pastors and other leaders, and provides them implicit assurance that they have the relational skills to carry out effective leadership.

❑ *Quiet Conversations: Concrete Help for Weary Ministry Leaders*. Alan and Cheryl Klaas share the results of a research study results in an imagined series of conversations among a consultant, a pastor, and his wife.

Multiplied mediocrity

Because its biological consequences include diminished focus and limited capacities, "trying too hard" invariably results in frenetic activity and in less-than-excellent results of planning or action. The cruel irony here: Even as "trying too hard" pulls apart excellence, it requires continuing effort to achieve less-than-acceptable results.

A downward cycle of dysfunction is established: Weary and wary brains, not happy with the dreary results of too much work, are nevertheless compelled by other variants of fear and anger—for example, "What will become of this place if we don't keep at this?"—to keep at the unrewarded tasks.

In *Emotional Intelligence*, author Daniel Goleman summarizes the matter: "Stress makes us stupid." Facing the continuing stress of futile efforts barely rewarded, the brain has a difficult time responding except from continuing fear and anger.

Diffused or disappearing identity

When a congregation is moving too fast, working at the edge, and experiencing limited success, it is possible that its core identity can be described as "diffused" as best. Identity is forged in reflection, and congregations trying too hard may lack the will or the opportunities to engage in reflection. Because "trying to be all things to all people" is one of the corollaries of "trying too hard," congregations whose programmatic reach extends beyond their grasp may also find themselves with pieces of their identity thinly distributed.

Institutional fragility

One effect of institutionalized overexertion might be described as a kind of "fragility." It is possible that congregations that try too hard think of themselves as trapped in a supposedly frail state, and this attitude becomes a self-fulfilling prophecy. (The brain's capacity to operate according to self-suggestion is powerful: If you imagine yourself to be sick, you will become sick.)

Leaders in a congregation can inadvertently project their worried/hurried view about their congregation's "delicate condition," and eventually it will become part of the congregation's self-image. (The story is told of a pastor considering a call to a congregation. One member, when asked what especially characterized the parishioners as a community of faith, answered truthfully, "We don't like each other.")

"Trying too hard" can bring with it a sense of imminent collapse, or the start of a long downward spiral. The important word here is "sense," because the reality of "collapse" is first based on feelings, not facts. Congregations that experience the continuing frustration of futile labors may be more prone to that "sense" than congregations that correctly ignore possible symptoms of their supposed death and keep on with lively activities and attitudes.

Unachievable results from unassailable goals

The presumption that some congregational elements or goals are absolutely necessary—and hence unassailable—can result from and cause futile effects. This phenomenon is symbolized by the oft-heard plea, "But we can't have a church if we don't have a Sunday school, can we?"

To take the "unassailable Sunday school" example just a little further, you can imagine what other outcomes might be generated by this goal. "We simply must . . ." fuels resigned-and-dutiful motivation for a program or activity called "Sunday school." Duty replaces passion, loyalty trumps reality, and so dutiful, loyal leaders find barely excited teachers who cobble together the bare skeleton of a program whose results may be hardly noticeable or valued by the parents or children whose lives the program is intended to benefit.

The question here is not whether people should be loyal or exercise their sense of duty. Of course they should. Of course they can and do operate from these motivational bases. The real question, though, is how certain goals or outcomes got to be "unassailable," never candidates for serious evaluation or replacement.

Intellectual dishonesty

Sadly, this phenomenon in the life of churches is widespread and even honored. Here, "dishonesty" is an unwillingness to name, accurately and honestly, *what is*, in the hope that *what might be* will somehow overwhelm the present realities in which a congregation finds itself.

Again, "trying too hard" is both cause and effect of this connected behavior. The inability of congregation members to tell the truth in love may legitimate the setting aside of

◆

Judge persons by their questions rather than by their answers.

Voltaire

honest assessment and evaluation. "Vision" and "mission" may be pumped up as somehow more spiritually correct substitutes for truth-telling. A pervasive culture of false hope may prevent gainsayers from speaking their minds. Leaders and pastors (especially new ones) may go about their business imagining that capacities and volition are well planted in the congregation, and therefore work too hard to achieve what is literally not possible. In their overexertion they gain both the admiration and pity of members, who are prevented by cultural expectations from disabusing the leaders of their notion of what is possible. This pattern can be particularly hard to break if the congregation cycles new leaders or pastors through the same stages of behavior.

Disinvestment by high-quality leaders

Another sad result of the "trying too hard" phenomenon can be the gradual pulling-back of talented and committed leaders from the congregation as institution. Precisely because they are gifted and experienced in leadership, they see the congregation's dysfunction as danger, a waste (bad stewardship) of their time and energies, or both. And so the very people who might break the pattern of behavior are not available to the congregation at the time when they may be most needed.

Here we're talking about the time-honored "20/80 Rule," among whose variations is the idea that 20 percent of the people will do 80 percent of the work. Other formulas of involvement peg the percentages at 30/70, and still others expand the notion to include measures of contributions of time and money, or expected levels of attendance. The "rule" is not yet a "strange attractor," but it tends to operate as such in the lives of many pastors and congregational leaders, or at least as "contagious folk wisdom."

Lack of value or significance in members' lives

Only a small percentage of members find high significance in their lives because of their involvement in the congregation's inner workings. The remainder of the members find primary meaning and purpose in their lives outside the church.

If the congregation has slipped into a "trying-too-hard syndrome," its preoccupation with its inner workings will likely render it less able to bring value or significance to the majority of members. However quietly or invisibly, the majority of members will reciprocate, not valuing the congregation as significant to their lives. In this way, "trying too hard" can touch off negative reciprocal actions that quickly affect most members.

Why this behavior continues

Like all dysfunctional behavior, "trying too hard" seems to bring some rewards to its practitioners, even if only in the short run. These behaviors are cyclical and feed on themselves. Just as piety is its own reward, and negativity becomes its own punishment, so overexertion may provide its own fuel or internal logic.

The martyr self-image

Some leaders' self-image can be described as "martyred" or "quixotic." The supposition in Christianity that pastors and other leaders are garden-variety "little Jesuses" is a long-standing tradition, one embedded in the hearts of many pastors and leaders. And so, in some faith traditions, Jesus' role as "prophet, priest, and king" is promoted as a likely model for pastors. (In those same traditions, the relatively short duration of Jesus' own public ministry is overlooked as part of the model.)

Short-term gain

Short-term rewards for overexertion are possible. Folklore is full of stories about a leader or pioneer who should have tried a little harder for just a while longer. (The late classical pianist and comedian Victor Borge used to speak of his grandfather as the ill-fated inventor of a soft drink he variously called "4 Up," "5 Up," and "6 Up," at which point he gave up the business.) And so there is the lure, especially for young and new leaders among us, that our hard work might occur just at the "tipping point" where a tiny tap on an impenetrable wall will bring it down (for example, the hope that one series of good sermons about generosity will finally be persuasive for a previously underfunded congregation).

The admirable risk-takers

Most leadership literature includes the mantra that good leaders are risk-takers. Risk comes from effort, and extra effort can overcome risk. Overexertive risk-takers are rewarded by the possibility of success and the admiration of their peers or followers. This encourages the most talented and energetic leaders to be most willing to "try too hard." How ironic that this affliction of excessive effort can cut short the ministries of those whom we might identify as the most promising.

Doing what we're supposed to do

Some leaders and congregations may think that overexertion is "the way it's supposed to be," or at least approximates the condition of congregations their size or shape. The congregations and leaders continue to try too hard because they know of no other way to behave. Their reward: behaving according to the expectations of those who have taught them.

Peer approval and belonging

Some leaders and congregations may be thoroughly convinced that "success systems" for church growth or health are universally applicable. They may also be so immersed in the principles or techniques they have learned that they cannot easily cast away what so many others seem so certain are worthy solutions for their problems. Their reward: The approval of successful peers, and the security of belonging to a "movement" that comforts and supports them.

One other factor that lacks any reward: Congregational leaders who try too hard may have become so demoralized by their present situation that they cannot trust deeper interior wisdom—what Aristotle called "practical wisdom"—which they have gained through life experiences.

How to start "trying less hard"

The body of this book is devoted to this matter, especially the latter chapters. But let's get a jump on some of those ideas right now, before you sink into some kind of quiet despair over the seemingly inescapable conclusion that your own "trying too hard" has rendered you an eternal victim of your own psyche. Let's approach the matter from the viewpoint of what you can do, while reading this book, to start to turn both attitudes and behaviors away from "ecclesiastical overexertion," the Sisyphean dilemma.

Let's start with some simple assumptions about you and the congregation you serve. Check to see how these statements describe your view of yourself and your congregation:

❑ You have more abilities than you know.

❑ Those abilities are sufficient for any changes you want to make.

❑ Inside you are passions for ministry that can't wait to get out and do something new.

❑ God's good news applies to your life right now.

❑ At some level, you accept and understand your personal power as a gift from God's Spirit.

Good. With those ideas about God's gifts firmly in your mind, let's start the discussion of "not trying too hard."

Ask the hard questions right away

"Ask me the right question and I'll give you the right answer," goes the aphorism. But the time for right questions is at the start of a process of planning and thinking. If you want to stop trying too hard, slow down any activity or process just enough to ask hard questions as a beginning step. Some of the best hard questions start with the word "why." Some of the best hard questions come from the people who seem the most irascible or difficult to lead.

Right now pick one area of your congregational life in which you are trying too hard, and mentally rehearse any five "why?" questions and your best answers to them. What do you notice starting to come apart? What gets clearer? What could you let go of?

Work at the basics first

Under every reality is a metareality, principles or basic values that are almost always true. Know what those assumptions are before you begin. Take the time to review their existence, to include them in goals, to honor their power and presence. So, for example, you may want to work at "strengthening your outreach program," but the metareality may be that your congregation is frightened by people in

◆

The toughest thing about success is that you've got to keep on being a success.

Irving Berlin

the community. In that case, you switch basic goals to work at diminishing their fear.

Stop reading for a few moments, and review the underlying assumptions that are driving the existence or liveliness of a program or activity where you find yourself trying too hard. How valuable are those premises? How do they match the stated purpose of the activity or program? How could you increase or make stronger the connections between the activity and its supposed purposes?

Insist on "two for the price of one"

One effect of "trying too hard" may be narrowed goals, so that you're satisfied with even the smallest change. For example, you work hard to construct the annual "funding appeal," whose stated purpose is to "provide funding for the ministries of this congregation." Because you are doing all this work for only one purpose, you are facing the possibility of minimally rewarded exertion.

An alternate approach: Name as your intended outcomes several additional goals—without lapsing into "function creep"—and ensure that you will realize both small and large expectations. As you work toward "two goals for the price of one," you're also practicing an economy of effort, lessening your workload and giving yourself the satisfaction any "two for one" bargain brings!

In the example of the annual fund appeal, your stated goals might also include:

❏ Providing new opportunities for service by new or younger leaders.

❏ Providing an outlet for event planners to use their skills successfully.

❏ Offering members a chance to rediscover themselves as "generous."

❏ Giving members an opportunity to evaluate their wider stewardship of money or possessions.

❏ Adding energy or excitement about the future.

❏ Providing the benefits of a congregational celebration for any reason!

In your mind, find one area in your congregation's life where you see limited results or narrow reasons for engaging in an activity. What other benefits could be derived from this experience? What other groups or leaders could work on this program?

Avoid "seeing too little" and "knowing too much"

The following two chapters detail the pernicious effects of culturally clueless and information-overloaded behaviors. You can start working against these twin difficulties by selectively paying attention to what is true and real in the culture around you and, on the other hand, resisting the temptation to "know fully" before taking action.

Just as your brain regularly and purposefully ignores most of the stimuli that it receives through sensory organs, so you can adopt behavior patterns that delimit or filter the kinds and amounts of information you are willing to accept.

Right now, consider how your ease-of-communication devices too aggressively seek your limited attention. Think what might happen if you watched less television, turned off your cell phone, did not answer your telephone every time it rang, or paid no attention to anonymous complaint letters. How would that feel? When could you get started?

Shed functions and "good ideas"

You will find yourself trying less hard if you deliberately shed supposedly required functions or roles, and regularly reject ideals whose only appeal is that they are somehow "good ideas."

Your body has known how to do this winnowing since before you were born. Between your eighth month as a baby-to-be and your birth, your brain sloughed off about half its available brain cells. In other words, your body made a decision to eliminate about half its inherent brain capacity. Brain theorists surmise that these cells are discarded by the brain because they are not needed or not used, or because your brain knows its own limits.

Think right now of one "good idea" that you will purposely not pursue in the next week, or one program, activity, or role you will prune from your expectations about yourself.

In his newest attempt to popularize and make available the sometimes mystical world of "brain science," writer, psychologist, and physician John J. Ratey (*A User's Guide to the Brain*) goes on to suggest that embryonic brain cells are pruned off because they were not used in utero, and did not survive the fierce competition for nutrients and functionality suggested by the "use it or lose it" mantra.

Start one new habit

New habits can displace old ones, and so one way to stop trying so hard is to replace dysfunctional habits by crowding them out with new ones. Take your pick: Stephen Covey's "seven habits," the "disciplines" of Roman Catholicism and other religions, or even a new habit involving the most mundane daily routines (e.g., your ritual around morning coffee). Start displacing behaviors that have become chronically deficient or purposeless.

Think about your morning coffee ritual, for example. Add time to this daily routine, make it a "rite" by adding time for prayer or conversation with a friend. Displace the hurried gulping of coffee by moving to a new location—perhaps a local coffee shop where members start their days. Bring along one page of the newspaper—yes, even the comics might do nicely here—as a conversation- or day-starter.

What will be displaced? A hurried gulping of coffee-as-drug-of-choice. What habit might take its place? Conversation, a shared "briefing" on the day's coming realities, an increase in conversational skill, a rush of endorphins or seratonin in your brain—pleasurable conversation might just help that happen—and a time for prayerful reconnection with your God.

Be satisfied with small steps

The small-step approach to change is at the heart of most current approaches to "transformation" or "organizational change." Because most systems—including the ones in which you find yourself trying too hard—are complex, a small change in one part of the system affects all other parts. This makes the small-step approach a reasonable alternative to whole-system change. (We'll look at this approach in detail in chapter 9.)

The key here is to be satisfied—and thankful and affirming and appreciative—about your taking small steps. One easy way to think and act in that way: Consider each small step as the beginning of a long journey that you may never finish but get to start anyway. Or think of each small step as a kind of behavioral seed that you are planting. My own favorite thought pattern: Consider every "ordinary action" as uniquely sacred.

While you are reading, review several "small steps" you have taken in the past year, perhaps ones that blossomed into

◆

A nail is driven out by another nail. Habit is overcome by habit.

Erasmus

entire journeys on which others joined you. Try to remember at what point you were fully satisfied with the size of the step and the first outcomes.

Plan and think with "assets" in mind

You'll hear this plea repeatedly in this book because its opposite—needs-based thinking—is nearly habitual in the minds of too many church leaders and pastors. Even some best attempts at "asset" or "gifts" approaches still look, waddle, swim, and quack like needs-based approaches.

This asset-based approach is sprinkled throughout this book and summarized in chapter 8. At its heart is the assumption that God has endowed you with capacities—assets—by virtue of your genetic and environmental legacy. And that's the place to start your planning and thinking about your work as a congregational leader.

The shortest way to express the matter: Start all your planning and crafting of programs and activities with two questions: "What are you good at?" and "What do you like to do?" The first question unveils assets, and the second calls out your passions or pleasures. Each is framed by the reality that you live for God's purposes, not your own, and that your stewardship of God's will is at the heart of your identity.

Quick, now: What *are* you good at? And what *do* you like to do?

Pastor and ethicist Karen Lebacqz writes about the gift of a slower-paced life. In *Word, Worship, World & Wonder*, she suggests that, in the slowing of our movements through life, we experience *kairos* moments when God's quiet stills our souls, when our senses bring into our inner being more of what God is saying and doing. A slowed pace allows time for thinking, for observing, for humble waiting on God's will.

Slow down and maybe even stop

You knew this was coming sooner or later, right? It's an unavoidable topic, this matter of the speed at which you move through your life. And eventually "slowing down" leads to the question of "stopping."

If you really want to stop trying too hard, you will need to take action of some kind. One of the simplest actions is to change pace, or just stop doing something for a short while.

Let's try this right now. After you read this paragraph, put down this book, go outside, and sit quietly for five minutes. Keep track of what you observe—in nature, among people, inside yourself. At the end of five minutes, come back to this page and write in the margins as much as you remember about the experience.

There is something to be said for doing nothing at times. Philosopher Anthony O'Hear's crisp logic in this matter: "It is one of the great illusions of progressivist thought that there is always something to be done, that there is a solution for every problem that faces us, that we can discover that solution by reason, and that the solution consists in doing something, either politically or individually" (from his book *After Progress: Finding the Old Way Forward*, p. 237).

Redefine and remeasure "success"

Finally, you can begin to calm your expectations if you examine the way you define "success." No matter how many books they sell, and how many thousands of devotees crowd their touring schedules, most success merchants are actually selling the proposition that by your hard work you can achieve phenomenal success, not unlike their own or the people in their strangely similar stories. By their definition, "success" is rooted inside you, and by that definition you are tricked or trapped into becoming the cause of your own effect. Thus you are lured into "trying too hard."

You can re-measure success in a more patient way if you keep in mind both sustainability and legacy-leaving. (See Chapter 7 for more detail about "legacy.") "What will last after I am no longer here?" measures both matters. So does the question, "What flourishes because of my work?" Although you may have to wait for years to hear the answers, by your patience you also measure your willingness to keep at this task.

TRYING TOO HARD
A Checklist for Leaders

Directions: Check the responses that most characterize your ideas about each question. Tally your answers with those of others and see what you can learn from your patterns of response.

Strongly
Agree

Strongly
Disagree

☐	☐	☐	☐	☐	1. Most of the time I enjoy being a leader.
☐	☐	☐	☐	☐	2. I don't ever try too hard as a leader.
☐	☐	☐	☐	☐	3. My work as a leader is meaningful to me.
☐	☐	☐	☐	☐	4. I never think of my work here as futile.
☐	☐	☐	☐	☐	5. I feel like I am supported as a leader.
☐	☐	☐	☐	☐	6. When I lead, others usually follow.
☐	☐	☐	☐	☐	7. My work as a leader is manageable.
☐	☐	☐	☐	☐	8. I am not carrying any program alone.
☐	☐	☐	☐	☐	9. Our pastor is not trying too hard.
☐	☐	☐	☐	☐	10. If I stop leading, others would step in.
☐	☐	☐	☐	☐	11. I feel rewarded for my leadership.
☐	☐	☐	☐	☐	12. I feel competent as a leader.
☐	☐	☐	☐	☐	13. I am accomplishing good things here.
☐	☐	☐	☐	☐	14. I would like to continue doing this work.
☐	☐	☐	☐	☐	15. My work here will continue without me.

Three words or phrases that describe the amount of work I do as a leader:

_____

_____

Using the Checklist "Trying Too Hard"

You can use this checklist as a tool for discussion or sharing in any of the following ways:

❑ Distribute the survey form as preparation for a planning retreat of your church governing board. As a first order of business, tally and interpret the results of the survey. Think together what patterns emerge, and what they say about over-exertion among leaders in your church.

❑ On a chalkboard or newsprint, list all the words and phrases written at the bottom of the survey. Try to group them in rough categories. Examine the kinds of words, the number and emotional freight of the categories. See what they say about "trying too hard" as descriptive of your congregation's core workers.

❑ Distribute the survey forms among all present and former congregational leaders, but ask them to complete the forms anonymously. Collect, tally, and interpret the forms using the suggestions above.

❑ Write and distribute your own survey on this subject, using more specific questions and allowing for a greater range of subjects to be covered—for example, specific congregational programs. One benefit: By writing the survey items with others, you will learn from each other.

❑ Distribute the survey at a congregational gathering, or in a mailing. Using as wide and varied a sample as possible, compare the results of the general membership with those of the leaders. (You can ask "ordinary congregation members" to answer the items "on the basis of what they think congregation leaders might answer.")

PARSING THIS CHAPTER

Spend some time with other leaders or pastors, thinking about and trying out some of the ideas that follow:

1. After reading this chapter, ask yourself how you're going to get yourself and others to be emotionally honest about this phenomenon in your lives.

2. In your journal or in some other way—shared e-mail?—note what you believe are the most memorable ideas in this chapter. Compare your thoughts with the written thoughts of other leaders.

3. Recall the range of emotions you felt as you read the chapter's several sections. How would you characterize each emotion? Taken together, what do they say about you as a leader who may be "trying too hard"?

4. What Scripture verses or stories have come to mind as you've read this chapter? How are you comforted? How are you warned?

5. On the basis of this chapter's contents, what will you add to your prayer requests in the coming days? What will you change? What will you remove?

6. Gather current resources—for example, magazine articles, Web sites—that treat this subject. Talk about what you read or see.

7. Tell each other about one person you've known whose life is an example of quiet, calm, and purposeful activity. What do you admire? What else characterizes this person? What advice would this person give to each of you?

3
SEEING TOO LITTLE

The eternally overexertive Sisyphus had one other problem with the Large Uphill-Bound Rock: He couldn't see around it. Think about it for a minute, imagining yourself in his place: Legs positioned for maximum lifting ability, shoulder and arms struggling to control the rock's movement, neck and face strained against stone, and eyes—well, your eyes would either be downcast or straining to see anything except the rock. Your vision would be limited by your contorted posture and, of course, by the rock itself.

In this chapter, you'll see how "trying too hard" can limit your ability to see things as they really are. I call this problem "seeing too little," a term that describes how futile effort both causes and is caused by limited vision and knowledge. In this chapter, you and I will look at this problem together, and think how you might bend your gaze around the futility you face. To accomplish those goals, we'll consider:

❑ What "reality" is or could be.

❑ The realities your congregation knows and proclaims.

❑ How you might be ignoring what's going on around you.

❑ How you might think about "evil."

❑ Where emotion helps or hinders vision.

❑ Ways your congregation can "get real" again.

What's real about reality?

Although it is sometimes elusive or hard to describe, "reality" is something you probably understand instinctively, because it's a way you:

❑ Establish worth of relationships, things, investment of time, emotion, or money ("You're a real friend!").

❑ Ensure believability or trustworthiness ("She's for real").

❑ Guard against ideas, people or schemes that might be harmful ("That fund-raising program sounds unreal").

❑ Find reasonable ideals in which to place your trust ("Forgiveness is as real as life gets").

❑ Understand success and failure. ("If I hadn't met you, I would have really been washed up as a teacher").

❑ Construct systems of ultimate value or belief ("God reveals reality through God's actions").

Savvy marketers, philosophers, politicians, and ordinary working folk like you understand that whenever you find "what's real," you hold on to it, sell it, proclaim it, or thank God for your discovery.

TOP TEN QUESTIONS TO ASK WHEN YOU'RE TRYING TO "GET REAL"

1. What is that supposed to mean?
2. Could you say that another way?
3. So what?
4. Where's this going to end?
5. How do you know?
6. Where's the value in all of this?
7. If you're right, what else is true?
8. What does God have to say about this?
9. What grabs my soul?
10. What difference will this make?

A real congregation

Because it has been created in the fire of the Holy Spirit and graced with God's own message, your congregation is always real. Not always as institution or cultural construct, but as the body of Christ, an invisible collection of believers, however it is named and however it is gathered.

You may recall, for example, past moments when, together with other believers, you knew intuitively that you were experiencing life in its deepest manifestation, times like these:

❑ Quiet or boisterous moments of spiritual beauty.

❑ Times when the authenticity or authority of your ministry was established.

❏ Moments when your personal witness or caring made a difference.

❏ Situations in which God's power in your life was undeniably present.

❏ Settings in which forgiveness—or grace or integrity—worked!

Because God is the "reality maker," God's own Word creates realities of every kind, even those you may barely understand, know only partially, or rarely talk about. The forgiveness of sins, the power of God's Word to change lives, the victory of Jesus over death, the blessings and gifts of the Holy Spirit—these substantive truths do not originate with you. Instead, by their own authenticity these realities of God make your congregation real. These are the places where "the church" is most effective, most necessary, most welcome in people's lives.

How congregations can ignore reality

You don't purposely try to ignore realities around you, but "seeing too little" can become a normal way of approaching ministry, especially if you're trying too hard. That's when "reality" is primarily the rock and its requirements. It may seem that if you try to peer around the rock, you won't solve the problems right in front of you. So you don't look at much more than your Sisyphean task.

You might also approach this rock-pushing metaphor from the opposite direction, and see how a limited vision of reality can contribute to the torturous quality of overexertion. It may be that "seeing too little" was a major reason why you got into the rock-shifting business in the first place. How does that work? For example, you might work at tasks with a limited view of their eventual cost or benefit. Or you might toil endlessly to fill a need that, on closer examination, actually does not exist in this congregation. You might gather opinions or data from a select group of members, and so work at something important only to that group.

Even the best intentions may not protect you from seeing too little. In your search for and proclamation of God's deepest realities—grace, forgiveness, the gift of God's gathered

Consultant and philosopher Peter Block considers *authenticity* as a core component of "flawless consulting." In his books and seminars by the same name, Block encourages aspiring consultants to "put into words what they are experiencing with a client as they work." Block asserts that authenticity is a key to consultants' success in helping people achieve their goals. You can see the analogy to God's own "authenticity": In Christ Jesus the "words of God" are made authentic for all times, for all situations. In a sense, your authenticity is always derived from God's Word.

If you and I were to speak in *lingua Sisyphea*—the new language we are learning here—we might also wonder whether "seeing too little" causes you to move the wrong rock in the wrong direction on the wrong hill.

people, Word made flesh, the awesomeness of God's own nature—your congregation might still miss some garden-variety realities, such as:

❑ Economic justice for your own staff.

❑ Spiritual growth of all your members.

❑ Your institutional affluenza.

❑ Ignorance about the "ordinary members" who populate pews and programs.

In the next few pages we'll spend some time visiting three groups where you might find "seeing too little" taking place:

❑ Leaders and congregations that still believe that the congregation and its programs are at the center of most members' self-identity or the major focus for their energies and commitment.

❑ Leaders, congregations, or churchly enterprises that issue edicts, discuss with a knowing air, or otherwise communicate supposed life-truths even though they may be ill-informed about these same matters.

❑ Leaders and congregations whose language is less-than-real, consisting mainly of specialized vocabularies from antiquity, platitudes, clichés, or euphemisms.

Let's look at these three matters in detail, recalling how each might show a congregation's incapacity to "see around the rock."

An imagined center of identity

Because you're a leader in your congregation, you may carry within you the imagined idea that this congregation is a primary focus for most members' identity, purpose, or meaning in life. Surrounded by like-minded clergy and laity, you might be blind to the fact that most of your constituency—as many as 80 percent of church members in some formulas—is walking, skipping, and hopping to tunes completely different from the ones you dutifully play or sing.

The 80 percent consider themselves Christians, "religious," or "spiritual," but outside the ways your congregation may measure these matters. They see their identities marked by their careers, families, relationships, hobbies, or other measures of lifestyle. They do not share with you or other congregational leaders any sense that the church should be a central feature of their lives. They do not find great joy in the prospect of learning much more about the language and practices of this congregation, engaging in its priorities, or volunteering their considerable gifts and time to its programs.

You may think of these fellow believers as "dropouts" or "inactives" because of their low participation in your congregation's institutional standards—for example, contributing, communing, worshiping, volunteering. This image creates a considerable problem: Although these standards are necessary for your congregation as an enterprise of human activity, leaders and members can ignore the spiritual activity and engagement of this institutionally invisible group and its faithful witness in Christ's name outside the walls of the church. What is even sadder is the possibility that your congregation is oblivious to the unique ways in which God uses these members for the fulfillment of God's will. This mutual disregard might be a sad reality for your congregation, one way in which you may be "seeing too little" and therefore trying too hard.

> Would you like to answer a really difficult question? Try this one: Name more than five biblical characters who were "good church members," and cite biblical references to support your answer. *Hint:* The concept of "good church member" might have changed between then and now.

Ignoble communications about noble matters

Unless you've been hiding under a rock most of your life, you've probably experienced a humbling moment when you were embarrassed to discover that you didn't really know what you were talking about.

What made the moment painful—as you spotted the knowing, disdainful glance of someone who had expertise in the matter on which you were discoursing—was that you realized in a flash that you had no way of saving face or crawling behind a plausible excuse for your error. Despite all your real or imagined authority, your authenticity among your peers, or your validity as a source of wisdom, you were at that moment reduced to the state of a shamefully naked emperor.

This phenomenon can sometimes be seen in the church's witness within the contemporary culture. Think about the times when a pronouncement from a local or national church

**ONCE AGAIN, BROTHER JENKINS'S RHETORIC
CAME UP SHORT**

leader was sadly inaccurate or hopelessly outdated in terms of current theory or practice. Or recall a time you've been rebuked by a congregation member who possesses a genuinely authoritative voice in the world of science, commerce, or government because you had ignored facts, analyzed a situation simplistically, or demonstrated parochial blindness to differing viewpoints.

These moments of "seeing too little"—and saying too much—create more than embarrassment. They diminish the credibility of your congregation with its members and its surrounding community. Without credibility, you have to work harder to gain trust or authority among knowledgeable members or community residents. "Trying too hard" can occur if you remain ill-informed about the realities of the world in which you live, the world you want to change, or the people you claim to care about.

You may not be able—or choose not to be able—to see beyond your rock. And so, you may operate with old models of:

> You may have seen the same problem in "whole church statements." Here the difficulty lies sometimes within the leaders' own inadequate perceptions of contemporary reality. In other cases, the processes by which "official statements" are researched, negotiated, adjudicated, or disseminated can take so much time that their accuracy is severely compromised by the time the processes are completed. In still other instances, passion for a cause or ideal might limit an objective and fair examination of facts.

❑ Commerce ("Multinational corporations are evil at their core").

❑ Cultural movements ("Men are all basically pigs").

❑ Chemistry ("The atom is the smallest particle of measurable matter").

❑ Physics ("Chaos is bad").

❑ Psychology ("It's good to express anger openly whenever it occurs").

❑ Biology ("The brain is divided into two parts: the left and right").

❑ Systems ("The world can be organized into various discrete systems").

❑ Technology ("Computers are going to solve all of society's important problems").

Leaders who say such things are like adult Christians whose faith development stopped at the time of their confirmation. A sad state of affairs in both cases.

 ## 10 Ways to Keep on Top of "Reality"

1. Ask several trusted friends to breakfast once a week and have them tell you what they've been reading lately in their areas of expertise.

2. Give up reading ecclesiastical publications for one month.

3. Spend one hour a week watching a highly rated television program you find spiritually or morally empty.

4. Eat one meal a week at a truck stop, diner, local bar, or teen club.

5. Visit the Internet site for your county or city government.

6. Check out library books only from the "new nonfiction" shelf.

7. Expand the scope and language of your daily prayers.

8. When you host social gatherings, invite more than the usual congregational insiders.

9. Read the business sections of papers and magazines first.

10. Visit members of your congregation at their places of work or leisure.

Language that's real

Because language patterns mirror thought patterns, any use of language that avoids, masks, or twists reality is a possible sign that the speaker or writer may be trying to influence readers or hearers unduly. When people find that kind of language heading their way, they may react negatively, and unconsciously decide, "I'm not paying attention to you any more!"

Consider how in a nanosecond you can figure out that a speaker or writer is using language in less-than-real ways when you hear:

My current favorite: "intentional." This belaboredadjective is frequently used to add emphasis to a desired or supposed action. ("I want to be intentional about our response to injustice.") But the brain is *never* lacking intent or "motive," because it's always making sense out of inputs and preparing for action. Or, as rhetoricians might say, "All speech is persuasive." (For a fascinating examination of the brain's language functions, see John J. Ratey's *A User's Guide to the Brain*, especially chapter 7, "Language.")

❏ An off-putting, special vocabulary you don't normally use.

❏ "Drama" added to a story that isn't very dramatic.

❏ "Special" attributed to what is actually ordinary.

❏ Rhetorical pushes or pulls that try to persuade you of something about which you don't care to be persuaded.

❏ Questions asked to insert the questioner's opinion into a discussion.

Think how quickly you question the character, motives, or social intelligence of the speaker or writer. From that moment on, the less-than-genuine communicator will have to work much harder to gain and hold your attention or trust.

The same thing may happen in your congregation. When the messages you communicate are couched in inauthentic syntax or vocabulary, attention and trust may erode among members, and you may have to work harder to proclaim the Gospel, to influence people's lives.

One more problem with less-than-authentic language: When you are incapable or unwilling to discern basic inadequacies in your style of communication, you may be exhibiting subtle arrogance to fellow members or to the world outside the church. No one tolerates arrogance for long.

"Arrogance" doesn't mean that I think I'm better than you. It means that I think you don't exist!

Three examples of reality-challenged language follow. Although their use is not confined to the church, you may recognize them as painfully familiar coinages from your own congregation.

Platitudes. Defined as "simple truths too easily derived and too easily expressed," platitudes and their cousins (bromides and clichés) send a clear message: "What you are now hearing or reading may not be true because the person communicating with you doesn't care enough about this matter—or about you—to find exact words or phrases that fit this moment." (Examples: "Don't you worry, honey; your husband's in a better place" or "Stewardship is everything you do after you say you believe.")

Euphemisms. Whether because of partially buried disgust with Anglo-Saxon vulgarities or fear of offending with straightforward expression, the church has long favored "softer/kinder" phrases over blunt talk. This preference seems strange when one considers how the worlds of commerce, politics, and science reward those whose communications are straightforward and easily understood. (Examples: "I can't resonate with what you're saying" instead of "I don't agree with you," or "If life gives you lemons, make lemonade" instead of "Stop whining!")

Specialized vocabulary and verbal constructs. One of the most frequent errors of clergy and lay leaders is the subtle insistence that all those with whom they speak understand the language of the church—their language—above all others. In mainline churches the alphabet soups of judicatories and programs are a good example. In emerging church or metachurch cultures, the specialized vocabularies err on the side of cutesy and trendy. When speakers or writers frequently use code language, they risk leaving behind all but the "insiders."

Why do worn-out language patterns persist in the church? One simple reason: Leaders who use this kind of language are rewarded by those who admire them, by assent and participation in these communication styles. A biological reason: When it attempts to draw meaning from assorted stimuli, the brain searches through familiar neuronal circuits before doing the more challenging work of constructing new patterns. Biologically speaking, well-worn verbal constructs are easier for the brain to find and connect.

The reality of evil

Evil confronts you every day, and presents a foreboding challenge to your relationship with God and with other people. You find evil in your daily work outside the church, and you find evil in your work inside the church as well. Unchecked, unpunished, or unknown, evil can sap your energy, create overexertion in your soul, and shorten the life span of your congregation. As a leader, you soon come to terms with the reality that "besting evil" is part of your work.

Oddly enough, though, you can also "try too hard" in combating evil, and trip over your own best intentions. Let's spend a little time together thinking how that might happen, and how you might better deal with the question of evil. (See chapter 5 for further treatment of this subject.)

Yapping at evil or barking at the moon

As you relate to the world (sometimes automatically assumed to be "evil"), world, your congregation may use language that essentially damns anything *not* connected to the church. You may have experienced this scene firsthand, or seen it on television:

A preacher or teacher gets wound up, spewing the rhetoric of God's holy wrath, adding sarcasm to condemnation to pillorying to verbal pillaging of anything that stands in view. The scene becomes almost primordial as this leader and assenting listeners become a pack of wolves. Together they work up a sweat, verbally circling their prey. They yap, growl, and bark at things much larger than they can understand. After a while, you stop paying attention.

SAFE FROM EVIL, THE RIGHTEOUS FOLKS AT GRIMSLEY MEMORIAL CHURCH TALKED ABOUT THEIR FAVORITE SUBJECT.

When this sequence happens regularly in your congregation, great harm can be done. The long-term sustainability of your congregation might be compromised, or overexertion may be triggered by these possible effects of overactive evil-bashing:

❑ These emotions can attach to other subjects or people, including unintended targets.

❑ You may spend more time than you'd like putting out negative emotional fires that get out of control.

❑ Members and visitors may see your congregation, its leaders, and message as totally out of touch with the good that can also happen in their outside-of-church worlds.

❑ These same individuals might become cynical about your congregation when it limits "what is real or good" to the church itself, rendering the outside world as barely tolerable garbage at best, and "bad and unreal" at worst.

❑ They may drop out of the church—either in spirit or in body—or never visit again.

❑ Members may decide that to remain in your congregation they must check their brains at the door.

❑ You may eventually run out of willingly mindless listeners or adherents.

Besting evil every day

You and your congregation are certainly righteous when you name Evil to its face. But yapping at "the evil world" from behind the safe confines of churchly trappings doesn't strike most members as a complete description of what they see in their daily lives. They know that come Monday morning, they'll be out in the middle of that world, trying to remove Evil's disguises. They'll need their wits about them to outweasel the devil, the world, and even their own sinful selves. Those members who work and prosper out in the world also understand their capabilities in the face of evil. They know that they can:

❑ Bring God's will to bear on the world.

❑ Sometimes win against the evils of that world.

❑ Accomplish good—in small and large sizes—through their work as "insiders" or influential leaders in their daily worlds.

Some Christians hold the view that the best or only way to deal with Evil is to confront it. It is easy to overlook the proposition that "excellence"—in all its forms and expressions—is equally efficient in counteracting the sinfulness of the world. The following story illustrates that possibility.

An advertising executive who is a Christian was able to dissuade her customers from draping scantily clad young women over their products in a blatant use of sexuality for commercial purposes. Her method was *not* to wax eloquent about the evils of sexism or the exploitation of the body's beauty for commercial gain. Instead, the executive carefully detailed a better way to market the products, citing the benefits of approaches more effective than sin-and-skin. Her clients were dissuaded from their amoral approach and agreed to try her more effective method of gathering potential customers for the product.

This Christian outwitted Evil with her excellence. Had she not been truly professional, at the top of her career, or keenly sensitive to the realities of her customers' worlds, she would not have been as effective.

Author and publisher Gregory F. A. Pierce writes in *Spirituality@work: 10 ways to balance your life on-the-job* how "insiders"—those individuals whose excellence and personal power are well-established in their places of work—bring God's will to bear on their enterprises. Precisely because of their understanding of the systems in which they work, these individuals can shape the smallest and largest elements of their workplace. These individuals know their capabilities as "God's insiders" and exercise them regularly.

The reality of emotions and feelings

As you wrestle with the realities of contemporary culture, one of the most important questions you face is this: "What do I really know about emotions?"

The question is important both to the matter of "trying too hard" and to your congregation's sustainability:

❑ Emotions and feelings are primary ingredients in decision making, motivation, or volition.

❑ Your congregation's long-term viability is based on the quality of relationships among your members—which are based, in turn, on the emotional bonds between individuals.

❑ If you do not understand how emotions or feelings operate, you may inadvertently be working against them, or failing to take advantage of their qualities. Both actions are forms of overexertion.

In this section of the chapter we'll see how your congregation may be "seeing too little" about emotions and feelings, and how you correct that lack of vision.

EMOTIONS, FEELINGS, AND ACTIONS

For almost three decades, education professor Robert Sylwester has written about the implications of brain theory and research to the enterprise of classroom teaching and management. In Unconscious Emotions, Conscious Feelings, and Curricular Challenges *(Educational Leadership, Nov. 2000), Sylwester summarizes newer research on emotions and feelings (most notably Antonio Damasio's* The Feeling of What Happens: Body and Emotion in the Making of Consciousness*) and its practical implications. Condensed here, Sylwester's insights may be useful for your congregational leadership as well:*

Emotions are like your brain's unconscious thermostat. Reacting mostly to high-contrast (easily distinguished) information, your basic emotions help you maintain awareness about your physical and psychological environment. (For Damasio, the primary emotions are surprise, happiness, fear, anger, disgust, and sadness, and the secondary social emotions are embarrassment, jealousy, and guilt.) By these unconscious states of mind you tentatively assess the positive or negative realities your senses collect.

When sensory input is sufficient, the metaphorical thermostat triggers awareness of your emotional state regarding danger or opportunity, which you now name as feelings. Feelings allow you to step into the world of consciousness, and you now attend to this awareness by conscious actions. Aware of yourself and your surroundings, you choose how to respond to the environment, protecting yourself or taking advantage of realities around you.

Awareness of emotions and feelings helps determine the quality of your relationships. Because of the size of your cortex, you are capable of remembering the past and imagining the future. Freed from the minimalist emotional prison of knee-jerk decision making, you learn to be socially intelligent, and are able to create and redeem relationships with other people. Thus you can minimize the occurrences of emotional hijackings—for example, instances when emotions take control of your intellect—and broken relationships.

Sylwester suggests that attention to the arts, playful activity, and participatory decision making are necessary to help you grow more aware of your emotions and feelings. Like Daniel Goleman (*Emotional Intelligence*), Sylwester believes that if you remain unaware of how your emotional states contribute to your decision making, you will continually fall back on overexertive philosophies of leadership like "command/control."

The church's feelings about emotion

The church has yet to decide fully on its answer to a simple question first posed in the long-ago history of God's people, rephrased during the time of Christ, and reintroduced at the time of the Reformation: "So what do you Christians think about emotion?"

The answers have been mixed. For some of God's Old Testament people—psalmists, prophets, charismatic leaders—emotional outpourings were basically good. Expressing emotion seems to have been acceptable to Jesus. Paul favored a wary approach to emotions, except for the most noble emotions. With the exception of Luther and a few others, the Protestant Reformers thought well of a style of faith-expression that included their emotions.

In your congregation you may find a difference of opinions about the value of emotions or feelings in your life together. On the one hand, some members may advocate for "more emotion," citing the apparent success of rapidly growing congregations where piety and relationships are accompanied by open and frequent expressions of feelings, especially in worship. On the other hand, some members may more highly value experiences, programs, or messages that are logical, ordered, and circumscribed with procedure and propriety. This understandable ambivalence about emotions and feelings may make it hard for you to decide the place for emotions and feelings in your leadership style.

◆

Come and see the fearsome things our God has done.

Psalm 66:5

Looking at emotions from another angle

Perhaps the question about your reactions to emotion can be rephrased slightly to read, "How are emotions and feelings helpful or harmful to congregations?" Let's think about that matter in the next few pages.

There is no question that unconscious emotions and named feelings are real. Because you are hardwired to be an emotional being, you can't label emotions as innately bad or good. (Their expression may be harmful or helpful, but their existence in your brain is not.) And if you extend that biological truth into the life of your congregation, you cannot name the presence of emotion there as bad or good.

Both body and brain have to work hard to maintain high emotions for more than a few minutes. Continuing emotion taxes the nervous, circulatory, and limbic systems, sometimes to their long-term detriment. Hardwired into the brain, strong emotions enable us to fight and flee, respond to basic instincts and urges, and seek immediate comfort or safety. Once the stimulus has passed, though, the body and brain return to their preferred—and less taxing—states.

Emotions and feelings are helpful and necessary ingredients of your congregation's life. Positive or negative, emotions provide your brain a kind of chemical certainty about the lasting quality of decisions. Whether expressed or not, emotions and feelings help you assess whether foundational elements—trust, appreciation, integrity, love—are present in your congregation. Your congregation's collective emotions help you determine together when danger and opportunity are present among you. When they are understood and fostered, positive emotions forge the relationships that are necessary for motivation, shared decision making, and financial and personal support of the congregation.

The emotional content of experiences brings almost immediate pleasure or pain to the surface, where those two emotions bathe our personalities in joy or sorrow. Emotions and feelings can unite a group of people—at a time of danger, shared experience, or opportunity—and so bring with them the wonderful possibility of a congregation working toward commonly held goals and objectives.

The problems with emotions and feelings come, I think, when we begin to depend on them as *the preferred state of mind* in a program, event, or experience. In this way of thinking, emotions and feelings become the primary litmus test by which you generate ideas. make decisions, or authenticate experiences.

If you depend primarily on emotions or feelings as the primary standard of your congregation's worth, you are relying on their raw and pre-eminent power to attract and hold the attention of the human brain, even if only for an intense and brief period. That might be a problem once the emotions begin to subside.

The same problem exists with "intellect" and its derivatives. When "logical decision making" and "factual analysis" are the preferred methods of approaching any matter in your congregation, necessary emotion can be bottled up or disregarded. As you might imagine, this appeal creates its own kind of futile effort!

Because emotional responses are "the first intelligence" in times of stress—and overexerted congregations live in perpetual stress—emotions are easily aroused and for a period of time supplant the capacity of the brain to process logically or globally. Two emotions—fear and anger—are most easily aroused and most universally recognizable, and can easily become the primary content of the church's message.

"Expressing feelings" can become a kind of addiction, becoming its own reward, its own validation, its own reality. High emotion brings high pleasure to the brain, and so your brain seeks to duplicate the experience, over and over. An increasing cost is exacted for this state of mind: the neuronal superhighways of emotion require increasing amounts of nutrients and electrochemical energy to sustain the emotion. This is why emotion-instilling leaders have to work harder to bring congregants to an emotional peak each time a "highly charged emotional state" is the desired outcome.

Balancing emotion and intellect

You might consider the following items as you try to balance the emotional and intellectual qualities of your congregation's life.

❑ When the level or quality of emotion or intellect begins to define the presumed piety or godliness of a congregation or believer, then emotion or intellect may have moved onto the dangerous theological ground of "self-saving act."

❑ Neither intellectual assent—agreement with tenets of doctrine, Scripture, practice, or beliefs—nor emotional attachment to those tenets is complete by itself. Together, emotion and intellect involve the whole brain.

❑ When it is used to exclude people, truth, or each other, neither emotion nor intellect is true to the wider intent of the Christian gospel.

❑ Whether spiritual leaders manipulate others by emotion or intellect, they are still manipulators.

❑ If you depend on a narrow range of emotions, you are not taking advantage of the motivating, comforting, or uniting qualities of other emotions. You're probably working too hard.

❑ Neither emotion nor intellect can be its own proof. Neither the emotions of Christian piety nor the truths of Christian intellect are sufficient by themselves for nurturing a complete and mature faith.

Additional resources on the subject: Daniel Goleman (*Emotional Intelligence* and *Working with Emotional Intelligence*) popularizes the notion that the physiology of "fear and anger first" is at the heart of much of human behavior. He spotlights practical ways for retraining brains not to rely consistently on these primordial instincts. Rush Dozier, Jr. (*Fear Itself: The Origin and Nature of the Powerful Emotion That Shapes Our Lives and Our World*) takes "fear" apart, anthropologically and biologically, and then suggests how fear pervades the majority of human decisions and interactions. The inquiring reader might also wonder about the biological truth of John's statement, "A real love for others will chase those worries away" (1 John 4:18).

❑ "Boring" can describe a lack of either emotional or intellectual depth. Unchallenged emotionally or intellectually, the meaning-seeking human brain turns its attention elsewhere.

❑ "Immature" can describe a lack of either intellectual or emotional meaning in an experience or individual, because that individual is using only a portion of available brain capacity.

❑ Responses to emotional messages are seen more easily than are the responses to intellectual messages. This observation does not mean that the former are better or worse, just more obvious.

❑ When they are stifled or muffled by your congregation's message or actions, both the emotional and intellectual capacities of the brain will seek new messages or actions elsewhere.

HANDY CHECKLIST
About Emotional Intelligence

Directions: Use this checklist to see what you know about "emotional intelligence." Answers are at the bottom of the checklist.

     T F

1. ☐ ☐   Logic and language are the basic intelligence for all other kinds of intelligence in the brain.

2. ☐ ☐   An "emotional hijacking" happens without our control.

3. ☐ ☐   Our basic emotional intelligence is set by genetic predisposition.

4. ☐ ☐   Once we get past puberty, we cannot change our basic emotional set.

5. ☐ ☐   One hallmark of emotional intelligence is control over anger.

6. ☐ ☐   Emotional intelligence is more about physiology than psychology.

7. ☐ ☐   This congregation does not have a vital role in teaching this kind of intelligence.

8. ☐ ☐   The ability to delay gratification is a predictor of success in later life.

(The matter of "emotional intelligence" is best treated in the book *Working with Emotional Intelligence,* by Daniel Goleman. Another hope-filled source, *Descartes' Error*, by Antonio R. Damasio, calls into question the long-held myth that reason and logic are the basic intelligences of life.)

Answer Key: 1-F, 2-T, 3-T or F, 4-F, 5-T, 6-T, 7-F, 8-T

How your congregation can "get real"

To be effective, your congregation needs to "get real," to recognize the actual dimensions of your context before trying to change them. As you assay the world around you, your congregation might also find God's hand, working and stirring in places the institutional church has not previously been.

Before we get into specifics, let's review some basic principles about "getting real":

❑ Because it is God's own creation, Christ's church has always been real as it proclaims the Gospel in word and deed. The God you serve is as real as Jesus of Nazareth, as earthy as the first human being created by God, and as tangible as every one of the Spirit's gifts.

❑ To find a way out of the problem (of your sometime inability to be real) you can weave together history, the present moment, and a hopeful future. By its nature, reality is anchored in all three: past, present, and future. You engage reality when you avoid fixating on nostalgia and "correcting mistakes."

❑ You can learn about the world around you by taking action. Brain scientists who specialize in the development of learning say that your continuing behaviors—as a leader in your congregation, a parent, or a friend—shape preferred thoughts much more than your continuing thoughts shape your preferred behaviors.

❑ God invites you to engage the world as it is, as well as how God wants it to become. It would be hard to find scriptural evidence for God's intent that the church should be thought of as cultural roadkill or feckless farce. The Spirit didn't flood you with gifts only for them to be rendered useless in the lives of those you love and serve. A flesh-and-blood Jesus didn't envision his followers as incapable of handling reality.

If you're interested in encountering reality full-faced, consider the following behaviors as a guide for that new way of acting.

Volition—how you decide to do what you do—is a complex matter for the brain. The whole front half of the brain is organized for mental and physical action. Brain circuits involved with movement are also related to brain functions such as language, memory, emotion, and learning (from *A User's Guide to the Brain,* by John Ratey, especially chapter 4, "Movement").

Seek places where you're blind to what's happening

The gift of self-perception is something you can receive best in your contact with other people, those who resemble you and those whom you may not yet understand. By engaging them in authentic and affirming conversations, by "drawing outside the nine dots" in your relationships and in your experiences, you can begin to see the realities of God's world more clearly.

❑ Use the "reality check" tool later in this chapter—or one of your own making—to see the areas where you're completely clueless about the movements of God in contemporary society.

❑ Ask people you trust to talk about what's really important in their lives, and note carefully times when your honest response is, "I didn't know that!"

❑ Try one of those current events quizzes in popular magazines or newspapers, and note where you come up short.

❑ Find a teen who's willing to help you learn how you may be ignorant of the transitory world of teenage realities.

❑ Listen to a close friend, spouse or family member when he or she talks about a topic with which you are basically out of touch. Ask what you might do to correct this ignorance.

❑ Analyze your weekly schedule to find the times when you're much too comfortable roaming the same territory, or trapped inside the same small cage inside the same small zoo. Make one small change to find a new place to explore.

❑ In your congregational directory place a check by the names of all individuals or families whom you are avoiding. Make a point to change that behavior.

❑ If you're a pastor, review your sermons for the past six months to find all the times when you've spoken about elements of life about which you knew you had little experience or knowledge.

Any of these activities will give you a start on finding the blind spots or inadequacies in your perceptions of "what's real out there." Pray about this matter, and ask for open eyes, ears, and brain. Ask for forgiveness, too.

◆

The first hint that you may be clueless: always being "busy."

Anonymous office sign

Speak and write plainly

Psycholinguists have for years operated with the counter-intuitive principle "As you speak, so you think." (You may have assumed that thought influences speech and not the other way around.) As you matured from childhood, your patterns of speech gradually shaped the larger patterns of thought that now form the habits that characterize your basic personality. You can change the way you think about reality by speaking or writing plainly, avoiding the language noted earlier in this chapter.

❑ If you're a preacher, start with your sermons. Run your last eight sermons through a computer grammar-checking program, noting especially the analysis of vocabulary grade level. Keep a tally of places where your speech patterns seem to violate the common rules of communication. For example, polysyllabic utterances that you utilize to ingratiate yourself to congregational communicants. *Translation: The big words you use to impress folks.* Look for the times when "in-church only" vocabulary and code words fill the pages of your sermons.

❑ Use a simpler version of the Bible for your own devotional reading. Start with the Contemporary English Version (CEV), authoritatively translated using an approximately third-grade vocabulary.

❑ Ask one or two trusted congregation members to tally words and expressions that you overuse in oral presentations. These worn-out tics may be a sign that you're out of touch with reality, at least for the tic-moment. These trusted listeners can also help you look for platitudes. How fresh are your metaphors? How overused are your adjectives? How tired or passive are your verbs?

❑ If earlier analyses revealed places where you are blind to reality, go to those places—for example members' workplaces or their celebrations—and listen to learn how you could change the way you talk so as to be understood quickly and intuitively.

Try any of these ideas for several months. At the end of that period, ask someone whom you trust to evaluate the

◆

One suggestion with a spark of truth is worth a hundred repititions of sound platitudes.

Liv Binyan,
Argentine revolutionary

ways you have improved the clarity of your written or spoken communication.

Expand your own realities

One way to become aware of life's realities is to leave your crowded box and find some fresher air. The paradox of this behavior: your life gets less complicated because you gain perspective about the priorities for your use of time and talents. As Stephen R. Covey, author of The *Seven Habits of Highly Effective People*, has stated the matter, "[It becomes] easier to say 'No!' when there's a deeper 'Yes!' burning within." New realities breed new possibilities for God's own "Yes!" in your life. You can expand your realities by simple steps such as these:

❑ Add one new journal or magazine to your "must-read" list, and subtract one familiar or comfortable journal.

❑ Visit congregation members in places and at times when they are least in need of your comfort and care. Ask them to talk about subjects in which they are most expert.

❑ For a few weeks, listen to a different radio station.

❑ Listen to cassette tapes of books during your "drive time."

❑ Identify a few congregation members who are "trend-tellers"—people whose professional or personal lives put them in touch with current cultural phenomena. Trade these folk a breakfast for a conversation about what's on their minds these days.

❑ Read the editorial pages of your newspaper.

❑ Ask several members who are well regarded in the community to bring you important articles from newsletters, trade journals, Web pages, or memos they have read—items that encapsulate what's happening outside the perimeter of your property.

Whatever you do to widen your horizons, be careful to maintain an open attitude. Balance that spirit with your ability to discern wisdom from stupidity, fact from fiction, single opinion from widely held view.

Audit your congregation's behaviors

An audit is a marvelous thing, a work of science and still a piece of art! You can think about an audit as:

❑ An organized way to determine if everything is in its place.

❑ A way to answer the question "Are things actually the way we say they are?"

❑ A time to recount and recategorize for efficiency.

You can benefit by putting your congregation or yourself through some "reality audits" such as the following:

The child's view. Use a wheelchair to see your church property from the vantage point of a child's height. Tally answers to these questions:

❑ What lines of sight are impossible for people shorter than 48 inches?

❑ Which parts of congregational life are not really intended for children?

❑ Where could children be overlooked?

❑ Where are children's comfort and safety compromised?

The "manly man's" realities. Sometimes congregations elevate certain kinds of masculine behavior and quietly disregard others. (The "manly man" is a term for the kind of guy whose work and hobbies are stereotypically masculine, perhaps excessively so.)

❑ Tally the occasions in congregational life when physical labor or work is subtly demeaned, when you make few references to sports-related activity, or fail to affirm nonintellectual achievements in the world.

❑ Notice the ways in which you or other leaders subtly discriminate against people who are less highly educated or less "correct" in every way.

❑ Search your congregation's soul for your prejudices against men who are strong, strong-willed, or strong-smelling!

The "working woman's" realities. Another group easily overlooked—and sometimes consigned to wandering from group to group within your congregation—are the "less-than-idealized" women who are subtly disregarded for their incapacity to achieve society's ideals of "the perfect mother" or "the well-balanced woman." You might check your awareness of these women's lives by trying any of these activities:

❑ Have breakfast or lunch with a group of working women and talk about something other than "how you balance work and personal life."

❑ Check your congregation's women's group membership, to see if some women are subtly excluded by virtue of education, work, the behavior of their children, or other prejudices. Start a new group that welcomes these women.

❑ Audit your congregation's messages about women, looking for ways in which women are patronized by paternalism, idealized, or otherwise locked into role expectations difficult for most of them to achieve. (For example, how do your messages depend on the assumption that wives *and* husbands belong to your congregation together?) Make changes as needed.

People you're afraid of. Whether you find it easy or hard to admit, one reality you face is that there are people of whom you are afraid in your congregation and in the world outside your church. Whether for real or imagined reasons, you find yourself avoiding these people, and eliminate any possibility of learning from and about them. Think who these people might be, and consider one or more of the following actions:

❑ Listen carefully to the arguments and objections of seeming curmudgeons, with this filter: "What compels them to speak this way? What positive outcomes do they hope for?" Let them know what you discover.

❑ Think about how many elderly members you know well. If the number is low, consider how you might be afraid of some life quality among members in their 70s and 80s that quietly threatens or frightens you. Resolve to visit an older congregation member this week.

❑ For one week, tally the kinds of people you could but do not encounter. Pray about this matter, and then pick one person to phone with a word of encouragement, a question that requires the member's wisdom or advice, or a word of gratitude for his or her work or life. Next week telephone another person on your list; keep at the task until the list disappears.

❑ Spend time at a bus station, train stop, coffee shop, or public safety facility. Volunteer for some task, strike up a conversation, or ask the workers about the people you meet there.

Experts' eyes. Most congregations are home for "experts" of many kinds. These are people whose reputation, skill, education, or role is significant in the worlds outside the church. Their acknowledged leadership may be local, regional, national or international. Their expertise may transcend the realities of most people around them, at least in the areas of life in which they are truly expert. You can audit your congregation's connection to these people by engaging in these actions:

❑ Construct a simple survey that asks members to rate their expertise or level of knowledge on scientific, cultural, artistic, economic, or governmental matters. Include other areas of expertise as well, such as acknowledged or respected life- or job-related skills, life experiences, or other valuable personal excellences. Think of seldom noticed expertise, such as hobbies, collections, skills in coping under difficult circumstances, management, or human care. Count the occasions when congregational activities honor these experts.

❑ Ask these experts to recount ways in which the congregation benefits them. Ask them to tell you how they are honored, how they feel included, how the congregation understands their expertise, how you could work together on something truly significant or challenging.

❑ Invite these experts to tell you how the congregation's leaders and programs miss their worlds, undershoot their commitment to excellence, or miss the point.

◆

Excellence is to do a common thing in an uncommon way.

Booker T. Washingon

❑ Consider how these experts could renew your congregation's vitality if they were asked the right questions and affirmed for the right reasons.

❑ Repent of your own hyperinflated claim to knowledge or your uninformed opinions.

❑ Thank God for the gift of these experts.

Sisyphus redux

If you were to visit Sisyphus during a brief break from boulder-hoisting, and if you were to ask him what "seeing too little" had to do with "trying too hard," you might have a conversation something like the following:

SISYPHUS: *(surprised to see you again)* So, partner, what brings you to these parts?

YOU: *(in the spirit of the moment)* Well, hombre, I just wanted to ask one more question, about overexertion.

SISYPHUS: *(being a modest congregational leader)* Me? Why would you want to talk to just an ordinary person like me?

YOU: *(ignoring his modesty)* Look, I just wanted to know if you saw any connection between the fact you're working way too hard and seeing way too little.

SISYPHUS: *(momentarily stroking chin and assuming pose of Rodin's* The Thinker*)* Yes, I do, and I think I could describe it this way: If you see too little, you don't know enough to "work smart," and so you're always trying too hard.

YOU: *(not quite believing the simple explanation)* That's it? That's the connection?

SISYPHUS: *(not quite believing you don't get it)* You thought there was more to it? You want this to be complicated?

YOU: *(realizing you're making a very strong person a little angry)* Well, I . . . .

SISYPHUS: *(quickly blurting out more words)* Try this: "Trying too hard" is not about *how much* you know—you'll have to read the next chapter in this guy's book to find out about that. Trying too hard is about *the way* you know. *(Points at large boulder that is his life's work)* See that rock? That's "trying too hard," and it keeps me from

EXPERTS UNDER YOUR OWN NOSE

Just for fun—or perhaps out of necessity—see how many genuine experts are already part of your congregation. Use the additional spaces here to make your own categories. When you've checked all the categories of experts in your congregation, decide what you're going to do about all these gifts!

- Someone who has raised more than four children
- A person whose poetry has been published
- A scientist doing medical research
- A farmer whose farm attracts public attention for its excellence
- A well-known storyteller
- A present or former teacher or school principal
- Someone whose skill or hobby takes her or him out of town from time to time
- New members who are rumored to be "good at something"
- A musician whom people pay to hear
- Someone significantly featured in a local newspaper
- An acknowledged scholar (Don't forget children and youth.)
- Someone who's won an award and had it presented in a ceremony
- A person who can fix just about anything
- The most quietly powerful person in the community
- A company owner or CEO
- A person whom most kids in town know and admire
- An adult, teenager or child who is excellent at playing a sport or a musical instrument, or who engages in activities such as photography, chess, debate, interior decoration, or art
- A retail clerk, bank teller, postal worker, food server, governmental employee, or other person who serves the public with graciousness and efficiency
- An adult, teen, or child who is a good friend to less popular children
- _____
- _____

seeing anything else. And because I can't see anything else, I keep trying too hard. Do you get my gist? Do you see my problem? Do you know who I am? Can you even begin to . . . .

YOU: *(thinking maybe it's time for old Sisy to get back to work and you to move on to the next chapter)* Well, yes, I think I can feel your pain, but . . . .

SISYPHUS: *(heading toward rock and the resumption of his work)* No, you don't. How could you know unless you've walked a mile with my rock? *(Heading back up the hill)* Look, you're keeping me from my futile work, and I'm keeping you from your reading. Let's say good-bye for now, and let's talk another time, OK?

YOU: *(waving good-bye as Sisyphus grunts and groans his way back to work)* Thanks for sharing! "It's not about how much I know but the *way* I know . . ." What a fascinating idea. I can hardly wait to read ahead.

(The scene ends with you heading into the sunset, ready for the next chapter.)

Using "The Reality Check"

The last two pages of this chapter present a reproducible "reality check," a survey tool that you can use to understand the worlds around you. After you've established the answers that are correct for your specific setting—for example see item 15—use this checklist in any of these ways:

❑ Decide with other leaders what survey respondents' scores say about their perceptions of outside-the-church realities.

❑ Add items to the checklist to adapt it to your community or locale.

❑ Compare scores among congregational groups (leaders, staff, newer members, and so forth).

❑ Plan programs that deal with the realities your congregation members don't already understand.

❑ Identify members who are deeply knowledgeable about the realities of contemporary society. Use their wisdom carefully.

❑ Interject the survey into the curriculum of a Bible-study group, sermon-preparation team, or small support group.

❑ Use the survey as part of an annual stewardship or funding campaign.

❑ Use wall, display, or bulletin board space as a place to educate congregation members about the community.

◆

Faith is like radar that sees through the fog—the reality of things at a distance that the human eye cannot see.

Corrie Ten Boom

THE REALITY CHECK

This checklist will help you find out how much you know about the "realities" outside our congregation. This survey can also assist our congregation to respond to all the things God is doing in the world. The answers will be scored by a group of congregational leaders. Thanks for your participation in this effort!

Directions: Check the box that most closely matches your knowledge of each item. If you have no knowledge of an item, check the box "Am Not Familiar." Check the "Am Familiar" box if you have at least a passing knowledge of the topic. Fill in blanks with the currently accurate name, idea, person, title, date, amount, or location.

Am Familiar	Am Not Familiar	
☐	☐	1. The name of a band composed of local high school students _____
☐	☐	2. The approximate size of the county budget_____
☐	☐	3. The name of the state senator for this district _____
☐	☐	4. The number of teen gangs in the area _____
☐	☐	5. The name of the person who delivers newspapers in my neighborhood _____
☐	☐	6. The location of the nearest landfill _____
☐	☐	7. The date of the next local or state election _____
☐	☐	8. The leader of a local service club _____
☐	☐	9. The local service clubs that are still active _____
☐	☐	10. The name of the leader of a local boys' or girls' group _____
☐	☐	11. A denominational leader who has roots in this area _____
☐	☐	12. The most popular book section in the local library _____
☐	☐	13. The most popular television show among all ages currently is _____
☐	☐	14. Where youth are likely to be found on a Saturday night during the school year _____
☐	☐	15. The cost of a hamburger, fries, and soft drink at a local fast-food restaurant $_____
☐	☐	16. The approximate cost (tuition, room and board) for one academic year at the nearest college or university $_____
☐	☐	17. The location of the next scheduled parade in town _____

Am Familiar	**Am Not Familiar**	
☐	☐	18. The names of members of your police or fire protection force, including administrators _____
☐	☐	19. The location of the closest homeless shelter or food cupboard _____
☐	☐	20. The maximum monthly unemployment insurance allotment _____
☐	☐	21. The name of the largest employer in this town or county _____
☐	☐	22. The location of the nearest water purification or sewage treatment faciity _____
☐	☐	23. The method by which you first apply for Social Security benefits _____
☐	☐	24. The average annual family income for the neighborhood around our church $_____
☐	☐	25. The racial mix of residents in the neighborhood around our church _____
☐	☐	26. The most famous citizen of this town or locale _____
☐	☐	27. The location of the next Winter Olympics _____
☐	☐	28. The most important item on the agenda of the current (or next) session of Congress _____
☐	☐	29. The name of a product or service that is manufactured or headquartered here _____
☐	☐	30. The best thing that ever happened to this town (area) _____
☐	☐	31. _____
☐	☐	32. _____
☐	☐	33. _____
☐	☐	34. _____
☐	☐	35. _____

Your comments: _____

_____

Scoring

Number of "Am Familiar" boxes checked: _____
Number of "Am Not Familiar" boxes checked: _____
Number of correctly completed items: _____

PARSING THIS CHAPTER

You can take apart and reassemble the meaning of this chapter for your own life by trying out some of these ideas and activities.

1. Philosophers and theologians have a wonderful time considering the question of "reality." How do you identify "what's real"? Where do you get confused or disheartened?

2. Talk about a time when you thought you knew what was true, right, or good, but had your mind or heart changed by another person or an experience. Where do you think God was in this situation?

3. React to the statement "This congregation does better when we don't worry about what's real."

4. For one week, pay close attention only to other people. The following week, pay close attention only to the realities you experience in news, television, the Web, and other information-providing mechanisms of contemporary culture. Compare your two weeks' experiences and talk about how they affected your own sense of identity or life purpose.

5. What proposition in this chapter was the most difficult to accept as true for your congregation? Which was most hopeful?

6. Discuss this idea: This congregation is the place where we come to get away from the world's realities; this is where we see Jesus, not the world.

4

KNOWING TOO MUCH

How would you feel if I told you that you may "know too much"? Insulted, right? Maybe you'd feel hurt, or you'd wonder how I got to be so arrogant so early in life. Or you might even be angry enough to want to break off our relationship.

But that's just what I'm going to suggest in this chapter, and I hope that by the chapter's end you'll react with some understanding of the real problems you and your congregation might face when you try to know too much.

In the previous chapter, you saw how "seeing too little" can be part of trying too hard: If you don't see what's really happening around you, you're likely to live a life of overexertion. This chapter looks at the backside of this matter, "trying to know too much." Social scientists have called this phenomenon "information overload." It's a problem that runs through the lives of individuals and congregations, threatening to bury them in data. It's another variation of "trying too hard."

In this chapter, we'll consider the following matters:

❑ What it means to "know too much"

❑ How knowing too much is trying too hard

❑ Where "the information culture" might lead

❑ "Information toxicity" in congregations

❑ How to assess information overload

❑ How to reduce the glut of information

❑ How your yearnings match your capabilities

What it means to "know too much"

If "seeing too little" is a condition of uninformed leaders, then "knowing too much" is a state of mind among overinformed leaders. It's certainly not good for you to be unaware of what's happening around you, but it's also harmful for you to be constantly aware of what's happening around you.

Information overload exposed

What we're talking about here is "information overload," which is known by other names as well. Architect Richard Saul Wurman writes about "information anxiety," a vaguely fearful attitude about the information that bombards you almost constantly. "Toxic information" implies actual harm to your brain and to your enterprises from receiving information in amounts or at speeds beyond the brain's ability to process, store, and use data. *Data Smog*, media scholar David Shenk's stinging rebuke of a "culture of information," describes the overflowing information as a polluting blight. "Information glut" adds a sense of vulgar excess to the supposedly benign notion of "too much information."

By whatever term it's called, this condition of contemporary society may be readily apparent in your own life. How can you tell? Think honestly about how well you monitor and limit the amount of information you encounter each day. Think how your frustration grows when it feels as though everyone and everything around you is trying

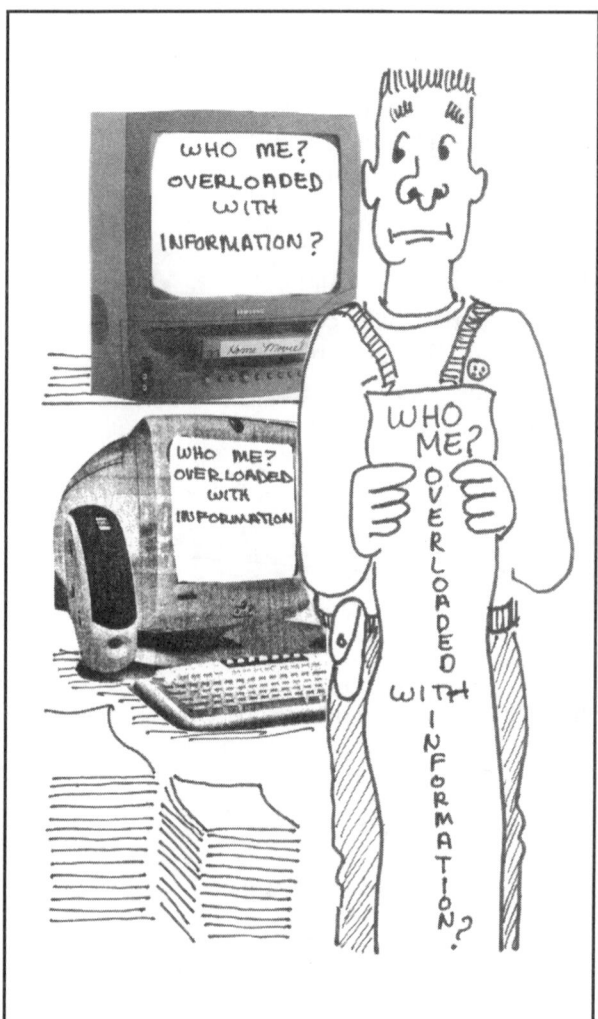

INFORMATION OVERLOAD CHECKLIST

Directions: Complete each of the items here as accurately and quickly as possible. Remember: Other information is waiting!

1. The average amount of junk mail you receive each day, *and* the amount you actually open
   _____ / _____ pieces

2. How much time you spend in essentially nonproductive Web surfing _____ hours per week

3. Your honest answer to the question, "Why is it, really, that you're 'so busy'?"
   _____

4. Your expectations—in your job or even in your relationships—about how quickly you will read and answer e-mail _____

5. How much television you watch (essentially alone) in an average week _____ hours

6. The purpose and duration of most cell-phone calls you receive or initiate
   _____

7. The number of magazines, journals, and newspapers you never quite finish reading each month _____

8. The average number of silly mistakes you make while trying to deal with "too much work" (read "too much information") per week _____

9. The number of times in the last week when you had trouble recalling a simple or familiar detail _____

10. How often you "multitask" during supposed moments of quiet or relaxed personal time (e.g., checking voice mail while brushing your teeth) _____ times per day

11. The amount of anger or energy involved in your reactions to phone solicitations _____ kilowatts

12. The places in your life where you participate as a willing "walking advertisement" (Hint: Check your "branded" clothing.) _____

Scoring: If you took more than five minutes to complete this checklist, you may not be working fast enough to survive in this information age. If, while completing this checklist, your blood pressure increased by more than 20 points, you may be overloaded with information. If you stopped reading the checklist or these scoring directions about halfway through, you may already understand the problem and how to solve it!

to get your attention. Or dig deep into your soul to see how often you wish for more quiet time, more time to read the Bible, more time to pray.

Let's switch roles and put you in the driver's seat for information production and distribution. Think how fervently you want to communicate with those around you, how often and at what length. How long are your memos or letters? What tricks or methods do you use to capture the attention of willing or unwilling listeners or readers?

Somewhere between those two positions—information receiver or sender—is another: information encourager. Think how you readily accept the presence of advertising. Recall the ways in which you allow telephone solicitors, e-mail joke senders, or denominational officials to barrage you with unwanted information. Think how dutifully you embrace the proposition that "information is power, and those who have more information have more power."

Unless you are reading this book from the deck of a raft moored off the shore of an unnamed lake where you have lived alone for the past three years, you are most likely a victim, enabler, and creator of information overload. If you're a participant in this information-oriented society, you're part of information overload.

I'd love to meet the folk whose job it was to produce all the legally required "privacy notices" I've received in recent months. By my last count, more than 20 fine financial institutions invaded my privacy with their lengthy assurances of all the steps they would be taking to protect me from information pirates. Most of them also included "just a few extra thoughts," presumably also for my benefit.

Information overload criticized

Critics of the "information revolution" include theologians, social scientists, educators, philosophers, brain scientists, and information technologists. Those who warn about the effects of technology-enhanced information-spewing avoid neo-Luddite behaviors—"Let's all throw our computers out the window and go back to writing with sticks in the dirt." Instead, these modern-day prophets encourage "technorealism"—for example, how we can realistically moderate technology's harmful effects. The first step: asking us to be aware of what our technologies are doing to us.

I want to do the same for you. I will ask how too much information might cause you to work too hard as a leader, diminishing the prospect for the long-term viability of your congregation's godly enterprise. I hope the questions don't overwhelm you.

Information overload analyzed

Let's take apart the idea of information overload and see how its dynamics relate to each other. This emerging branch of social science is based on the following premises:

There are limits. The human brain limits the amount of information it will process, and how quickly that will take place. Human organizations react to information in the same way. Personal or organizational "memory loss" may be evidence that brains or enterprises are handling more data than they can adequately process or recall. Richard Saul Wurman, in his *Information Anxiety 2*, calls this "overload amnesia."

Excess information is useless. Once the brain reaches its physical capacity to receive or process information, it begins sloughing off the additional information, treating it like background noise. Dispensed at increasing speeds and volume, information begins to clog both new and traditional delivery methods. (For example, both bandwidth and "guaranteed overnight delivery" are regularly overwhelmed.)

Attention is limited. Now "supply and demand" dynamics begin operating in this matter. Information overload creates its own cycle of inattention and attention-seeking.

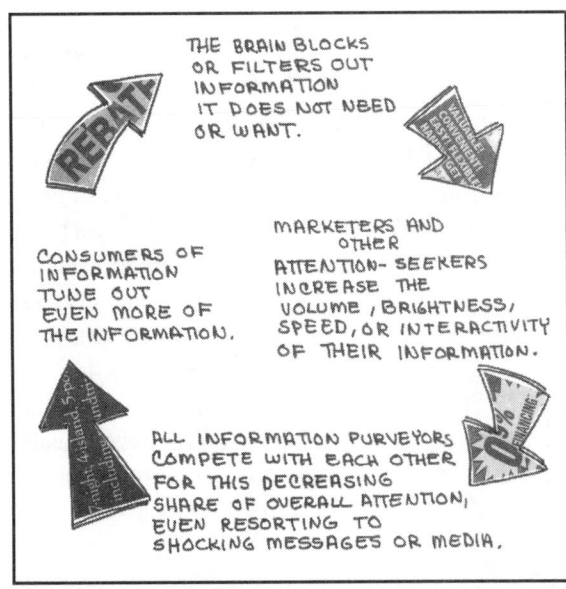

THE BRAIN BLOCKS OR FILTERS OUT INFORMATION IT DOES NOT NEED OR WANT.

MARKETERS AND OTHER ATTENTION- SEEKERS INCREASE THE VOLUME, BRIGHTNESS, SPEED, OR INTERACTIVITY OF THEIR INFORMATION.

CONSUMERS OF INFORMATION TUNE OUT EVEN MORE OF THE INFORMATION.

ALL INFORMATION PURVEYORS COMPETE WITH EACH OTHER FOR THIS DECREASING SHARE OF OVERALL ATTENTION, EVEN RESORTING TO SHOCKING MESSAGES OR MEDIA.

(Based on the essay "The Mother of All Howard Sterns," in *The End of Patience: Cautionary Notes on the Information Revolution*, by David Shenk.)

Stress has increased. By its overabundance, information crowds out other necessary elements for a pleasurable existence. The so-called information revolution has increased individual and societal stress and stress-related disease. The speed by which information is available also speeds up our expectations about how quickly this information will be useful. Impatience increases.

Brewster Kahle, architect of the Internet Archive that hopes to save lost or shut-down Web pages, estimates the average Web page life span at about 75 days. The Internet Archive presently consists of 8 terabytes (8 trillion bytes) of data. This project echoes (and dwarfs) H. G. Wells's 1937 proposal for a "world brain," a permanent world encyclopedia that would provide for "the intellectual unification" of humankind.

The quality of information decreases. Much of the "information" we are subjected to lacks intrinsic value or lasting quality. (The banner headline on my Web server at this moment announces, "Verdict Just In: Lopez and Pitt Have Best Bodies.") Advertisements and the Web work best as temporary conveniences.

Information is not value-neutral. The notions that "information is power" and "information is knowledge" are both false. The first proposition is false because the unmanageable volume and complexity of available information diminishes any possibility of "control"; the second is false when streams of information are not adequately integrated into larger constructs of meaning.

Attention is now a commodity. The control of information has shifted from institutions and bureaucracies to individuals and corporations. "Pay attention" now has a double meaning.

In *Blur: The Speed of Change in a Connected Economy*, consultants and futurists Christopher Meyer and Stan Davis suggest that attention is the primary commodity in an economy in which boundaries are blurred beyond recognition. Other intangible elements of a faster economy include services, information, emotions, intellectual capital, relational capital and organizational capital.

Information becomes complex. If you step back and look at the entire picture, you see that information sources tend to increase in complexity. It becomes harder, not easier, to find useful, relevant information. We may be running out of ways to keep things simple. "The Strong Law of Small Numbers" states that there are "not enough small numbers to meet the many demands made of them." We are running out of unique telephone area code prefixes, Internet domain names, short names for new medicines, titles, icons, and acronyms. (Richard K. Guy, "The Strong Law of Small Numbers," *American Mathematical Monthly* 95 (1988): 697-712, as recounted in James Gleick, *Faster: The Acceleration of Just About Everything*.)

In most descriptions of information overload, authors and social critics contend that what we are losing, individually and as a society, may be of greater value than what we think we have gained through information-dispensing technologies. The questions about information overload grow more universal and more insistent. Their answers may determine our future.

Presently, over 20,000 distinct Web sites address the subject of information overload. Ironically, they also contribute to the problem they name.

How knowing too much is trying too hard

"Knowing too much" is a variant of "trying too hard." The sheer volume of information seems to require you to respond immediately and continually. Contemporary methods of information delivery are exquisitely capable of bringing information to you in ways and in places where it is difficult to ignore. Therefore, if you attempt to "keep up with" the information available to your senses, you must work harder and harder to receive, store, and process the increasing volume of data.

Earlier in this chapter, I alluded to a second way in which information overload and "trying too hard" are related: what your brain does when the amount of information knocking at its door exceeds the brain's capacities. What happens? The brain relegates the information to "noise," and thereby eliminates the problem by not paying further attention. If your brain is on the receiving end, the process requires work because you're always operating at capacity. (To say it another way, even ignoring information is work!) If you are on the information-sending end, a nearly perverse irony prevails: Once receivers' brains stop paying attention to your information, you have to try harder and harder to get their attention.

Overexertion and information overload are related in some other ways as well, among them the following:

❑ "Stress" is another way of describing "brains working at capacity." Stressed brains are not smart brains, and so information overload requires you—and others working with you—to work harder to make wise and workable decisions.

❑ Time is finite. When you attempt to process ever-increasing volumes of information, at whatever speed, you push aside or compress the time you would have given to other activities. Either of those choices is hard work. For example, what qualities of life or necessary tasks get swept aside or accomplished too quickly in order for you to surf the Web or read your e-mail at work?

❑ Because there is so much of it, and it is so easily available, information seems to be more important for decision making than intuition or emotion. Your important decisions wait for more information, and decision making becomes tedious and drawn-out.

❑ Information (raw data) gets confused with knowledge (filtered and interpreted information). When you are overloaded with information and wearied by it, you may be content just to present accumulated data, passing it off as meaningful or important. Decisions based on that kind of "knowledge" often require that programs, services, or products be retooled, revised, or revisited. Extra work, hard work!

❑ The fundamental proposition of the information age is that you must know much more than you know now if you are to survive and prosper. If you accept the premise, you spend a great deal of time scurrying around, making up for what you perceive to be "an information deficit" in your life. You also spend large amounts of time learning how to use the just-updated information tools you have been told are "absolutely necessary."

One note: "information" is not the problem. (I am not suggesting that you "see too little," or I would have to rework the information in the previous chapter.) The matter of "knowing too much" has to do with the amount and speed of information and your false expectation that you can or should receive, process, and use most of it.

In *The Social Life of Information*, information scientists John Seely Brown and Paul Duguid write, "Attending too closely to information overlooks the social context that helps people understand what that information might mean and why it matters" (p. 5). My added comment: Any time you ignore social context, you are doomed to work too hard.

Where the "information culture" might lead

For social scientists, futurists, brain researchers and other observers of the human condition, the increasing pace of information overload creates short- and long-term problems. In their view, the effects of technology-inspired information overload may include the following:

❑ **Growing anxiety.** Generalized anxieties may increase in the general population, as human ambition collides with the limits of human capacity. At its basic level, "anxiety"—from a Greek word that means "to strangle"—is fear of the future.

Stress reduction will increase as an important pharmaceutical goal and a multibillion-dollar enterprise.

❑ **Increasing hysteria.** The occurrence and intensity of generalized hysteria may increase. Information-overloaded stock markets and information-empty urban myths illustrate the phenomenon of ready hysteria, albeit at opposite ends of the spectrum.

❑ **Collapsing economies.** The "information economy" may collapse when biologically necessitated inattention and "noise filtering" increase resistance to information. It is not difficult to envision a time in which too many information sellers will be chasing too few information buyers. We may already be there.

❑ **Multiplying mistakes.** We may see increased stress and resultant dysfunction in institutions. If "stress makes us stupid," it stands to reason that information-overloaded individuals and institutions are more prone to make mistakes in judgment or intent. Multiplied on the order of millions of flawed decisions each day, the costs of information overload to human enterprise are staggering.

❑ **Decreasing community.** A spirit of "community" may decrease as individualism increases. When anxious and stressed, humans tend to draw into themselves as a way of protecting or avoiding stressors. (In an ironic twist, even other people may be seen as threatening or avoidable.) The eventual effects of individualism can only be guessed at, but few of them are pleasant or hopeful.

In his brilliantly researched work *Bowling Alone: The Collapse and Revival of American Community,* sociologist Robert Putnam overwhelmingly illustrates how, since the mid-1960s, American culture has tended toward individualism in every element of life. He charts behaviors as simple as backyard-fence conversations and as complex as volunteerism. Putnam's conclusions are seemingly irrefutable, if only by the sheer volume of his citations. Among the possible causes: increased television viewing.

❑ **Blurring categories.** As noninformation and misinformation increase, it may be increasingly difficult to sort fact from fiction, news from entertainment, entertainment from advertising, or truth-tellers from truth-hiders. "Infotainment" and "infomercials" are easy examples of blurred information streams. One easy reaction of the human spirit is to ignore all claims of objective truth. This is now considered a bedrock premise of "postmodern thought."

❑ **Widening conformity.** In an age of increasing confusion about information and decreasing ability to sort it into meaningful constructs, conformity—to one's peers, to advertisers' branding, to exotic, erratic, or enigmatic leaders—

may offer a seemingly hopeful option. Nonconformity, creativity. and criticism may be considered "noisy nuisances." Neofascist movements may thus be popularized by their quick and powerful capability to order reality (knowledge) and settle confusions about meaning and purpose.

❏ **Deepening spirituality.** The information-sorting capabilities of religion may make churches especially valuable to the general society. Unfortunately, the most manipulative and coercive religious enterprises and leaders claim to offer the greatest help for finding the truth in the middle of information overload. Still, "providing purpose and meaning for life" remains one of the greatest benefits that congregations offer their members.

Science author Rush Dozier, in *Fear Itself: The Origin and Nature of the Powerful Emotion That Shapes Our Lives and Our World*, suggests that "by providing insights into the purpose and meaning of life, religion gives us a sense of control over the fear of death and the unknown" (p. 129). Because fear of death is the primary fear, the value of religion remains high.

❏ **Decreasing wisdom.** As I noted earlier, "knowledge" and "wisdom" may be in short supply, since both require prolonged time and uncluttered brain space. In a society overloaded with information, simple "remembering" may become a highly valuable skill.

❏ **Disappearing data.** To increase the speed at which we receive and process information, data disseminators will cram increasingly smaller bits of information into smaller windows of attention. This will decrease the amount of actual information available to observers or consumers. (For example, have you noticed the decreasing time given to "sound bites" in political rhetoric on television news?)

❏ **Diminishing effort.** As information whirls around us, individually and collectively, and as our anxiety about "keeping up" grows, we may eventually give up trying to keep pace. (This might explain the alarming lack of knowledge so often seen nowadays in general surveys about current events, geography, or politics.) "Too much information" may result in "too little knowledge."

❏ **Clustering power.** Information purveyors may grow more cynical in their approaches, playing on easily aroused emotions—fear and anger are the most basic and universal—or combining into large monopolies the means by which information is generated and disseminated.

❏ **Growing appreciation.** Those who sort or otherwise order information may be considered more valuable than those who generate the information. Advertising copy increasingly touts the worth of products or services that help sort financial and medical information. Some dot.com companies are built on the premise that they make it easier to engage in information-laden tasks such as choosing the right book, finding friends, or shopping for groceries.

❑ **Deepening yearnings.** Deeper yearnings for meaning, connectivity, and intimacy are becoming evident. The ubiquitous cell phone, used mainly in individualized and isolated situations, may be emblematic of these yearnings. According to James Gleick (*Faster: The Acceleration of Just About Everything*), cell-phone use may indicate how deeply people yearn to be connected. By their cell phone use, he suggests, "people may be checking on their existence."

Among the hopeful conclusions presented in futurists William Strauss and Neil Howe's *The Fourth Turning: An American Prophecy* is the idea that cross-generational learning and influence will increase as the world approaches a period of economic calamity. Wisdom and knowledge will be preserved as grandparents and grandchildren engage each other in mutual appreciation.

The future of the world's economy and other cultural constructs is, of course, in God's knowing hands. If social scientists and futurists are correct, the church-as-institution may be God's partner in shaping that future in a hopeful way.

"Information toxicity" in congregations

Your congregation cannot sustain itself if any kind of toxicity saps its vitality. Information overload and its connecting anxieties may be good examples of life-diminishing toxicity. In this section we examine the question of how information overload may exhibit itself in your congregation or in your leadership as a potentially lethal force.

The place to start

Where to begin? With the people you serve. As you plan and engage in activities based on your shared sense of mission, keep the following ideas in mind:

❑ By virtue of their participation in contemporary culture, the people you serve are most likely afflicted with some form of information overload. Examples: hurried children, their taxi-driver parents, and "retired" people who are busier now than when they were working.

❑ A significant percentage of people in your congregation may be "techno-junkies," whose toys include marvelous "time-savers" that require more and more time for their use or maintenance.

❑ As they participate in your congregation, individuals behave and think no differently from the way they behave or think in other spheres of involvement.

❑ With few exceptions, those who participate in your congregation's mission are giving their most precious gift: their attention. Their contributions of time and money follow naturally.

❑ In these times, neither loyalty nor duty is strong or prevalent enough to motivate the majority of members to engage in the congregation's work.

❑ Your congregation may be an unwitting part of the information-overload problem. It will take all of your wits to be part of the solution.

❑ Through your congregation, God offers a message of good news for harried and hurried people. You already have the capacity to ameliorate information anxiety for the people you serve.

What you might see in your congregation

Because information anxiety already exists in people's lives, they will bring to your congregation virtually every element of this toxicity. You will do the same as a leader. Therefore, you might expect to find these phenomena in your congregation:

❑ Most people ignore, filter out, or forget most information they receive from the congregation or from you.

❑ You experience a decrease in ready participation in congregational programs, events, or other activities, across all age and income groups, but especially among younger, more affluent generations.

❑ You see decreasing knowledge (and wisdom?) about religious or doctrinal matters. This state of affairs is sometimes described as "biblical illiteracy," and its critics usually suggest some "new" variety of information overloading as a corrective.

❑ You carry with you the vague sense that the decisions you make with others—especially those made quickly, under duress, or with some anxiety or fear—are really not all that wise.

❑ With other leaders, you find yourself harboring the gnawing suspicion that you are overlooking, or giving minimal attention, to what really matters—long-term or basic fundamentals like trust among members, understanding of each other's daily lives, and having fun together.

Your logical reactions

Because you don't know how information overload is affecting anyone beyond you and your congregation, you may begin to believe that it is somehow caused by something you are doing (or not doing). Most likely this is not true, but you can't shake the possibility that you're at fault. Like any other leaders who want or need their constituents' attention, you may react in any of the following ways:

❑ You increase the frequency, intensity, or volume of information you send members. For example, your newsletter now moves to an 8½ x 11-inch size, and your "announcements time" before worship frequently takes up to 10 minutes.

❑ You find yourself irked at "inactive members" who don't attend congregational events, and you find your frustration leaking into the information you generate and disseminate.

❑ You push harder to persuade people to "volunteer," using techniques that resemble "the hard sell."

❑ You make sure all information (about events, programs, ideas) reaches members "at least seven different ways."

❏ You use sermons as a subtle device to feature or foster congregational activities, programs, or mission.

❏ You set up telephone trees, "circles of caring," or other mechanisms by which "everyone will be kept informed of what's going on at the church."

❏ In an attempt to "involve everyone in decision-making," you inform all members, usually through mailings, of each step along the way of an important decision. Although desirable from the viewpoint of collegiality, this information may be unwanted or unneeded and may therefore be ignored.

❏ You decide to be "clever" with information presentation, spending time and money on enhanced computer capabilities, humorous skits, or improved presentation technologies.

In each of these cases, you are succumbing to the notion that "more communication" will enable information to reach members more easily, or that its increased frequency and volume will somehow assure some receptivity and an attendant response. You may instead be adding to the "noise" in members' lives, and becoming increasingly susceptible to their filtering out the information you so dearly hope will grab their attention. Unless somehow ameliorated, this cycle will repeat itself, requiring increased energy and creating greater frustration.

Assessing information overload

Before you rush to judgment—"Alas, this Great Affliction hath visited our house; we are worms and thus doomed"— you might assess the extent to which information overload may be overwhelming your congregation. Use any of the following questions or tasks to begin the process.

Conversing

Select a small group of members—for their honesty, connections with others, or critical judgment—and ask them questions such as:

❑ How much of our newsletter do you actually read?

❑ What elements of this congregation's life are you unsure about? Which would you like to learn more about?

❑ When do you feel "put upon" by the information you get from this congregation?

❑ What/whom have you stopped paying attention to?

Make sure to allow enough time for each conversation so that you thoroughly understand the information you receive. Consider having the conversations somewhere besides the church facilities.

Observing

You can learn about people's thoughts by looking at their actions and the artifacts that come from those behaviors. You might:

❑ Watch how quickly worshipers read (or ignore) bulletin inserts or items in the pew racks.

❑ See how many members consistently arrive for worship *after* your standard pre-service announcements.

❑ Look at people's behaviors as they enter and exit the church buildings. What information do they pause to read?

❑ Station yourself by an information-dispensing place such as a "tract rack" or "information table." Notice what is taken or read. How would you characterize the conversations that take place about the materials?

❑ During times of fellowship or light conversation, see who talks with whom. Watch for folk who are ignored or who avoid conversations. These two behaviors might tell you which members are most likely to spread information informally, and which members are least likely to receive information in this way.

◆

You can observe a lot just by watching.

Yogi Berra

Counting

"Assessment" is a kind of counting, and you can easily count behaviors that might suggest information overload.

❑ Include simple response surveys in several newsletters. Count the responses you receive as a measure of attention.

❑ Spend some time counting *all* the members, of any age, who participate *in any way* in the congregation. (These individuals are less likely to need formal and repetitive information.)

❑ Count the "information purveyors" in your congregation, individuals who consistently originate or disseminate information. How diverse is that group? How well respected? How skilled?

❑ Tally the mailings (including e-mail) members receive in a month. See how that number has increased or decreased over the past year.

❑ Pick any congregational activity (for example, the end-of-summer picnic) and see how many times the same information about that activity is presented to members.

❑ Count the average number of words in each article of your newsletter. To see patterns, keep track of verbiage—sentence length, vocabulary level, and so forth—for about four months.

◆

*Where is the wisdom
we have lost
in knowledge?
Where is the knowledge
we have lost
in information?*

T. S. Eliot

Looking more closely

Sometimes the smallest matter can reveal the most significant truth. To see information overload in its slightest manifestations, you might observe:

❑ How many members wear pagers as part of their daily work or life.

❑ How many "hits" you get on your congregation's Web site, or some other measure of its usefulness.

What a Web-Site "Hit" Tells You

The World Wide Web provides the best examples of minimalist information, and the "hit" symbolizes what happens when data masquerades as knowledge.

The "hit" is one of the Web's supposed measures of utility or worth. At face value, it makes sense: If a user clicks on your Web page, you have the user's attention. But experience and consistent data suggest something else: The average time spent on a page is measured in precious few seconds, even milliseconds in some cases. (One urban myth tells of high school students being paid to click on selected Web sites repeatedly to artificially inflate the supposed interest the site generated.) Actually, clicking on a site (one hit) may be the electronic equivalent of leafing rapidly through a book.

Measuring the worth of a Web site by the number of recorded hits may be analogous to measuring the quality of readers' interaction with a book by how quickly they flip through the pages. (And calling these fleeting moments of attention "visits" is analogous to categorizing a waving hand as a meaningful social call.)

This near-puffery raises a difficult question: How else might you determine the quality of attention a Web-surfing visitor gives to your site? An even more difficult question: How does your Web page justify its cost in time and money besides numbers of hits and visits?

❑ How quickly Internet-wired members respond to e-mail originating from your congregation.

❑ The number and type of books, videos, tapes, and journals checked out of your congregational library.

❑ How many children or teens regularly carry cell phones.

❑ How long it takes to schedule the next meeting date at the end of a committee meeting.

Surveying

Although they raise the critical question, "Aren't you making the problem worse?" surveys can help you assess how information overload might affect your congregation. A sample reproducible survey—in bulletin insert format—is included here for your use.

You might use other kinds of "surveys" as well:

❑ In a sermon that relates to contemporary life, ask for a show of hands in response to questions like "How many of you use your cell phone more than five times a day?" or "How many of you have taken your names off junk-mail or phone-solicitation lists?" This survey method is informal, but it gives you a general picture of the worshiping congregation's encounters with information overload.

❑ Use a bulletin board as a survey response tool: Frame a simple question on the bulletin board—for example, "How frequently do you read our church newsletter?" Provide note cards, markers, and thumbtacks or stickpins for respondents to use in answering the survey.

❑ As a warm-up activity during fellowship time, do a quick "values voting" exercise, using a line on the floor—for example, a rope or masking tape. Ask participants to stand along the line—a kind of continuum of responses between two poles of opinion—at the place that most closely characterizes their response to questions such as: When you think about the information you receive each day, do you get too much or too little? Are you an information junkie or an information avoider? How much do you know about (our denomination, this congregation's mission)? Which would you rather have, more time or more money? Which most describes the pace of your life, "hurried" or "slow"? If we sent you information about this church's activities, how many times would you like to be reminded?

Decluttering the physical landscape

Walk around your congregation's facilities, looking for places where information assails the senses. The questions to ask yourself:

❑ How much information is competing simultaneously for the attention of the viewer?

❑ Whose best interests does the information serve?

❑ How might it be made more visually appealing?

SURVEY:
How Much Information Do You Want?

Directions: We want to know how information about this church affects your life. Complete as many of the following items as possible, and return this survey as directed or to the church office. ("5" indicates "Strongly agree" and "1" means "Strongly disagree.")

5 4 3 2 1

☐ ☐ ☐ ☐ ☐   1. I enjoy whatever information the congregation sends.

☐ ☐ ☐ ☐ ☐   2. I understand most of what I hear or read.

☐ ☐ ☐ ☐ ☐   3. In my life, I am basically in charge of what information I choose to pay attention to.

☐ ☐ ☐ ☐ ☐   4. I know how to use most information technology effectively.

☐ ☐ ☐ ☐ ☐   5. I feel overwhelmed by the amount of information that comes to me every day.

☐ ☐ ☐ ☐ ☐   6. I use the Web only when necessary.

☐ ☐ ☐ ☐ ☐   7. I know enough about this church.

☐ ☐ ☐ ☐ ☐   8. The church newsletter is valuable to me.

☐ ☐ ☐ ☐ ☐   9. I welcome "announcements" as part of the worship experience.

☐ ☐ ☐ ☐ ☐   10. I ignore lots of the information that comes my way each day.

☐ ☐ ☐ ☐ ☐   11. I ignore lots of the information that comes from the church.

☐ ☐ ☐ ☐ ☐   12. I would pay more attention to church information if I received it only once.

How I like to receive information:

_____

Visit these places in your church, asking these questions or undertaking these tasks:

Pew racks. How many items do you think people will actually read or use during worship? After these items have been in the rack for a few weeks or months, how eye-pleasing are they?

Worship bulletin inserts. Which inserts are really nothing more than ecclesiastical junk mail or advertising? Check the pews and wastebaskets after worship to see how many inserts have been discarded immediately.

Bulletin boards. How much information does any one bulletin board (or display area) present to the passersby? How much time do you expect viewers to spend at the bulletin board? How attractive is it?

The entryways or narthex. Count how many congregational or denomination events, functions, or programs you are trying to push onto people. On several Sundays, watch entering and departing worshipers to see how much time, if any, they spend glancing at or otherwise paying attention to tables, standing easels, short videos, displays, leaflet/tract racks, or booths.

Signage. How redundant are your signs? How many styles and sizes are used? (Contrary to the mantras of some church-growth formulas, there *can* be too many signs, and they can communicate the subtly off-putting message that this congregation is trying too hard to get or hold your attention.)

Banners and thematic decorations. How do they enhance the visual beauty of a space? Where do they distract the viewers' eyes from the sweep of architecture, lines of sight, or a sense of "sacred space"?

Examining use of time

Excessive information can rob meaning from otherwise enjoyable times. The following examples might help you understand where information overloading occurs:

Quick "meetings." Some leaders use pre- or postworship time to conduct short "meetings" instead of participating in the fellowship of the moment. This may seem an efficient use of time, but it can also contribute to the deterioration of your congregation's hospitality to visitors and new members.

"Just a few announcements." Among the most toxic elements of information-floods are the announcements given before, during, or after a time of worship, learning, or fellowship. The spirit of the moment—joy, quiet need, anxiety, prayerful devotion in God's presence—is destroyed by spoken words of information, usually duplicating what is already provided in a bulletin or program. The message is implicit: These bits of information and those who wish to share it with you are more important than your own needs.

◆

Don't worry about tomorrow. It will take care of itself. You have enough to worry about today.

Jesus

Reducing the glut of information

Has all this information about information overload convinced you of the problem? Have these pages helped you see yourself working too hard to push information to resistant congregation members? Did you find yourself described in some of the futile behaviors I've outlined? Are you more aware how "more information" can result in "less attention," and how that's a prime example of "trying too hard"? Do you have any questions that I haven't already anticipated? Are you getting tired of my curious probings here? Good! It's time to look at correcting these problems.

Back in the early years of the environmental movement, the aphorism "The solution to pollution is dilution" summarized a universal truth: If something harms you, avoid it, change it or get rid of it. The same may be true of the surfeit of information that hangs on you like excess weight. "Dilution" means either weakening or reducing the problematic substance—in this case, information. Therefore, the solution to information pollution is to weaken or reduce its presence. You are the only one who can regulate the amount and speed of information that washes through your own life.

Likewise, you may be the only leader who decides to stop overwhelming your congregation with information. These broad ideas and specific actions may help you do that.

Install and use filters

One way to reduce the volume or speed of information is to use "filters" that keep the amount or kinds of information to a manageable level.

Filters can be of any size or shape. They can be made of a variety of materials. They can take advantage of a variety of physical and chemical realities. They can be easily installed or embedded inside an organism, process, machine, or enterprise. Because there are many kinds of filters, each can regulate the flow of specific materials.

Filters do important work:

❑ They keep out what can't be used at the moment, or what might be harmful.

❑ They let through what is most necessary or vital.

❑ When they are well maintained, filters work with nearly automatic ease.

❑ Part of the maintenance of filters includes emptying and discarding what the filter collects.

"Information filters" work in the same way. Once you've found them, you can use information filters to keep to a minimum the information that is not relevant to what your congregation is doing. You can maintain these filters by first recognizing their existence, and by making sure you discard what they winnow out.

Some possible filters—or filtering mechanisms—in your congregation might include the following:

❑ **Funding.** Information overloading costs money (for equipment, supplies, staff time).

❑ **Efficiency.** The "cost/benefit" ratio applies to information as well, based on this question: "What will we gain and what will we lose if we choose to add this information [technology] to our work?"

❑ **No-nonsense members.** The members whose straightforward approach to everything cuts right through euphemisms and frilly-edged "visions" can help you filter

Psychological, moral, and ethical filters help diminish information overload. "Technology has given me the power to create the life I want for myself. And what I've got to do now is disengage from certain behavioral programs that are in place in my own brain, like 'Earn as much money as you can,' 'Get as much work as the world will give you.' The bad thing is when people feel compelled, like they have to know things." (telephone conversation with Douglas Rushkoff, author of *Ecstasy Club*, *Playing the Future*, and *Media Circus*, recounted by David Shenk in his critique of the "information culture," *The End of Patience*).

out unwanted or overextended streams of information. (Hint: Don't overlook "inactive members," children or youth.)

❑ **Goal-oriented time-management systems.** You and your pastor might benefit from using a time-management system that always connects life mission and roles with what matters most.

❑ **Insistence on fundamentals.** One of the best filters: your insistence that all information helps sustain your congregation. The building blocks for sustainability include intangible elements like good will, collegiality, trust, hope, optimism, commitment, and joy. How information builds these qualities of life in your congregation may be the most important filtering question.

The "First Things First" (now "What Matters Most") seminars and writings of the Covey Leadership Center (Steven R. Covey, A. Roger Merrill, Rebecca R. Merrill, et al.) suggest that much of the information anxiety we experience comes when our present activities are disconnected from our overall life goals. The Franklin-Covey systems of habituated time management insist on establishing this connection, affording adherents the satisfaction of goal-directed living.

Engage in creative ignorance and inattention

You can diminish information overload by encouraging and practicing a kind of caring and creative inattention to information. ("Caring" and "creative" are important, because they guard against arrogant indifference.) You might find some of the following "purposeful ignoring" helpful.

❑ For part of every day, live inside an "information-free zone" by turning off televisions, cell phones, beepers, radios, and e-mail/Web-based communication; by not taking telephone calls; and by staying away from magazines, newspapers, professional journals, and denominational mailings. Instead use the time to develop or strengthen one relationship.

❑ Keep your information technology at a manageable minimum. These toys have value, certainly, but their costs—in dollars, and in the time it takes to learn how to use them and manage their glitches—may far exceed their benefits.

❑ Cancel all subscriptions and remove your name from all mailing lists—including e-mail groups—whose information is available elsewhere, not often helpful, or too time-consuming to process.

❑ Whittle down your e-mail correspondence list to about five of your closest friends (or whatever number of friends you could reasonably and pleasurably manage if they were close at hand).

❑ Take the necessary steps to remove your name from all junk mailing lists.

❑ Each time a telephone solicitor calls, ask the caller to remove your name and number from the company's list.

❑ Evaluate the content of the newsletters, announcements, magazines, and mailings you receive from your denomination, association, or local judicatory. Where possible, ask that your name be removed from optional mailings.

❑ Do the same with all "friends" who graciously forward e-mail jokes, conspiracy theories, and news-crumbs to you and scores of others. (Option: Find new friends without this penchant.)

❑ Learn to value being "the last to know." Relish the freedom from responsibilities you do not need to assume because you are not the first to know. Think about the joy you can give others who have a zest to tell what they know. Think of this role as a "ministry of receptivity."

❑ Inventory your daily schedule to see what information is necessary and what information is noise. For example, is it necessity or "noise" to watch and read "news" several times the same day? Guard the necessary, and shut off the noise.

❑ Talk with other leaders and members who purposefully limit the level of information they pay attention to; ask them for other suggestions.

Simplify information

Every good writer collects and organizes large amounts of information into logical trains of thought. The "good writer" is made an excellent writer by an excellent editor. (The editor excises unnecessary verbiage and eliminates confusion.) An excellent writer and editor garner readers' attention because of a good designer. (The designer's work attracts readers' eyes to the page, so that the reader can make quick decisions about where to go and what to do.) Writer, editor, and designer have the same goal in mind: simplifying information for the benefit of the reader.

◆

Everybody gets so much information all day long that they lose their common sense.

Gertrude Stein

As you examine how to diminish the glut of information that weighs down your congregation, consider how you might "write, edit, or design" in some of the following ways:

❑ Try to eliminate redundant information streams. For example, consider asking members *not* to follow along visually while a Bible selection is read aloud. (They might just close their eyes and listen with imagination!) When you lead people through an activity, give instructions only once, after you have informed people that this will now be your preferred style.

❑ Use the simplest technology possible. This may mean newsprint or the spoken word; it may also mean a succinct PowerPoint presentation. ("Bells and whistles" may communicate more about the presenter than about the message.)

❑ Where possible, "visualize" information. You can accomplish this literally by using charts, drawings, or flow charts, and metaphorically by inviting the imagination of listeners or viewers. (Hint: "Eye candy" attracts only the eye, detracts from information, and may communicate to viewers only your deep need for their attention.)

❑ Check sentence length, vocabulary levels, and syntactical complexities that diminish the effect of your writing. (Use your computer's grammar-checking function to practice on the previous sentence.)

❑ Rely on conversation as your primary medium for information spreading. It builds relationships, communicates emotion as well as information, establishes trustworthiness, and is relatively low-cost.

Pleasurable conversation may also bring physiological benefits to the brain. Seratonin levels increase, calmness is restored, the healing effects of laughter are made possible. This most basic human activity gives great pleasure to brains.

❑ Add interactivity to your writing and oral communications. For example, when presenting information as a printed conversation, use a "dialogue with the reader" style of writing, and ask for comments and questions (and provide easy access for commentators and questioners). If the presentation is oral, schedule as much time for group questions and discussion as you do for your presentation.

❑ Use "silence" as a part of your communication. Silence allows time for respondents to work through information before encountering new information. Visual "silence"—that is, white space on a printed page—provides the same opportunity for the eye.

❑ In spoken and written communication, provide "path markers"—a verbal or visual progress report—so that listeners and readers understand where this information fits, where the thoughts will lead, and where they have been. (Another way to think of these thought-markers: as informational equivalents to "YOU ARE HERE" signs in shopping malls.)

Your yearnings match your capabilities

Before you close the pages of this chapter and try to digest what you've read, permit me these personal observations, which may help you make sense of this chapter:

❑ Don't wait to do something. Reducing the glut of information does not require extensive planning. You can begin to diminish your information overload anxieties by the simplest actions, most of which include the words OFF or NO. Any step you take will predispose your brain to take further steps, and increase your resolve to diminish the effects of information overload in your life and that of your congregation.

◆

Intuition becomes increasingly valuable in the new information society precisely because there is so much data.

John Naisbitt

❑ Find someone who agrees with you. Although you may think that information overload is a problem "for other people," it may be harder to admit your own addiction to information, its technologies, and the speed at which the "new" runs through your brain. To sidestep this dulling disregard, find one other person whose yearning to combat information overload matches your own. Start with conversation; then move to one shared action. That may be enough to start a continuing process.

❑ Remember that you are never alone. As you begin this work of deconstructing the elements of your own Babel story, you will find solace in God's presence. As you pray, read the Scriptures, and meditate, you will find the Spirit of God there beside you. The voice and touch of God's hand will calm and encourage you.

PARSING THIS CHAPTER

Use the following questions and tasks to cement the content of this chapter into your thinking and acting. A hint: Consider these matters in the company of other believers.

1. How severely does information overload affect your daily life?

2. Which elements of this chapter increased your anxiety about the world? About your congregation?

3. Where did you find encouragement or comfort?

4. Tell a story about a time when you avoided information anxiety.

5. What do you think is at the heart of our society's desire to "know more and more"? Give reasons for your answer.

6. Read a Sunday newspaper, especially the advertisements, to see the degree to which "information" and "information technologies" are being pushed at you.

7. How does your understanding of God's nature inform your views of information overload?

8. How is your relationship with God affected by the "information culture"?

Part 2
WHAT'S AT THE HEART?

Now that you understand the fundamental problem with "trying too hard," it's time for us to move into the second section of this book. In the next three chapters we'll back up a bit and examine some practical and philosophical basics that are necessary for resolving overexertion in your congregation.

In this section you'll find:

- Support for the proposition that "the world" is a good place for God to operate, a good source for God's working wisdom.

- Ideas about "what pastors are for."

- Strong encouragement to value your legacy as a leader.

In these chapters we'll talk more about you. Our conversation will get a bit more personal, and perhaps more insistent. But if you're going to stop trying too hard, that kind of conversation is necessary.

5

FINDING WHAT'S GOOD

You probably don't believe this, but Sisyphus' cousin was Don Quixote, a noted church leader in the Middle Ages. (You don't believe it because it isn't true. You must admit, though, that this sentence makes a good grabber for the opening of a chapter.) To recap your memories of Cervantes' classic novel, let me characterize the story: Don Quixote dreams admirably impossible dreams, but his daily adventures seem to circle back to his belief that his life purpose is battling evil. Whether windmills, knights, royalty, or common folk, Quixote's protagonists are defined by his imagination that they are dangerous or evil, and therefore problematic for an ideal world.

The expression "tilting at windmills"—engaging in a medieval jousting match with an inanimate object—symbolizes Quixote's futile conflicts with "evil" that does not exist.

If Don Quixote and his squire Sancho Panza had been church leaders—OK, OK, I made that part up—they could easily have been described as people "working too hard." The nature of their overexertion: overimagining the presence of evil and being blind to the possibility of good. Instead of fanciful "adventures," however, they would have been engaged in a futile existence fueled by admirable-but-mistaken intentions. Something Quixote would have learned from his cousin. . . .

In this chapter we'll examine the "evil world and good world" propositions a little more closely, focusing on two major premises:

❏ The distinction between "sacred" and "secular" may inhibit congregational sustainability.

❏ God works well in the worlds outside the institutional church.

My invitation to you: Stop your work for a few hours. Dismount from your trusty steed, take off your well-worn psychological armor, and settle into this chapter. I hope you'll find in its pages what's good for you.

"Sacred" and "secular"

The first idea we need to examine is the continuing distinction God's people have made between "sacred"—pertaining to God—and anything else, which we will call "secular," less for historical accuracy than for economy of understanding. We'll look at what some people describe as the "dangerous world," in the light of Scripture and the church's usual understandings. Then we'll circle back to Scriptures' oldest wisdom: God has embedded good in that supposedly dangerous world.

> In the history of this false dichotomy, "secular" has collected other synonyms, including "profane" (literally, "outside the temple"), "worldly," and "temporal." You will easily notice how each term carries a subtle negativity about anything other than "sacred," which seems to allow the easy next step: labeling anything "not sacred" as "evil."

It's not safe out there

The history of the people of God, including their gathering for worship or service as "institutionalized church," has always included the setting apart of God's people. This stream of thought finds its source in the idea—perhaps even the fear—that the world is just too dangerous for spiritual health.

You can easily spot this theme in Old Testament stories, personalities, and writings:

> "Sacred as dangerous" runs throughout the premonarchical period of Judaism, but seems to diminish as the Temple cult develops. Old Testament scholar Richard D. Nelson (*Raising Up a Faithful Priest: Community and Priesthood in Biblical Theology*) says that because of their position, priests "insulated worshippers from direct contact with sacred space and holy things, yet priests also provided the connections that brought divinity near and made life with Yahweh possible" (p. 85). For an example of this role being carried out, see Numbers 16:46-48.

❑ The nearly cryptic story fragment in pre-Deluge Genesis 6:1-5, where the corruption of humans is somehow contrasted with the righteousness of the Nephilim (heroic figures descended from the marriage of angels and beautiful human women).

❑ Abram's rejection of and removal from Ur, in response to God's call or in reaction to the pantheism of that society.

❑ The Wisdom literature of the Hebrew Scriptures.

❑ The concept that the early priests' roles were as much about the awesome power of God as they were about sin forgiven or Law interpreted.

❑ Prophetic insistence that "obedience to God"—including cultural purity embodied in the law—sets God's people apart from all surrounding nations and peoples.

❑ The emergence of the Chassidiim—literally "the pious ones"—during the Babylonian captivity, whose synagogues and personal lifestyles preserved not only ritual and Law, but the cultural constructs (for example, the Hebrew language) that supported faithful living in a hostile world.

❑ The possibility that much of the Old Testament was written in the context of the continual struggle between prophets and priests, each group having its own viewpoint about how separated-out God's people should be.

The "dangerous world" theme continued into the time of Jesus and the establishment of the New Testament church. You can find evidence of this stream of thought in places such as:

❑ Three of the four branches of Judaism at the time of Jesus—Zealots, Essenes, and Pharisees (who were the cultural descendants of the Chassidim)—believed that separatism was essential to faithful piety in the face of the Roman occupation.

❑ Jesus' own life and preaching about "the world," at least at first glance, seem to suggest a near-asceticism. For example, in Matthew 20:25ff, see his comparison between the way "rulers of the world" treat their subjects with the servanthood of his own followers.

❑ Transformed Pharisee Saul/Paul consistently writes about "the world" in terms that echo his spiritual forebears and the Old Testament prophets. (Romans 12:2, for example, exhorts against conformity with the people of the world. The first chapters of 1 Corinthians are equally specific.)

❑ The writings of James, Peter, and John are especially insistent that the people of that time—"the world" and its people—are at war with God's intended purposes. (1 Peter 4:3ff contrasts believers' former lifestyle with their now-faithful living; James 4:4 warns that "love of the world" is the same as "being God's enemies;" and John insists that "the rest of the world is under the power of the Devil" [1 John 5:19b].)

Several Greek words can be translated as "the world." In Pauline literature, for example, "world" might include *kosmos* ("world," used 47 times); *aiòn* ("age," especially "this age," used 31 times); *ge* ("earth" or "land," used 14 times); and *oikoumene* ("inhabited world," used once). The first caution about "evil world" readings: Look for accurate translation, especially in older scholarship.

In summary, this theme—the world is a dangerous place—carries its weight throughout the Scriptures, for a variety of purposes. That theme was important for the establishment and sustainability of "the church," which we will examine next.

How the church understood the problem

The church didn't form as an identifiable human institution until centuries after God's first revelations and actions among human beings. Eventually, God's people assembled into the Old Testament temple cult, a "national church" of sorts. The temple's rituals and relationship to the government helped establish a sustainable identity, as God's chosen people, that included purity-by-separation. Later, that purity was broken by the apostasy of polytheism and the commingling of Canaanite influences with the Law's requirements. The punishments of the Assyrian and Babylonian captivities seemed to prove the point: God's people must separate themselves from the world, for their own good and because Yawheh requires it.

In captivity, the faithful formed faith-sustaining synagogues, and garnered identity and purpose from their removal from the world. The Torah's codes—at least for the Pharisees—favored "purity" over "justice" and resulted in avoidance of what was unclean or profane. The nation's viability was thought to be dependent on obedience to this interpretation of the Law.

◆

No problem can be solved from the same level of conciousness that created it.

Albert Einstein

The New Testament church soon moved in the same direction, especially after the first blush of quick emotions at Pentecost. Although the Jewish understanding of ritual purity was put into disarray by the Jerusalem Council, Paul and the apostles still had to remind their followers that to be part of this new church, they must forsake what was worldly and evil. Congregations needed to be held together, believers matured, dangers avoided. To sustain these new enterprises, believers avoided the dissembling influences of the sometimes barely civil first-century world.

During the 200 years after the establishment of the church (and well before the "conversion" of Constantine), the church-as-institution faced another question: How could the church stave off the onslaught of misshapen doctrine and practice that came from rapid growth? Possible pollution threatened the message of Christ and the apostles. Part of the answer: professionalized clergy, whose training and set-apartness would equip them especially well to be preservers and sustainers of the Gospel and of the institutions that proclaimed it. Constantine's nationalizing of the Christian faith sealed the matter into Roman law.

"The matter" now became the distinction between "lay" and "clergy." By the time of Constantine, "lay" denoted wildly secularized (or barely tamed former pagan) Christians—a threat to the stability of the church-as-institution. "Clergy" had come to characterize people who were more responsible for what was truly sacred. In a convenient dualism, Constantine saw himself as the highest authority in affairs of the world and the pope as the highest authority in matters of the spiritual realm.

By the Middle Ages, the church had established clearly the distinction between temporal and eternal, sacred and profane, the church and the world—and had developed a complex system of governance by which to ensure what was most desired: the sustainability of the institutions of church and state. In the minds of church leaders, both were the province of the church; in the minds of political leaders, the matter was a little more complex.

> The second chapter of Roman Catholic scholar Russell Shaw's *To Hunt, To Shoot, To Entertain: Clericalism and the Catholic Laity* summarizes the history of clericalism, including the notion that its beginnings were benign. My take on the matter: Church leaders feared that "sustainability" was not possible unless a professional clergy ensured it. (As to "clericalism," we'll explore that in depth in chapter 6.)

The problem with this "problem"

As Cousin Quixote demonstrates, demonizing "the world"—one way to describe avoidance of spiritually dangerous influences—is not a complete or useful description of God's view of the world. "The problem of the world" may itself become a problem, creating nonsustainability and overexertion in the following ways.

Limiting God's intent

In the beginning of time, God's creative intent was that creation, including its creatures, would be good. God's original intent continues to this age. Without papering over the existence and power of evil in the world—and inside the human spirit—you can shortchange God's intent for the world and its eventual course when you concentrate too heavily on the matter of the "evil world," especially as the major focus for your life as a Christian. God certainly asks you to pray and work for deliverance from evil and strength under temptation. But God's entire nature cannot be narrowed to "the jealous God who visits iniquities."

If you paint God primarily in dark and somber tones as "punisher of evil," God remains only watchful and vengeful. If you worry only about "what would Jesus do?"—would he wear expensive jewelry with that question emblazoned on it?—you might not see Jesus as Savior but only as accuser. If you view God only as evil-hater, you focus only on God's demands and miss the gifts.

Your admirable intent for godly living can be worn down by a too-strong emphasis on God's work as judge. God's grace can be trumped by your worries about evil. Preoccupation with God's wrath over your sinfulness results in overexertion because you're responding only to one part of God's intent and God's nature. (Seeing only one element of God's nature is "seeing too little," which we examined in chapter 3.) Working too hard to "please God," you eventually run out of gas. And when most congregational leaders think this way, your entire congregation might end up trying too hard.

Underestimating God's power

You might also increase your workload by minimizing the power God exerts. God battles evil in powerful ways, but you might not know when or how God is victorious.

◆

Real love isn't our love for God, but God's love for us.

St. John

Martin Luther's life can be described as an attempt to deal with that matter. As characterized by Luther biographer Heiko Augustinus Obermann (*Luther: Man Between God and the Devil*), Luther lived in tension between the power of God and the reality of evil in the world. More than a superstitious medievalist, Luther wrestled with matters of "power" as he saw them in Scripture and the political developments of his own time.

For Luther, God's power was all-encompassing, moving not only within the realm of spiritual matters (the church and its work) but also in the wider realm of the world. Thus, all that exists is part of God's realm. God continues to create, Jesus the Christ is eminent evidence of God's love for the world, and the stuff of creation—however ordinary it may be—is the stuff by which God accomplishes the divine will.

Without falling into traps of determinism (God's will is already completely planned, God's power unquestionable), pantheism (the created world is God), or idolatry (the creature is made into the Creator), you can nonetheless maintain a spiritual mind-set that accepts God's power in the world around you. When you trust God's power, you are free to turn over to God what you have previously imagined as your sole responsibility, and thus resolve the problem of trying too hard. When you see some of that power given to you—for example, the power to forgive freely—you are less likely to undertake your work thinking of yourself as powerless. When you discover God's constant and continuing faithfulness in empowering your congregation, you can extend your vision of the congregation into the long-term future.

Ignoring history

If you ignore the lessons of the past, you are likely to consider all situations as new, and try too hard in your responses to them. If, on the other hand, you know what people much like you encountered in their strangely similar lives, you can avoid a sense of generational superiority and overexertion, and save time and effort by applying to your life what you learn from the wise people who preceded you.

Take a little historical side trip with me now, and look at some history that might help you understand how your spiritual ancestors encountered "the evil world." We'll start with Martin Luther and John Calvin.

Luther and Calvin participated fully in the world around them—in the minds of other reformers, perhaps much too fully—and so disagreed with the idea that a reformed Christianity should wall itself off from its surroundings. The theological streams of Protestantism begun by these two reformers have continued through the centuries.

Some of their spiritual descendants didn't pay close attention, though, and took up "avoidance of evil" as their primary identity. This institutionalized world-avoidance reappeared in a variety of "awakenings" in Europe, and later in the Americas. Communities of believers sprang up as ideal places for Christians to live: separate and isolated from the world. The utopian dreams of these communities were rarely realized, however, and their hopes were dashed when "perfect systems of social order"—usually developed and taught

Luther's appreciation of "the ordinary," including "ordinary people," is summed up in the Latin phrase *Finitum est capax infiniti*, or "the finite is the vehicle of the divine." This is why bread, wine, water, shoemakers, and scrubwomen are no longer "ordinary," but serve the will of God in extraordinary, even sacred ways. Luther also described the "happy exchange" between Christ and humankind in Holy Communion, as a time when "Christ takes on everything that we are and we take on everything Christ is." (Luther would have fun today with theses of genetics and brain science, such as "Every seven years, every atom in the human body is replaced," or "You are what you eat.")

by charismatic leaders—ran afoul of human nature or biological principles.

The pattern of early growth and eventual decline can be seen in an 18th century Pennsylvania utopian community, the Ephrata Cloister. Their strict moral codes included the unfortunate provision of celibacy—perhaps their idea of avoiding completely all that was evil. Although married families within this group carried a small German Baptist denomination into the 20th century, celibacy ensured a dwindling number of adherents. Righteous removal from the world's evils ended in the righteous disappearance of this group as a potential power for changing the world.

Although fundamentalist notions of Christianity and other world religions will never disappear as legitimate strains of belief, history teaches that the problems these groups encounter with "the evil world" can become the seeds of their own destruction or disappearance. Absent the fervor of the charismatic leader or the challenge of separatism, these groups seem destined to rise and fall within the span of a few generations.

(To be fair to history, I should also note that other faith families have disappeared into the backwaters of history primarily because they took the opposite approach to evil, losing their identity by completely blending into the culture around them.)

Narrowing the "gene pool" of possibilities

A simple biological principle might describe one reason why avoiding or shunning the world could present problems for sustaining your congregation: "Monocultures"—only one species living and growing in one place—don't last very long. Because narrowed gene pools put the organism at risk—for example, by producing lowered resistance to disease—the organism is less likely to survive. Continued viability is more likely when a diversity of genetic material (within a species) or symbiosis (among species) allows or encourages the interdependence and strengthening of organisms.

If you accept the view that "the world is evil and we must avoid it because it poses danger to our spiritual lives," you can easily conclude that "certain parts of the world, best identified by us, are evil and thus not worthy of inclusion in our fellowship." And so your congregation might not welcome people of other socioeconomic classes, ethnic origins, political persuasions, sexual identities, races, or ages. Your pool of possible members shrinks, and your congregation's future is sorely threatened.

Even if you have diminished those excluding behaviors, you might still limit your membership by including people of only one class. Demographers know that the most thoroughly descriptive predictor of lifestyle or personal preferences is a person's daily work. Could you measure your congregation's sustainability by the diversity of occupations—and therefore, socioeconomic classes—you find "acceptable"? Conversely, is "occupational monoculture" a sign that your congregation is losing its long-term viability?

If your congregation walls out "the world," it can become a kind of monocultured organism—think of the ethnic enclaves of previous centuries—and is therefore less likely to sustain itself except through massive effort. "Avoiding the evil world" might result in "trying too hard."

Misunderstanding relevance

One of the most compelling desires you hold as a leader is to be relevant. You want your leadership to make a difference, to mean something for other people's lives. The people you serve feel the same way about your congregation. You know that if together you lack relevance—or "significance"—you miss the opportunity to proclaim God's grace: "Good News" that means something.

But if you or your congregation base your identity or mission on the false relevance of avoiding evil—or on shrill criticism of the evil world—you ghettoize yourselves and soon find that you have diminished your capacity for doing God's will.

If you try to find relevance through avoidance, shunning, or universal condemnation of the world-beyond-the church, you will quickly find yourself in a cycle of attention-seeking. (See chapter 4 to review how overexertive attention-seeking causes inattention, and thus increases your work.) Because the emotional energy required to maintain fear or anger about "the world out there" is high, you must work harder and harder to keep others' attention and focus your energy.

Sadly, you can find support for the false relevance of world-condemnation and avoidance by placing on a high pedestal the office or person of the clergy. By regarding a pastor as the highest example of the godly life, you may think you have found an encouragement for avoiding evil. The logic is simple: The gifts or wisdom of the pastor embody the highest values of faithful living. The pastor is a beacon of virtue, a counterweight to evils outside the church. Unfortunately this "support" lasts only as long as that pastor—perhaps including spouse and family—can sustain an exemplary lifestyle. The likely life span of that kind of encouragement is one generation, or one pastoral call.

◆

A cynical young person is almost the saddest sight to see because it means that he or she has gone from knowing nothing to believing in nothing.

Maya Angelou

Decreasing mission and vision

Just as you most fervently wish to engage in mission and to perceive a vision for your own life, you want to lead your congregation toward a purpose-driven existence. Condemning or avoiding the world decreases the variety of congregational purposes or identities. To illustrate how this might happen, let's look at four seemingly admirable elements of "mission" or "vision" and see how each might become weakened when the "our response to the evil world" is considered to be the primary ingredient.

"Telling the Good News." In the Christian lexicon, this activity is usually considered an "ultimate good" that can come from congregations' mission, or from individual believers' lives. Nonetheless, you may encounter some difficulties if you presume that "Gospel-sharing is essential Christian behavior," especially when it is founded on consistent condemnation of the world.

❏ "Telling the Good News" can easily deteriorate into hackneyed platitudes or formulaic repetition of key phrases that may take on the character of talismans to ward off the dangerous thoughts of others.

❏ When it is based on the assumption that the whole world outside the church is rotten to its core, "sharing the Good News" may be motivated primarily by the attitude that the only involvement God's people can have with the world is to help God save it.

❏ Adherents may learn techniques of "how to share the Good News" *before* they have encountered the exquisite worth of God's attributes and actions in their daily lives. Skills may take precedence over the reasons that believers would want to share in the first place.

WHAT'S SO GOOD ABOUT THE GOOD NEWS?

If you want a group of faithful Christians to examine more closely what they're all about, talk together about the question, "What's so good about the Good News?" Because this question is one whose answers are presumed already to be known, it may never get asked.

Among evangelical Christians, for whom "salvation" has essential importance, the question is easily answered in the contrast between behaviors before conversion and the blessings of life after Christ enters believers' hearts. For these members of the Christian family, the "Good News answer" starts there and continues wonderfully into the rest of life.

But for many Christians, the answers are unknown, unfelt, and therefore unexpressed. Especially among Christians in middle and upper socioeconomic classes, there may be no real "good" in "Good News" because these believers don't know how they may been "lost and now found." (They may overlook isolation, normlessness, chaos, self-estrangement, and lack of meaning or purpose as part of their own lost identity.)

This is not a good situation for the church's future. Lacking any sense of emotion about the "goodness" of God's grace in their lives, many Christians have little or nothing to share with others except formulaic—and often quasi-heretical—statements such as, "Well, Jesus died to save my sins."

How would I answer my own question? God's Good News starts with God's action in Jesus Christ and moves to the following:

● I don't have to be "God." It's already taken care of, all this "God work." I'm not ultimately responsible for everything.

● I don't have to be greedy, selfish, or stupid. There is another choice for my brain, another way of living besides "grab it all [or mate with everyone]." Jesus' life proves it; the Holy Spirit empowers the better choices.

● I don't have to be afraid. My brain can do more than run away or fight. God fights for me. "Perfect love casts out fear." I have more important things to do with my life.

● I'm not alone. (Satan's temptations—in the Garden and in Jesus' wilderness experience— included the subtle notion "You're the only one.") By God's grace, "aloneness" is a lie; I am surrounded by people who, blessed by the Holy Spirit, face the world together with me.

● I'm forgiven. I don't have to justify myself, to God or to other people. I can depend on forgiveness as an ultimately good element in all my relationships.

● I can forgive. Because of Christ's example and the gifts of discernment that come from the Spirit, I have another, better choice than violent conflict or subtle vengeance. Forgiving takes less energy and lasts longer.

● I have a purpose for living. God's wide will for the world gives me a variety of choices about how to serve as a partner to God in accomplishing that will. (Recreating, redeeming, and making holy are three large arenas of possible purpose.)

● God's grace permeates all the "good" that comes to my life. I'd hate to have been given what I actually "deserved."

If you try this most basic question with a group of other believers, be ready for some surprising answers about how "what is good from God" for these folk is also Good News for others.

Certainly, there is delight and joy in salvation's goodness. But when the motivation for sharing is rooted in a deep disdain for the world, that attitude will reveal itself in the message and messengers as arrogance or paternalism. People who perceive these attitudes will not readily receive any news, good or not, and so you may need to work harder, not only to share but also to overcome the pre-existing perceptions that exist among those with whom you want to share good news.

"Making disciples." Currently enshrined in the mission statements, programs, and structures of many congregations, the task of "making disciples"—defined as leading believers through a maturing process—can also be limited if its attitudinal core is primarily a variant of "shunning the evil world in order to find safety in the church."

WHO ARE DISCIPLES?

"Disciples" are certainly more mature believers than "children" or "sheep," both New Testament antecedents for contemporary "seekers." But the first-century Greek term for disciple is *mathetes*—literally "learner." It may actually denote a slightly less mature believer than current usage suggests. Disciples (or "followers," from *akolouthous*, "those who walk behind") were usually part of a company of students led by a single teacher. Sociologically, disciples were, along with robbers, emigrants, Zealots, vagabonds, and prophetic groups, characterized by renunciation of possessions, a life of wandering, and virtual homelessness. They lived in a codependent relationship with their teacher and found meaning in their ability to understand and integrate the teachings of their master into a meaningful whole. In this relationship, "disciples" were not known for their mature self-differentiation or individual interpretations of their leader's teachings. Instead, they were seen as faithful when they adhered closely to what they had been taught. In short, "disciples" were always students, dependent on and controlled by their teacher; obedient learning was the behavior preferred by their teacher.

Outside its specific usage to name the followers of Jesus in the Gospels and Acts, *mathetes* is not mentioned after Pentecost. Terms such as "believer" or "member of Christ's body" seem to supplant "disciple" in the rest of the New Testament. The verb form, meaning "to make into a disciple," is seldom used and "discipleship" does not occur at all. "Disciple" is hardly used outside of the literal and specific sense described above.

In their description of stages of maturing relationships with God (*Seasons of Strength: New Visions of Adult Christian Maturing*), Roman Catholic developmental psychologists Evelyn and James D. Whitehead value the relationship of "disciple" with God as more fully developed than that of "child," but suggest that the maturing of faith eventually leads to "steward."

The mission-mindedness of "making disciples"—or the verbed-noun, "discipling"—is admirable and necessary for the church to undertake, especially in a supposedly post-Christian, postmodern, and postinstitutional era. But the goal can become questionable when its primary motivation is rooted in distaste for the world, and its eventual end is to remove people from the world to the church-as-institution. In an oblique way, the necessary and admirable "disciple-making" work of mature believers can be undermined by the oxymoronic removal of new believers from the world which, after extensive "training," they will eventually be asked to re-enter as supposed "disciple-makers."

"Taking care of hurting people." A third supposed "primary activity" of the church can be described as "servanthood" or "ministry to the whole person." Modeled on Jesus' own life of healing and care, activities and programs of congregations attempt to ameliorate the effects of injustice, poverty, "isms" of every kind, and other garden-variety sins.

These admirable venues of Christian ministry can become limited in their effectiveness, however, when they are based on the assumption that "most people are needy most of the time." This variant on the "evil world" theme may gain some of its motivational power from Christian abhorrence of evil (or neediness born of evil), which jump-starts a variety of justice-seeking actions and activities. In this way of thinking, as long as the world is basically evil, there will always be a need for Christian care-giving and justice-bringing work.

When it is rooted only in a subtle dislike of the world outside of the church, "taking care of others" can defeat itself. Consider, for example, the tensions you experience as you try to decide how to confront evil or do good in the world. If the world is always and completely evil—and therefore always and completely dangerous—you have first to decide whether to fight or flee. These two emotional reactions are not long-lasting, and hardly contribute to a sustainable attitude toward helping others. "Approach/avoidance" psychological mechanisms snap into place, and suddenly necessary motivation for "world caring" is hard to find. This biological reaction may explain, for example, the consistently low preference for "social ministry" activities among members of many congregations, or the "donor fatigue" that has continued to bedevil organizations trying to alleviate poverty, injustice, or hunger in the world.

THE DILEMMA OF FIGHTING THE EVIL WORLD

The hard work here? Lacking a long-lived emotional base (love, generosity, or hope) you might have to work harder to overcome the fearful or angry emotions about the world that instantly demand your response and then quickly leave. If you are the leader of a caring ministry, you might have trouble maintaining a pool of volunteers whose primary motivation is anchored in dislike of the world.

"Taking care of each other." The final mission-minded view of the church is that its primary purpose is to care for its members. But the effectiveness of this "mission" can be delimited if your congregation members all quietly agree that "out there" is not interesting, valuable, or especially safe for this group of God's people. "This is why," the logic goes, "we have no choice but to take comfort and find worthwhile mission primarily in caring for each other." Extensive programs of crisis care, fellowship, or education; organizational shufflings; or recurring construction projects become a kind of organizational opiate, deftly distracting congregational members from the world around them, even their own neighborhoods. These kinds of congregations can be characterized (unfairly, perhaps) by their supposed "lack of mission," and by the underlying fear or disgust with which they face the world around them. Sustainability can be difficult when mission is narrowed to this monoculture, and self-care deteriorates into small-minded squabbles or personality conflicts. Extensive effort is required to repair small or lasting problems in relationships. Even greater effort may be needed to guard against creeping individualism or self-absorption.

Where is the "good" in God's "good world"?

What's the antidote to the possible poison of world-avoidance or condemnation? It's seeing how God accomplishes great and continuing good in the world through the lives of individual Christians, and incorporating what you learn into the way you organize your congregation.

In the following pages we'll examine some of the places where "good" may occur in God's world, and how what happens there might be instructive to you. As you progress through these ideas, keep in the mind the following:

❑ Not everything that happens in the world is good.

❑ It is not always easy to see that what is good in the world is God's doing.

❑ Still, God is active, perhaps most powerfully in the lively work of individual Christians whose influence helps tip the world toward doing God's will.

"STEWARDSHIP" IS DOING GOD'S WILL

New Testament theologian John Reumann, in his incisive work *Stewardship and the Economy of God*, translates the Greek root word *economia* as something more than "the household rules," its usually accepted translation. Instead, Reumann strongly suggests, *economia* has to do with the larger plan of the owner, not just the rules derived from the plan. That larger plan is what the *economos*—the steward— fulfills, anticipating the will of the owner and thus not waiting to be told what to do. The steward is not slavishly "following the rules."

For Reumann, "stewardship" begins with God's will for the world. (This is no minor matter, this "will of God," nor can it be easily encapsulated as "making disciples of all nations" or "loving as you have been loved.") An almighty God, who continues to create, redeem, and make holy the entire world, certainly has a vast intent for the world.

Therefore, "stewards" serve any and all parts of God's will as they find their place in that overall scheme of God's activity. Followers become stewards as they find themselves especially gifted (by the Spirit) to carry out their part of God's creating, redeeming and sanctifying will for the world.

Gathered together in communities of faith, stewards provide funds and workers for collective ministries whose scope or duration vastly exceeds the capacities of individual stewards. Contributions of money and time are pooled to sustain these institutions so that stewards are equipped to engage their daily ministries with God's grace in their hearts.

❑ The "good" in an enterprise (for example, arts and entertainment) does not necessarily redeem the rest of its character.

❑ The examples included here, although current at the time of publication, may have been supplanted or sullied by the course of events. Think of these examples as illustrative of the good that can happen in God's world, and find examples from your own experience.

It is easy to get caught in the trap of evaluating the world's actions before we have first assessed or understood what is taking place. Like other participants in the temporal world, Christians can rush to judgment about what they observe, and thus can misjudge intent, long-term benefits, or costs to society. In the examples that follow, I have begun with the assumption that God is accomplishing something good in these places in the world, enough that we would do well to pay attention.

Rather than arguing whether, for example, the music industry is good or evil, let's admit that both may be true at one time or the other. And let's admit to an even more powerful possibility: that God works through the activities of the music industry to bring good to the world. We may even have something to learn from that good.

How can you and your congregation learn from the "good" that's happening in God's world? Since answering this question is hard work, each of the following subsections ends with questions that might give you ideas for what to do with what you've read.

Business

The world of buying and selling is a good place for Christian leaders to begin a search for God's good work happening in the world. In the past 20 years, changes in the business world have included more than just efficiency, increased profitability resulting from technology, and longer work weeks. If you look closely at business today, you may also see some of the following:

❑ **Cause-related marketing.** In this slice of the marketing pie, entrepreneurs bring together organizations doing civic or social good—for example, food banks—with companies

---

In his book *The Seven Habits of Highly Effective People*, author and consultant Stephen Covey talks about "seeking first to understand before seeking to be understood." This habit of daily living parallels Jesus' insistence that we remove logs from our eyes before we criticize specks of sawdust in the eyes of others. This "habit" is a good one for individuals and congregations, too!

What is "God's job," you wonder? A classic work in the field of ministry in daily life is Robert Banks's *God the Worker: Journeys into the Mind, Heart and Imagination of God.* The former Fuller Seminary professor lays out fascinating biblical metaphors for "the work of God." Moving past the theologically described "Creator," "Redeemer," and "Sanctifier," Banks enriches the metaphorical mix with descriptions of God as performer and composer; metalworker and potter; garment maker, gardener, and orchardist; farmer and winegrower; shepherd and pastoralist; tentmaker and camper; builder and architect.

that want to get rid of surplus inventory. Mutual benefit is arranged, material or food is not wasted, and thousands of people are fed.

❑ **Redefining the "bottom line."** Although companies have bleated the standard mantra, "Our people are our most important asset," it is not until recently that economists have started to measure things like "knowledge capital," trust, or job satisfaction as ultimately more important than short-term gains on balance sheets. "Sustainability" is now seen as a measure of "profitability," given the high cost of employee turnover. In businesses that do more than mouth the words, such "people assets" are developed and stewarded by purposeful care for workers and their collective interests.

Consultant Peter Block, in *Stewardship: Choosing Service Over Self-Interest*, cites the significance of survey results that consistently show workers preferring the awareness and affirmation of peers and managers as the reward for their work. Block asks managers how their attitudes about the worth of individual workers might add value first of all, to the workers, then to customers, and eventually to the value of the company. The "value-added" formula may work in congregations as well.

❑ **Collegial working styles.** One of the outcomes of the so-called feminization of the workplace has been the increasing success of collegial styles of management and work. In a chaotic and fast-changing workplace, top-down management styles that diminish the worth of individual workers and business ethics cannot keep pace with overflowing information and necessary levels of expertise. "Wisdom from the corner office" has been replaced by "collective wisdom."

❑ **The spirituality of work.** Within the past decade, American enterprise has shown an increasing interest in the spirituality of work. More than Bible discussion groups at lunch, "spirituality" also includes an insistence on ethical practices, forgiveness as a necessary element in business, the calming and healing effects of prayer and meditation, and the fostering of a sense of purpose for the enterprise.

Some of us may have forgotten—and others simply overlooked—the fact that the earliest manifestations of the "megachurch movement" were based on church leaders' early appropriation of godly wisdom in the business world. The Willow Creek phenomenon is one example.

In their summary of types of spirituality in the workplace, researchers Ian Mitroff and Elizabeth Denton (*A Spiritual Audit of Corporate America: A Hard Look at Spirituality, Religion, and Values in the Workplace*) showcase a few examples they found in a narrowly cast research net. They provide another lens with which to examine the changes taking place in American business. One inescapable conclusion: "spirituality" is washing through corporate boardrooms and shop floors as part of "a new way to do business."

Putting business wisdom to work

How might the good that God is doing in the business world affect your congregation's way of doing its work? Using the simple illustrations here, you might ask yourself:

❑ How might your congregation participate in cause-related marketing, in addition to inventing and maintaining your own programs for social ministry?

❑ How collegial, really, are your ways of doing "church business" together? How much value do you add to the lives of your members?

❑ How "spiritual" is the work you do together as leaders? In your meetings, in your conversations and writing, how do you make "congregational leadership" something spiritual?

Philanthropy

One of the premier organizations that train fund-raisers is Indiana University's Center on Philanthropy (www.philanthropy.iupui.edu), headquartered in Indianapolis, but offering courses throughout the nation. Their quarter-century of experience has yielded a solid base of information about donor behaviors and fund-raising skills, as well as a highly ethical approach to giving. Although their courses are crammed with effective techniques, their dedication to ethical fund-raising is what makes their work an evidence of God's own good work.

Rooted in "love of humankind," the enterprise of fund-raising outlasted decades of uninformed criticism. Many of us are still surprised to find out that this part of American enterprise is not only effective; it is also guided by ethical and philosophical principles that could be termed "spiritual." These few examples may give you a hint.

❑ **Ethical, joyful funding approaches.** The assumption of "success" in fund-raising has moved from the simplest aims—fulfilling a budget or achieving a goal—to deeper and more lasting outcomes such as "developing a spirit of generosity," "donor-driven fund-raising," and "transparent record-keeping." A body of philosophical work has emerged that provides fund-raisers with specific codes of ethics and the reasons for those kinds of behaviors.

❑ **"Appreciative inquiry."** As a theory and method of human development, appreciative inquiry, according to its founder, David Cooperrider of Case Western Reserve

University, pays special attention to "the best of the past and present" so as to "ignite the collective imagination of what might be." Philanthropy has taken this approach to heart and, by a variety of designations, incorporated this way of thinking into the science and art of fund-raising. Inquiry about donors' life goals is the starting point, and the fund-raiser's tasks are to honor (appreciate) and actualize the donor's cherished objectives for humanity. In *Appreciative Management and Leadership*, Cooperrider and his colleagues promote a management theory that draws together the insights of social biology, brain science, complexity theory, and garden-variety optimism. They believe that "positive imagination" is a necessary feature of human enterprise. Thus Cooperrider joins the wave of philosophers, business leaders, and other seers who decry needs-based thinking, planning, and management as a "natural way of doing business." For an eye-opening and persuasive look at this quiet room in the edifice of social science, see www.appreciative-inquiry.org. Or type "Pygmalion effect" into your search engine and see what turns up!

❑ **Skill in asking.** One universal principle of philanthropy is simple: People give to people who ask. Anecdotal evidence and research in philanthropy bolster this truth. Jesus understood the matter well: "Ask and you will receive." The very act of asking serves as a kind of gateway for acts of generosity, not only in prayer to God, but in relationships with each other. In God's case, the generosity is already there; in the case of humans, God-graced generosity is strengthened by asking.

Putting the wisdom of philanthropy to work

You can incorporate some of the God-given wisdom of philanthropy by thinking about questions such as these:

❑ What, really, are the principles and values that underlie the ways in which you fund God's mission through your congregation?

❑ How do you come to know the deepest and most hopeful yearnings of members, for their lives and for the directions your congregation might take? How do you honor and affirm those yearnings as you construct programs, build "budgets" or ask for members' contributions of time and money?

❑ When it comes to soliciting member's contributions, how might you conduct those interactions face to face?

Social critics

At first, "social critics" may seem a loosely defined category of "God's good work." But when you read editorial pages, scan book lists, or watch commentators on television, you may recognize social critics as contemporary prophets. These truth-tellers of our times include educators—yes, your child's teacher is a kind of prophet!—philosophers, humorists, media critics, historians, politicians, columnists, cartoonists, consultants, and environmentalists. Their message and methods may differ, but their core work remains the same: to warn us about too-easy analysis, too-quick reactions, and too-narrow viewpoints, and to suggest alternate ways of living and thinking.

> Yes, politicians can be truth-tellers. Our frequent mistake is to require of them constant agreement with our truth alone. We too readily label them "dishonest" when we misunderstand the necessity of compromise, "the greater good," and a vision that may transcend our own.

The kinds of social criticism are as varied as the categories of human endeavor and relationships, so it is difficult to characterize "social criticism" streams of thought. Citing four of my favorites might help you recall some of your own.

❑ Law professor, television commentator, and prolific writer Stephen L. Carter (*Integrity; Civility; The Culture of Disbelief;* and recently, *God's Name in Vain: The Wrongs and Rights of Religion in Politics*) exposes the ways in which the behaviors of our society may lack intellectual honesty, and how they may work to the degradation of our personal and cultural future.

❑ Educator and writer Neil Postman has, over the course of his distinguished career, moved from analysis of schools and the education process (*The End of Education: Redefining the Value of School*) to deeper probings. He continues to examine matters that undermine effective education (*The Disappearance of Childhood; Amusing Ourselves to Death*). My favorite among his works is *Technopoly: The Surrender of Culture to Technology.*

❑ Several years ago economist Jeremy Rifkin wrote a hopeful analysis of how our society might ameliorate the continuing effects of the displacement of workers by machines. In *The End of Work: The Decline of the Global Labor Force and the Dawn of the Post-Market Era* he outlines the possibility of a work force realigned for the delivery of important human services to at-risk segments of our population. The wisdom of his analysis is slowly revealing itself in the reshuffling of workers in the "new economy."

❑ Consultant and philosopher Peter Block (*Flawless Consulting; The Empowered Manager*) deftly exposes commonly held beliefs about "the way business works" and offers evidence that principle-based approaches to workplace relationships help bring about business goals more effectively than the usual ways of working. He continues to inspire high-level managers to practice their highest sense of calling in principled decisions.

Putting the wisdom of social critics to work

Your congregation probably already includes a variety of self-appointed "social critics," but you might also benefit from the godly good of other critics. Use these questions as a way to start discussion or action:

❑ How could you learn from social critics ways to encourage thoughtful, helpful, and caring criticism within your congregation?

❑ In what areas of life—economics, stewardship, relationships, consumerism, time management, parenting—could your congregation find and share critical insight with your members?

❑ How could the work of social critics help you add vital thinking skills to your leadership style?

❑ Where, outside your congregation, can you find criticism especially helpful for your leadership?

Government

While it may seem strange to include "government" in a listing of how God's good work occurs in the world—especially given the continual pejorative targeting of politicians and governmental workers—it may be that in the enterprise of governance we might find especially poignant evidence of God cutting through our individual selfishnesses to bring about the greater good. A few examples might help here.

❏ **Restraining rampant individualism.** Our brains tend toward an individualized—even selfish—view of the world around us. One of the most important works that government does is to keep that narrow view of reality from overwhelming the greater good, and through the rule of law to keep us mindful that we are best served individually when we best serve others.

❏ **Making possible safety and well-being.** Where evil and danger abound—and sometimes when they are only imagined—government exists to assure the safety and well-being of its citizens. As simple as a neighborhood park or as complex as the product-liability laws, the work of government is best evidenced in continued safety and health among its constituents. You have only to look at places in the world where danger and dysfunction grow daily to see where governments have forsaken this basic function.

❏ **Keeping power in check.** When the powerful forces of wealth, weaponry, or majority threaten to overwhelm a society, government holds in balance these and other manifestations of power so that the rights of all its citizens are exercised. Especially in governance systems where "checks and balances" are codified and practiced rigorously, this function of government can be strong evidence of God's intent to care for the weak and lowly.

Brain scientist Paul McLean proposed the concept of "the triune brain" over 30 years ago. His analysis of brains of various organisms yielded the idea of three interacting—and even competing—brains within humans. The "reptilian brain" was most capable of fight/flight mechanisms. The nearly instinctual behaviors of the "mammalian brain" focused on satisfying basic needs, notably eating and mating. The outer layer of the brain, the neocortex, was the "thinking brain," where language and logic made higher-order activities possible. From McLean's analysis, it is possible to name two parts of the brain as essentially "selfish." *Note*: Subsequent to McLean's work, other researchers have refined descriptions of the brain, including discussions of innate capacities for love and altruism.

Putting the wisdom of government to work

As you examine your congregation's governance—its rules, guidelines, and procedures—you might find good wisdom in how the good work of God continues in local, regional, and national government. Use these questions to start your work together:

❑ Where are "safety" and "well-being" reflected in the ways you lead this congregation? What could you learn from governance matters such as zoning, liability, or environmental laws?

❑ How does your congregation keep in check the power of a few? How do you determine who is "powerful"? What could a politician or government worker teach you?

❑ How does your congregation restrain the impulse for individualism that can lay waste your processes for decision making? Where in the world of government could you learn about effective ways of doing this?

Entertainment and arts industry

Another seemingly odd venue where you might find God's hand is in the worlds of entertainment and the arts. Because of our endless interest in lifestyles unlike our own—and the media's gracious willingness to provide us with every detail—we can easily characterize these two areas of human work as "basically ungodly," "modern-day Babylon," or "Satan's backyard."

But here again, it is helpful to understand God's abilities to bring about good in unlikely places. (Old Testament readers should always keep in mind the story of the angelically verbal steed of the questionable prophet Balaam. New Testament readers might recall the stories of wisdom that came from supposed fools or outcasts.) In fact, one of the quiet changes in the arts and entertainment industries has been the emergence of a principled, value-based work force, people who care deeply about the impact of their vocations for the good of God's world.

Once I experienced the righteous anger of a colleague who wanted to know "why the church isn't doing anything about the ungodly movie and television industry." My reply: "I don't think you have to worry, because this morning hundreds or thousands of Christians—'the church'—went to work in those industries, and their personal mission includes precisely what you are asking for." To check out this premise, ask your friendly Web browser to search categories such as "Christians in entertainment/arts/sports" and see what comes up. You'll have to skip the obvious—"Christian radio stations"—and play around a little, but the information is there.

❑ **Films and books with "a message."** It is no accident that in recent years, many popular films, novels, television shows, and even cartoons promote ideals that are strongly moral, thoughtfully spiritual, or encouraging of a godly view of reality. My favorites include author Anne Lamott (her poignant *Traveling Mercies* tells the story of her struggle for faith; it brings knowing laughter and tears to any of us who were lost—or found!) and the television series *The Simpsons* (whose episodes can justifiably be seen as contemporary morality plays). These message-laden art forms are especially powerful because their intended audience is the general population.

❑ **Proliferation of "Christian entertainment and arts."** Although their exponential growth has slowed somewhat, these enterprises continue to use music, sports, and art forms (for example, puppetry, comedy, sculpture) to encourage and sustain Christians in their daily living. The strongest example can be found on your radio dial, where "Christian radio" is now reaching into mainstream markets.

❑ **"Hero" worship.** It may seem that the qualities of "hero" are severely diluted in our society—pick your favorite "bad boy" sports figure or loose-living entertainer. But it is also true that hero worship is maintaining its hold on the psychology of adolescents—and the adults whose development was arrested in their teen years. This transference or finding of identity in the lives of others has ennobled many public figures to re-examine their responsibility to model values-laden living. Their numbers may be few and their witness overwhelmed by the media glare given to their opposites. Still, some actors, sports figures, entertainers, entertaining politicians, television celebrities, and others find great satisfaction in the role of embodying what is good and right in God's world.

Putting entertainment industry wisdom to work

Members of your congregation consume many hours' and dollars' worth of "entertainment" each month. Part of your ministry of leadership is to help members be wise critics of what they encounter. But you might also help them learn from the behaviors and messages of people in the arts and entertainment industries.

❑ What messages of great and godly worth are available to you each day, in television shows, films, new kinds of toys, or sports? How do you share these messages?

❑ In what ways might you take advantage of "hero worship" as a way of mentoring young people or learning life lessons? (For example, which 80-year-olds in your congregation could be legitimate "heroes" for teens?)

❑ How can you take advantage of the media-savvy work of artists, filmmakers, actors, and writers who are Christians?

Science

The vast enterprise of science within the human community is replete with examples of how God's work gets done. I spotlight several here, with the caveat that in these few examples I do injustice to the size and scope of what God accomplishes through scientific endeavors.

❑ **Complexity/chaos theory.** At first blush, complexity theory may look like part of a quasi-idolatrous attempt to unify all knowledge into singular theories. In fact, this branch of scientific inquiry is evidence of the ultimate inability of humans to explain or control much of anything. Of special interest now is the spread of chaos/complexity theory into other areas of human enterprise, including change theory, systems thinking, organizational development, group dynamics, and learning. In a world beset with confusion, overloaded brains, and widespread dysfunction, it is humbling to understand that both chaos and order are good, and that God is working within both essential states.

Exploring Complexity Theory

Where to start with your exploration of chaos theory? It's a complex question. You can begin with basic texts about the subject, written toward the end of the 20th century. Or you can move immediately to works that begin connecting complexity theory with human enterprise.

My own journey in this area of thought began with *Chaos: Making a New Science*, by James Gleick, a book whose inner complexities required a long period of reading and digesting. Classic texts on the subject include *Who's Afraid of Schrödinger's Cat: An A-to-Z Guide to All the New Science Ideas You Need to Keep Up With the New Thinking*, by I. N. Marshall, Danah Zohar, and F. David Peat. If you want to move to "applied complexity theory," Zohar's *Rewiring the Corporate Brain* attempts to apply complexity theory to organizational development. *Blur: The Speed of Change in the Connected Economy*, by Stanley Davis and Christopher Meyer, takes complexity theory into account in its free-wheeling attempt to explain "change." Story-laden *Surfing the Edge of Chaos: The Laws of Nature and the New Laws of Business*, by consultants Richard Pascale, Mark Millemann, and Linda Gioja, offers explanatory romps into the world of commerce. The journals *Scientific American* and *Discover*, which seem to include periodic references to applied chaos theory, are written in a popular style.

Your local library, middle-school science teacher, or obliging Web browser can also help you begin learning about chaos theory. By the time you read this book, someone may already be categorizing congregational behaviors according to specific concepts of chaos theory.

❑ **Medicine.** The medical sciences may exemplify God's sure and guiding hand in human existence. Because humans will always be concerned about their own health, medicine is one field where people of good will work to eliminate or ameliorate disease and life-threatening conditions. One historical example is the persistent and embattled work of medical researchers who found the correlations between cigarette consumption and ill health. Environmental health, increased ability to prevent of disease, improved technologies, the widening scope of pharmacological treatments, and renewed interest in diet and physical fitness—each of these is an example of how the enterprise of medicine works to make available God's gift of health to the world's peoples.

❑ **Genetic "miracles."** Freakish headlines about cloning and cryptic warnings about neo-Nazi applications notwithstanding, genetics reveals a beautifully complex web of protein and chemical interactions that, at their reductionist levels, can describe "life." God's hand may most clearly be seen in the abilities of geneticists to help parents make difficult decisions about bringing a child into the world, and in the gradual discovery of genetic connections to life-threatening or life-diminishing physical and mental conditions. Not yet an "exact science," genetics nonetheless provides an exquisite window into the existence of disease and promises increasing relief from conditions that a scant five years ago would have been "incurable" and "unknown mysteries." As this field of human endeavor gathers ethical protection around it, we can expect to see marvels whose miraculous nature can lead us only to praise a God of complex ability for miraculous origination and care.

❏ **Brain science.** You've already been introduced to the implications of applied brain science for the workings of organizations such as congregations. Here let me add a few other possible evidences of God's working through this branch of science. First is the emerging field of "neurotheology," in which the spiritual (and anti-spiritual?) activities of the brain may be measured or observed. Another is the work being done in "information-overload science," which is based more on the biology of the brain than on plaintive pleas for "simpler living." (Chapter 4, "Knowing Too Much," noted this connection.) A third: As brain science moves toward understanding mental conditions such as Alzheimer's disease and autism, we will see some of life's most vexing problems begin to be solved. A fourth: Brain science may help integrate areas of study such as genetics, social science, philosophy, ethics, psychology, and education so that practices and techniques for enhancing human potential are readily available. Finally, like all sciences, brain science uncovers thousands of questions for each "answer," thus compelling creaturely humility toward our Creator.

In their new compilation of information about a "spiritual brain," researchers Andrew Newberg, Eugene D'Aquili, and Vince Rause (*Why God Won't Go Away: Brain Science and the Biology of Belief*) probe this proposition: The brain is hardwired for belief. Two quotations put the matter into perspective: "Neurology makes it clear: There's no other way for God to get into your head except through the brain's neural pathways." And: "Whatever the ultimate nature of spiritual experience might be . . . . all that is meaningful in human spirituality happens in the mind. In other words, the mind is mystical by default" (p. 37).

Putting the wisdom of science to work

You can bring "scientific wisdom" into your congregation's structures and behaviors with questions such as these:

❏ What new ways of thinking about the complexity of your congregation might be helpful? (for example, the less-than-adequate "order" in your congregation's structure).

❏ What can you learn about the way people think—in brain science, for example—that might be helpful in explaining how and why congregation members do (or don't) respond to specific programs, events, or invitations?

❏ Where would you turn to find out how best to explain the connections between faith and science?

❏ Where might you look in science for reasons to praise and thank God?

❏ What should leaders like you know in to be conversant with the high percentage of members who work in fields of scientific endeavor?

Social sciences

The social sciences can provide your congregation with insights and wisdom that you may have overlooked in reading about ecclesiology. For example, a social psychologist working on motivational psychology may have much to say about "why people give." Although mystery and wonder remain part of the social sciences—even in the face of intricate and extensive social surveys and sociometrics—social scientists know enough about how groups of people behave and think to give you clues about how to be a leader in your congregation. A few examples might start your own thinking and searching.

❏ **"Change theory."** We looked at this idea briefly in chapter 1, noting that its nature is also changing. As it now stands, "change theory" can be helpful as you try to understand whether and how to "change" your congregation's ways of doing business. Inextricably connected to complexity theory, the concept of "change" today describes many ways in which people change. If the burden of "change agent" or "inevitable change" is removed, you may find yourself less frantic about "keeping up" or even "leading change." (Chapter 8 explores this subject further.)

❏ **Generational theorists.** In their two high-profile works (*Generations* and *The Fourth Turning: An American Prophecy*), social theorists William Strauss and Neil Howe provide new windows into the possible interactions between generations. Although sometimes answered by individuals who view life with dark foreboding or immature generational self-importance, the question "How do specific generations interact with others?" has been helpful in describing the differences and similarities among generations. The "science" part of "social science" has always been "soft" here, but generational theory has nonetheless been instructive for congregations that wrestle with cross- and intergenerational ministries.

❏ **Historians.** In a world where "new" sometimes runs amok, it is easy to forget that what was once true may yet be true again! Historians invite us to consider the benefits of long, humble backward looks. If "hindsight is always 20/20," then the views of historians can help us resist the temptation to cast off the old as we are distracted by the bells and whistles of the new. Sometimes assigned a curmudgeonly role in society, historians instead ask us to maintain respect for our roots, the inevitable material from which our experiences are formed. "Postmodern" or not, the world is sometimes most carefully and accurately interpreted by historians.

❏ **Real power.** One final example of the good work of social scientists is the wisdom of a single author, Janet Hagberg, whose propositions about "stages of personal power" (*Real Power: Stages of Personal Power in Organizations*) are enduring descriptions of human interaction. Her stage theory holds in loving embrace what you might want to know about your most basic concern: Am I powerful? How? Hagberg names "power" as good and essential and proposes that "real power" exists only as it is "given away" to others. Rising above the overused metaphor of "empowerment," Hagberg is specific about how, at each

◆

We are members of a great body...
We must consider that we were born for the good of the whole.

Seneca

stage, power is found, engendered, or learned. Perhaps the most compelling element of her work is her description of "masculine" and "feminine" forms of power.

Putting the wisdom of social scientists to work

Since it may be argued that "ecclesiology" is a branch of social science, you may find the following questions readily applicable to your congregation:

❑ What views of "change" motivate your congregation's work? What part of "change" do you need to learn more about? From whom?

❑ Where could you go to learn about the fascinating possibilities in "cross-generational influence" that have been suggested by generational theorists? What would you hope to learn?

❑ What discipline of historians could be most helpful in plotting the "history" you would most hope for your congregation?

❑ As you wrestle with "power" questions in your congregation, what would you like to understand better? From whom could you learn?

Journalism

The field of journalism is sometimes accused of being its own worst enemy, when "sensational" and "journalism" are combined, and a dash of "sloppy" is thrown in. But here again, godly good happens when the highest aspirations of this profession are lived out in the faithful work of purposeful journalists. These few examples might help you find good where you've been otherwise tempted toward cynicism.

❑ **Exposing sinfulness.** In many ways, journalists are a working-class variety of "prophet," as they continue to tell the truth about what they see. (Sometimes that kind of vision is not possible for the rest of us.) Corruption is rooted out, injustice exposed, shame heaped on those who are selfish or dishonest, or the weight of the law is leveraged to correct a continuing wrong. Seeing and saying what we may have overlooked (or are afraid to tell), journalists also leverage the will of the people toward eventual good.

❑ **Elemental honesty.** It may be so simple that we miss it, but most journalists daily provide an example of what it means "to be honest." In a world where subtle untruth is ubiquitous, professional journalists can provide a trustworthy and consistent model of basic honesty.

❑ **Finding inspiration.** Although the startling news of "man bites dog" is sometimes assumed to be the bread-and-butter of journalism, it is also part of this craft to find the ennobling and inspiring stories of human perseverance, *noblesse oblige*, and other "random acts of kindness." Think of a local reporter who spotlights an inspiring individual whose selfless service would otherwise go unnoticed, or a factory owner who keeps his employees working after a devastating fire wipes out half of his production capacity. Think of the times you've noticed a welling up of your "gratitude for people like that" when you've read or seen a story about a person or group whose life is a song of human dignity and worth.

◆

If you tell the truth, you don't have to remember anything.

Mark Twain

Putting the wisdom of journalists to work

You deal with "truth" and "honesty" in your work as a congregational leader, so you can benefit from the example and skills of journalists. Here are some questions to move you in that direction.

❑ As you look at the way you disseminate "news" about your congregation (or your denomination), where could you learn how to find and tell stories that might inspire others? Where could you find those stories in your own congregation?

❑ How honest are you in your communications with congregation members? What could you learn from journalism about courageous truth-telling?

❑ If your congregation needed to help expose an instance of evil nearby (or inside your fellowship), where could you go to learn how to "tell the truth in love" effectively?

Law and law enforcement

One of the most comforting images of the Holy Spirit, "Paraclete," is derived from the Greek *parakletos*, loosely translated as "comforter" or "helper." Further etymological work reveals the subtlety that the *parakletos* can also be an "advocate," one who stands to the side of, or accompanies, the one calling for help. Only one passage in Scripture (1 John 2:1) uses the term in this way, and here it refers to Christ. We always need his advocacy because of Satan's constant lies and accusations before God. Therefore, since lawyers are "advocates," it might be comforting for them to see Jesus Christ as one of them!

Another frequently maligned arena of human enterprise is that of the law. Its practice (by lawyers), its enforcement (by police and other public servants), and its judgments (in the court system) are all easy targets of disparaging remarks or humor. But God's work as law-giver, and God's insistence on justice-by-law are part of the Almighty's work in the world. Think through these examples as you find God's good work inside the legal system.

❑ **Deliverance from evil.** Every time the Lord's Prayer is prayed, Christians ask for deliverance from evil. The legal system answers that prayer. Law-enforcement officials, lawyers and judges face down the power of evil in individual lives and in society. They take on this potentially dangerous task every time they put on their badges, open their offices for business, or don judicial robes. By their work your prayers are answered.

❑ **Injustice restrained.** Blatant or subtle injustice must also be restrained or eliminated in our society. One thankless task of workers in the legal system is to ferret out injustice, apply the remedies of the law, and enforce sustained suppression of injustice. This work is "thankless" because of the subtle nature of injustice and its tenacious hold on the human condition.

❑ **The weak and oppressed defended.** Defense of those accused of wrongdoing is also a godly work, given especially to lawyers. Sometimes supposedly "guilty criminals" may be discovered to be victims of too-zealous law enforcement. People with legally weak or inaudible voices are given their day in court, and their reputations and character defended vigorously by lawyers. An impartial law is applied equally to each defendant. At the other end of the spectrum, officers of the law and judges arrest, prosecute, and punish those who oppress or prey on people who are weak. God's work as defender is thus carried out every day through the legal system and those who work in it.

Putting the legal system's wisdom to work

What could you learn about your congregation's work by paying attention to the legal system? Perhaps questions like this can get you started:

❑ What evil faces your congregation? How could a lawyer's advice or presence bring comfort to you?

❑ Where could members of your congregation learn how to advocate for each other, or for those around you who are weak or oppressed?

❑ What injustices operate inside your congregation? How do you restrain them? Who could teach you?

❑ In what ways does your congregation's ignorance of the law put it at jeopardy as an organization? Who could help you change that situation?

Social justice groups around the world

I conclude this section with an obvious example: organizations and enterprises whose godly work helps bring God's justice to bear on the world close at hand and beyond the horizon. In the examples that follow you can get an idea how these organizations echo Jesus' own ministries.

❑ **Hunger alleviated.** Organized programs by which hunger and poverty are diminished have been part of most denominations since the middle 1960s. Although you may not hear this statistical summary often, hunger and poverty have decreased over the past 40 years. A simple way to

◆

If we do not maintain Justice, Justice will not maintain us.

Francis Bacon

state the matter: Fewer people go to bed hungry every night. Micro-enterprise projects are growing, infant mortality has decreased, efficiency multiplies in rebuilding war-torn or disaster-ravaged countries, sustainable technologies for health and agriculture are working in more places, reforestation efforts are expanding. The prevalence of sin, greed, war, and natural disasters or those of human origin suggests that the work of these organizations will continue into the coming decades. But the godly good news is that these efforts are working.

❑ **World health.** The dismal reality of continuing epidemics of AIDS; recurring episodes of typhoid, polio, malaria, tuberculosis, and hepatitis; and environmental degradation and persistent malnutrition still plague the state of the world's health. At the same time, we cannot overlook the work of medical personnel whose selfless devotion to their professions—usually at some personal risk—is an example of the healing of Christ and recalls the early Christians' selfless living.

❑ **Asset-based planning.** This exciting bit of applied social theory serves as a good example here of how social-service organizations have been a godly force in Third World development efforts. You will recall from chapter 1 that this way of approaching community development first anchored the work of nongovernmental organizations overseas. In communities where perpetual neediness had characterized people's self-image and daily living for generations, the applied principles of asset-based thinking gave rise to increased rights for women, just and equitable distribution of community resources, and increased capacity for self-help. The simple proposition of God-given capacity helps move entire communities from dependency to self-reliance. Thus God's blessings are multiplied in a stewardship of newly discovered abundance. (We'll revisit this subject in depth in chapter 8.)

Putting social-justice wisdom to work

"Overseas development philosophies" might also apply to the dynamics of your congregation.

❑ What motivations and what techniques have social-justice organizations used to call God's people to extend themselves in service far beyond their comfort zones? How might those motivations and techniques work in your congregation?

❑ What have you done to thank donors and servant-volunteers in your congregation's partnership with social justice organizations?

❑ What could you learn about asset-based planning that could inform the way you "do church"?

❑ How might the term "ministry of health" characterize your congregation's identity or mission? Where could you learn about that?

A final note on this matter

In these pages you've examined how avoidance of evil—although seemingly justified by scriptural evidence and the presumed state of the world—may not be a helpful way of thinking or acting. You've also waded through pages of "evidence" that God is doing something good in the various human enterprises outlined here. You've pondered questions about your congregation, and wondered how you might learn from the godly good you've examined.

Whether or not you have agreed with each example of godly good happening in the world, you have seen the truth of the basic premise: God works in the world through people. In every arena of life, Christians invest their God-given gifts in the promise that what they do in Christ's name—no matter how small it might seem—can be multiplied in God's surprising mathematics.

By your participation as a worker in God's world, you are a partner in God's work. You can certainly find "godly good" in that joyful promise!

**UNCLEAR ON THE AGENDA FOR THEIR MEETING,
THE WITNESS AND SERVICE TEAM DECIDED TO FIND
"WITNESS AND SERVICE" ON THE WORLDWIDE WEB.**

MORE PLAY TIME ON THE WEB

You've probably realized that I've prodded you to try playing on the World Wide Web, to see what's going on in the world. Use some of the following activities to extend this learning experience.

● Try combinations of "Good News" and other words, such as medicine, law, automobiles, environment, education, or relationships. (I had fun with "toys"!) On newsprint or chalkboard make a quick listing of all the Web sites you find. See what you learn, what patterns you find, what "good news" means to Web denizens and their search engines.

● Find sites established by organizations that want you to know the most recent developments in various fields of human endeavor. Try the categories in this chapter first—law, business, journalism, etc.—and then branch out to some wildly exciting places to find "godly good." (Some I'd want to check out are nutrition, farming, housing, parenting, counseling, prosthetics, preventive health, volunteerism, and alternative fuels.) Again, chart what you find, especially the surprising places. How could you construct new kinds of Sunday prayers from what you find?

● Insert news of godly good into sermons. Each week, discipline yourself to use examples from only one field of human endeavor, and insist that the examples be positive and illustrative of what the lessons tell about God's actions. (For an easy example, for a Sunday service that features a story of healing, search the Web to find current examples of how God heals today in the actions of medical researchers, doctors, and psychologists.) Try this for two months, and then adjust the content of your searching and preaching on the basis of hearers' reactions.

● Do something similar—but shorter—as devotional material for all your committee or task-force meetings in the next two months. See how this habit changes the way you do business, the way you feel about the world, or the way these bits and pieces of godly good connect with participants' lives.

● Follow the "rabbit trail" of one Web site's many directions. (How does "surf the Web" make sense, if waves run in only one direction?) Meander through subdirectories, inner workings of the site, and the all-important links to other sites. On your electronic trip, "shop" for evidence of godly good news, jotting notes about anything interesting you find. If you do this as a group activity, talk about what you find. If members of your group do this individually, report to each other what piqued your interest, what sparked ideas, what you want to thank God for. (A place to start: type *safety* into your browser, pick one site, and start your rabbit-hopping!)

HOW TO KNOW
IF YOU'RE BEATING ON THE WORLD
A Checklist for Leaders

Directions: This checklist helps our congregation leaders see how we think about the world around us. Answer all items by checking "yes" or "no."

YES NO

☐ ☐   1. I regularly get angry about what I read in the newspaper, see on television news, or find on the Web.

☐ ☐   2. Most of the people I know are evil in some way.

☐ ☐   3. My basic view of politicians is that they're in politics mostly for their own good.

☐ ☐   4. Most of the people in the entertainment industry don't live morally upright lives.

☐ ☐   5. Most people I know don't tell the truth unless they're forced to.

☐ ☐   6. I think it's the church's role to let us know how to wall ourselves off from the evil world around us.

☐ ☐   7. I like this church because I feel safe from the evil I encounter outside this place.

☐ ☐   8. I'm worried that "good" is losing the war with "evil."

☐ ☐   9. If I had my choice, I'd ask God to punish evildoers instead of trying to change them.

☐ ☐ 10. Most of the Bible was written to teach us how to live the way God wants us to live.

Scoring the checklist: If you checked more than three "yes" boxes, you may want to think carefully about how "evil" affects you. You may want to read this chapter again more carefully.

PARSING THIS CHAPTER

The preceding pages may have been a "long drink of water all at one time." Taking in what you've read might be easier if you think about such follow-up items as the following:

1. After you read about all the "good" that I think is happening out there in the world, take a newspaper or newsmagazine and try to make a quick chart of some of the godly goods you see happening in your world. Right now, in front of your appreciative, God-thanking eyes!

2. What in this chapter pricked your conscience? Explain your thoughts to those around you.

3. When you think about your own daily living, for whom are you (or is your work) some kind of godly good news? How do you know? What does that make you want to do next?

4. Pick one or two areas of human enterprise outlined in this chapter. Find a good example of God's good work. Ferret out the name, title, and address of an individual to whom you could write. After a time of thankful prayer, compose and send a letter of thanks for the work of this individual, company, or organization. (One easy place to find addresses: The fine print on product wrappers or containers.)

5. Where in this chapter did you find yourself being asked to fly or flutter with joy? Where did you experience an "aha!" moment that you'd like to share?

6. In what ways has this chapter made you even more grumpy about the condition of the world? What does that make you want to do next?

6

EQUIPPING WHO'S HERE

If you're like me—and I know that I am—reading the previous chapters has felt like looking through a telescope's big end: big subjects have been made smaller so you can see them all. Now I'm going to switch ends of the telescope and bring closer some things that may have been far away. The first thing we'll look at is "the pastoral office," the role pastors assume in congregational behaviors and structures. Whether you're a pastor or not, the ideas in this chapter may help you bring new life to a role or office that may have become unnecessarily overexertive.

In this chapter you'll:

❑ Look at the nature of clericalism and anticlericalism.

❑ Think about how to redeem the role of the pastor.

❑ Play around with ideas about how the members of your congregation can be "equipped."

I like to crumple "pastoral office" matters into a simple, foil-ball question, "What are pastors for, anyway?" And sometimes I set it next to two others: "What are members for?" and "What are congregations for?" The nice thing about these questions? Their grammatical form invites answers that include active verbs!

Clericalism and anticlericalism

By whatever name you give them, the behaviors and attitudes of clericalism (and anticlericalism) are probably well known to you. For the purposes of this chapter, let me define them this way:

❑ "Clericalism" is any behavior that comes from the assumption that the church equals its clergy.

❑ "Anticlericalism" is any reactive behavior that is based on the assumption that the church is better off without clergy.

Both clericalism and anticlericalism operate in the psychology of most congregations. They exist as two opposing viewpoints about the congregation's structure and mission. On the one side, some members and leaders may view these times as chaotic, and in need of ordering. According to this viewpoint, a well-established and highly regarded class of spiritual leaders is necessary to ensure the integrity of the congregation-as-institution. In the view of others, the congregation may die slowly from within when misused clerical power contradicts the prevailing societal trends of inclusion, democracy, and collegiality.

A little deeper look

The term "clericalized laity" describes people whose devotion to the pastor—or to that role—is so great that they unconsciously define all other elements of the church by their high regard for clergy. Clericalized laity may work alongside clergy as devoted partners, counselors, and friends. They may think and behave in ways similar to clergy. They may see the greatest good—or deficit—of a congregation personified by its pastor. In some congregations, this attitude may be an unwritten qualification for congregational leadership.

Clericalism can be described as any attitude, behavior, or structure within the church that presumes that the subject of the church is its clergy, that laypeople are the object of the church, that the clergy are responsible for the church, and that these truths are historically and everlastingly true.

Sociologically, clericalism is one variety of classism, in which one class of church members—the clergy and clericalized laity—holds greater power than other classes of church members.

Anticlericalism is a reaction against the power or the office of the clergy. Sometimes it is associated with a virulent populism that disallows any authority. Sometimes anticlericalism is connected to a generalized disregard for the church's orthodoxy or history. Anticlericalism is usually a reaction, however, and not self-generating.

Because they seem to feed off each other, clericalism and anticlericalism can be considered "twinned evils" in the life of the church. Both begin with fear and anger—a subject we'll visit in chapter 7—and draw people into conflict within themselves and with each other. Both clericalism and anticlericalism can develop into insidious behavioral patterns or emotional states that are easily aroused. Both can build inflexible institutional structures that are easily justified only by their own logic. Both claim righteous histories and righteously imagined futures.

A short history

Within a hundred years after Pentecost, the early church created a separate class of the laity, called "clergy." Because of the rapid infusions of new, formerly pagan Christians (and their beliefs), the authority and quality of the apostles' teachings were being threatened. Professionalized clergy were authorized not so much to exhibit power over "ordinary Christians," but rather to offer believers the comfort and security of established doctrine and practice. Given the chaotic alternatives, the office of clergy was a welcome development.

By the time of the first millennium, a churchly classism had become permanently established. New theological explanations asserted that "the spiritual estate" (the institutional church, its leaders, and workers) was in charge of the temporal estate—the government and commerce. Thoughtful leaders agreed that separation from the presumably evil world increased spiritual purity. Those holding clerical offices were due certain rights and privileges in society.

As a reactive pattern of thought, anticlericalism grew more slowly than clericalism. The collapse of the Roman Empire delayed serious challenges to the church's authority. But there was not universal agreement about the presumed power of the church. Kings and emperors, as well as leaders in commerce and some theologians, questioned the shaky logic that established singular power in the offices of church leaders. In repeated ecclesiastical rebellions throughout the Middle Ages, early and late reformers suggested or demanded that the church-as-institution pay attention to its constituents, and to other sources of power in the church. By the time the Reformation ran its political course—including several lengthy wars—the mind of the church was evenly split between the choice of chaotic equality among Christians and the idea that general order was best established and maintained by the church.

Anticlericalism flourished during the Renaissance. Not only the reformers of the church, but also newly independent scholars and political authorities openly questioned the basic assumptions that had allowed the church to run roughshod over the affairs of families, businesses, and nation-states. The political power of the church continued its decline in the ensuring centuries. By the 19th century, political leaders, philosophers, and Reformed theologians had thoroughly disabused people of their notions about the power of the

Health, education, and civility were in short supply during the Dark Ages. The church and some nobility were the acknowledged repositories of knowledge and wisdom. Science, philosophy, medicine, the arts—all necessary elements for an ordered civilization—were both preserved and developed by members of the church's orders. Thus, anticlericalism was muted in favor of the greater good, the emergence of civilization from these difficult centuries.

church and its clergy. Nationalistic movements in Italy and Britain sparked virulent anticlericalist activities in the rest of Europe and in the United States.

What causes clericalism and anticlericalism

To understand how these twin evils originate and continue, let's look at some possible sources for these sets of behaviors.

Emotional triggers in the human brain

The attitudes and behaviors of clericalism—and its reactive twin, anticlericalism—begin in the human brain, probably in the danger-sensing structures and mechanisms that cause fear, anxiety, or anger. In the case of clericalism, the perceived dangers may have to do with threats to the clergy's financial well-being, success, family relationships, or a preferred future. In the case of anticlericalism, the anger or fear are easily triggered by even the slightest stimulus that suggests an imbalance of power between the "too-powerful clergy" and the "powerless laity."

Possible neuroses

Clericalism may also be rooted in such neurotic phenomena as:

❑ Distorted attempts to heal childhood dysfunctions (such as abuse or severe feelings of inferiority).

❑ Obsessive craving for self-importance.

❑ Obsessive-compulsive disorders.

❑ Living primarily within "the false self," an imagined persona.

The scriptural story

Another possible source for clericalism and anticlericalism is biblical history. Scriptures seem to support the centrality of the clerical role or office. For example, the Bible uses the metaphor of "shepherd and sheep," which has been misappropriated into a contemporary mythology that describes the laity primarily as sheep and the pastor as shepherd.

Anticlericalism shows up almost invisibly. Some of the religious tensions in the Old Testament could be seen as the battle between institutionalized clericalism—the priestly class, which included Levites and other religious workers—and charismatic leaders like Amos, Jeremiah, and David, who questioned the authority of the religious leaders.

Jesus' witness and example

One of the most plaintive motivations for clericalism may be the "little Jesus" phenomenon. Here, expectations about the office of pastor include minor-Messiah roles patterned after Jesus' functions as "prophet," "priest," and "king." This overemphasis on Jesus' divine work sets up unreal expectations for clergy behavior. You can easily see how "trying too hard" could result from this variety of "what would Jesus do."

On the other hand, Jesus' diatribes against the spiritual miscreants of his day could be seen as anticlerical. His treatment of the pious Pharisees—and the Gospel writers' inclusion of the ruling Sadducees as fellow culprits—seems consistent with a view that "professional religious leaders" were a primary source of the problems within Judaism.

The larger church

Large regional or national expressions of the church can be both primary and continuing causes for clericalism and its reactive twin, anticlericalism. Just as "racism" is institutionalized prejudice and injustice, so "clericalism" is institutionalized classism. It is easily fostered by the assumption that the good of the larger church depends on clergy well-being and care. In its operations, the larger church might foster clericalism in these ways:

❑ Judicatory officials (who are probably former parish pastors) reward clergy for clericalist behaviors.

❑ Decision-making bodies are made up primarily of clergy and clericalized laity.

❑ Most rules, procedures, and rituals are clergy-focused.

❑ Clerical opinions are more often expressed—or more highly valued—than lay opinions.

When the larger church encourages clericalism, it also provides imagined reasons for anticlericalism to arise in reaction to the alleged abuse of power by clergy within the larger church structure. Thus highly visible clericalism can beget highly visible anticlericalism.

Generalized narcissism

One other disturbing reality may lie at the core of both clericalism and anticlericalism: generalized narcissism. It is easy to see what may contribute to excessive self-love among clergy:

Citing their previous research, psychologists Brad Bushman and Roy Baumeister ("Violent Pride," *Scientific American*, April 2001) propose that people with low self-esteem are not prone to aggressive responses. Instead, Bushman and Baumeister warn, we might all beware of "persons who regard themselves as superior to others, especially when those beliefs are inflated, weakly grounded in reality or heavily dependent on having others confirm them frequently. Conceited, self-important individuals turn nasty toward those who puncture their bubbles of self-love." Their name for this phenomenon is "threatened egotism," which could equally describe clericalism or anticlericalism.

❑ Continual adulation and praise ("Nice sermon, Pastor!").

❑ Overabundant gratitude for clergy presence at times of deepest need ("We couldn't have faced Dad's death without you, Pastor!").

❑ Absence of qualified critics ("You're the one with the seminary training, Pastor").

❑ Relative lack of measurable objectives for job performance ("What *is* a good sermon, anyhow?").

It may be harder to see how anticlerical laity could also be infected with excessive self-love. Remember, though, that for decades both the church and the culture have perhaps overemphasized self-esteem and self-worth. This trend may have encouraged many people to hold themselves in artificially high estimation. When the thin veneer of their excessive self-regard is threatened or exposed, they may react with the verbal violence of anticlericalism.

Is It Like This "Out There"?

Pastors who deal with their members' clericalism—yes, laity can be comfortable living inside the clericalist world that they have constructed—and with undeserved forms of anticlericalism may wonder whether these problems exist outside congregations. Most likely they exist in any organization where the management style centers on the manager.

Congregations may differ from other human enterprises in one important way, however: Congregations can draw psychologically needy people together in one place, reward and care for those needs, set up consuming codependencies, and ease out of their comfortable nests any others who threaten the "healing place" nature of the congregation.

These behaviors can be cemented into a congregation's foundations. In such places a higher-than-average percentage of members may depend on the church to meet their psychological needs—"This is the only place where I'm understood and welcomed, Pastor." When a congregation becomes a needs-filling place, a caring pastor and other members might reinforce this "cowbird effect" by loving and caring for those with perpetual needs, even to the detriment of the congregation's well-being.

In the world outside the church, hurting and needy people are diffused among the population, and their concentration in clinics, helping agencies, and doctors' offices is matched by a concentration of skillful professional care.

When congregations behave primarily as "healing places," "refuges for the weary," "safe havens," or other varieties of "hospitals," they may run the risk of attracting a disproportionate percentage of people who have made the sad error of identifying themselves by their dysfunction. In those places, pastors and members inevitably try too hard.

The clergy's search for significance

In their most honest moments, few clergy are certain that they have personal significance in most aspects of their parishioners' lives. They certainly understand and value their leadership in institutional matters, their skill and knowledge in churchly constructs, and their ability to add meaning to the lives of leaders, hurting people, and members of "inner circles." Some clergy may feel separation from members who:

❑ Are highly successful outside the churchly world.

❑ Have superior skill or knowledge.

❑ Are wealthy or otherwise well-off.

❑ Do not depend on the congregation for their self-worth or identity.

❑ Do not pay attention to clergy activities or leadership.

The "80/20 Rule" holds that about 80 percent of the congregation's work is accomplished by about 20 percent of its members. Another arrogant correlative is that the 80 percent who are doing 20 percent or less of the work are "inactive." Why is this assumption arrogant? The term "inactive" implies that because of their inactivity in the congregation, such people do nothing to change or otherwise affect God's world outside of the church. The term "inactive" may be most used by clergy and congregational leaders who have problems with their significance or who don't see past their own self-defined views of "active in God's work."

The separation is not antagonistic or disrespectful on either side. Instead, it shows that the pastor's role has relatively low importance in these members' daily lives. Depending on how you define or identify these individuals, they may constitute as much as 80 percent of the congregation.

Some clergy accept this limited emotional connection as a given in their ministries; others live with the dull pain of bruised egos; still others fight for any shred of significance they can gather around their naked-emperor souls; and some give in to blatant clericalism. For all of them, though, the question remains: How can I find significance in this role, outside its own institutionally defined measurements? Many of them may try too hard to correct the situation.

The "power" of clergy and laity

Clericalism and anticlericalism may also have their roots in the legitimate wish of clergy and laity to be powerful for God's purposes. (For these well-meaning people, power is defined as the ability to change something.) So both clergy and laity seek ways to be powerful in their congregations. Clericalism and anticlericalism occur when clergy and laity differ about the distribution or direction of their power.

It can be hard for clergy and lay leaders to keep a balanced perspective about power. In her book *Real Power: Stages of Personal Power in Organizations*, business consultant Janet O. Hagberg shows how individuals develop "real power"—an ability to link inner purpose and reflection with capacity for action. In her "stage theory" description of power, the first stage is "powerlessness." She describes the next two stages, still far removed from real power, by their sources: "power by association" and "power by symbols." Later stages, "power by reflection" and "power by purpose," characterize the personal authority of leaders who are skilled at giving away power.

This theory of power helps explain how clergy can get stuck in less-evolved, less-powerful relationships—having no power, or using the symbols of the office to exert weak power. Hagberg's work may also explain how clericalized laity add to the pastor's false view of significance.

Seeking authentic relationships

Both clericalism and anticlericalism might be energized by ordained ministers' search for authentic relationships with laypeople. (Authenticity consists of shared perceptions about important matters; integrity among emotions, intellect, and actions; and personal competence.) If clergy lack authenticity, they may substitute clericalist behaviors for authentic relationships. Some lay folk react negatively to this inauthentic replacement, and push back against the clerical power they feel pastors exhibiting. Strangely, both clergy and laity still desire deep and authentic relationships with each other.

How is this behavior "trying too hard"?

I see three ways in which clericalism (and reactive anti-clericalism) may result in overexertion that threatens the sustainability of congregations and their leaders.

A cycle of growing exertion

First, let me suggest a downward spiral of behaviors that works like this:

❑ Most clergy are aware that their members find personal meaning also in places other than the church.

❑ This awareness may leave clergy with the false perception that their significance is reduced.

❑ Thus diminished, clergy may think that their only choice is to try harder to achieve special excellence or to exercise control in their own sphere of influence, the church.

❑ This behavior may heighten anticlericalist emotions and actions.

❑ The pastor's feelings of separation or insignificance increase.

These behaviors result in a self-perpetuating cycle that sucks energy and goodwill out of a congregation and damages its emotional well-being.

The hard work of exclusivity

Next is the matter of exclusivity. One effect of clericalism is that clericalized laity are more likely than other members to be appreciated and rewarded by clergy. Over time, increasing numbers of congregation members are excluded from the inner circle. Important decisions are predigested by this tight group of the pastor's friends or followers. Other members are persuaded or motivated to accept or participate in decisions they did not make. Like participants in any cycle of codependency, clergy and clericalized laity may grow insensitive to the effects of their behaviors. Eventually their mutual admiration society cannot carry out all the decisions that have been made. Subtly excluded members reciprocate with their own disregard, and the congregation suddenly faces the prospect of "not having enough volunteers." At that point, clericalized laity and their pastors start working too hard, either to persuade, cajole, or shame other members into action, or to undertake more and more tasks themselves. Entrepreneurial leadership decreases, the pool of leaders grows smaller, and the congregation seems apathetic about its own programs or activities.

Anticlericalism can also be exclusive, especially as congregations move toward conflict. Those who oppose the pastor's authority or power can form their own mutual-whiners societies. These groups exclude other members who don't strongly dislike clergy in general or the present pastor in particular. Members who harbor continuing anticlericalism in their souls always have to work hard to experience a positive and hopeful attitude about their congregation.

The seeds of conflict

Because their behaviors can engender anticlericalism, pastors and laity who think of the congregation as "pastor-centered" always risk sowing seeds of conflict. Congregations whose decisions and identity are clergy-centered are places where "personality conflicts" are likely to emerge. Those who accept or welcome "clergycentric" attitudes find themselves in sharp disagreement with those who do not accept the assumed power of the pastor. These small differences can easily evolve into full-blown hostilities—between pastors and members, and between groups of members—which consume enormous amounts of energy, emotion, and financial and spiritual capital.

How to spot clericalism

A first step to removing both clericalism and anticlericalism is to identity clericalism when it manifests itself. (Remember that anticlericalism is usually reactive, so eliminating clericalism is usually a first step in reducing its twin.) The easiest way to spot clericalism is to ask, "Who benefits most from a particular behavior, structure, or attitude in the church?" If clericalism is at work, both the obvious and subtle answers point at clergy and clericalized laity.

Because attitudes result in actions, lay leaders or pastors can demonstrate clericalism in such behaviors as these:

❑ Emphasizing strongly the importance of ordination rites.

❑ Equating the worth of a pastor's ministry almost exclusively with preaching skills.

❑ Creating or maintaining a personality cult centered on clergy.

❑ Denigrating or disregarding those who criticize clergy.

❑ Willingly offering or accepting special privileges.

❑ Behaving in a controlling way, or participating in controlling structures.

❑ Preferring clergy's role as sole caregiver among many care receivers.

❑ Emphasizing fulfillment of laity needs; de-emphasizing the affirmation of laypeople's gifts.

❑ Relying on ecclesiastical symbols—clothing, titles, judicatory positions—that emphasize the set-apartness of the clergy.

One hidden anguish among regional and national judicatory staff members is the high percentage of their waking hours devoted to congregational conflict resolution. The cost in time and wages (or consultant fees) is considerable. Their anguish is deepened by the sense that "this time could be better used."

◆

If the decline in pastors continues, it is impossible to imagine our congregations growing!

Anonymous seminary fund solicitation letter

❑ Consistently deferring to imagined ecclesiastical authority or procedure.

❑ Subtly disregarding "secular" knowledge, attitudes, or skills.

❑ Fostering passivity or codependence among lay leaders.

❑ Choosing hierarchical decision-making styles.

From outside your congregation, clericalism is easily visible. (The parodies and stereotypes of clergy in popular media are a familiar example.) People in the world beyond your congregation see clericalism as a reason to disregard or dishonor you and your ministries.

Inside the church the prejudices are reversed, and anticlericalism sticks out. What members of the congregation see: a small group of untamed or uncivilized laity whose disregard for clergy and institution threatens to destabilize the congregation's fragile balance of power. Anticlerical members are viewed as nonproductive or dangerous.

Dr. Billy Poobah's
SUBTLE CLERICALISM CHECKLIST

Directions: Read each of the items below, checking those that apply to you or your congregation.

❑ I never address my pastor using his or her first name.

❑ Our pastor runs most meetings in the congregation.

❑ Our pastor talks about this congregation as "my church."

❑ Out of respect, I do not question the pastor's judgment in congregational matters.

❑ When looking for another pastor, I'd want to find someone really likable.

❑ Important events in our judicatory always take place during the week rather than on weekends.

❑ We insist on having our pastor's name on the outside church sign.

❑ It would be hard for me to name my pastor's faults.

❑ I appreciate our pastor especially for caring at every imaginable time of need.

❑ Without a good pastor, a congregation will fall apart.

❑ In our congregation, "the buck" stops at the pastor's desk.

Scoring: If you checked fewer than three items, you're probably just a nice person and you like pastors in general. If you checked as many as six, you may need to think about how much emotional baggage you're attaching to the role of "pastor." If the number of checked boxes approached nine, you may want to read these pages one more time.

Dr. Billy Poobah's
SUBTLE ANTICLERICALISM CHECKLIST

Directions: Read each of the items below, checking those that apply to you or your congregation.

❏ I would never address my pastor without using his or her first name.

❏ It makes me angry that our pastor runs most meetings in the congregation.

❏ If our pastor says "my congregation," I fume inwardly or correct the language.

❏ Out of respect for other leaders, I feel free to question the pastor's judgment in congregational matters.

❏ The statement "We should like our pastor" doesn't make any sense to me.

❏ Important judicatory events always take place on a weekend.

❏ We would never allow our pastor's name to be put on the outside church signs.

❏ I am painfully aware of our pastor's faults.

❏ I think our pastor would do better *not* caring for everyone at every imaginable time of need.

❏ Without a pastor, this congregation would probably do better than we're doing now.

❏ Our pastor doesn't take responsibility for what a pastor should.

Scoring: If you checked fewer than three items, you're probably just a nice person who happens not to like your present pastor. If you checked as many as six, you may need to think about how much anger you're attaching to "pastor." If the number of checked boxes approached nine, you may want to read these pages one more time.

Redeeming the role of the pastor

In the pages that follow, we'll look for thoughts and actions that might correct—or inoculate against—clericalism and anticlericalism.

One kind of solution

Absent some new kind of vicarious atonement—one pastor in some large parish is publicly shamed in the national media, or a pastor is elected president of the United States—the solutions to pastoral powerlessness or insignificance seem predictable:

❑ Work harder.

❑ Work smarter.

❑ Be clever and charismatic.

❑ Work harder and smarter at being clever and charismatic.

❑ Rely on the whistling magic bullets of metachurch formulas.

❑ Work harder at putting into practice the magic bullets of metachurch formulas, while being clever and charismatic.

❑ Die while working on the items above.

❑ Hope for the Second Coming, or a bodily assumption into heaven.

In all these "solutions," the cost of redeeming the pastor's role seems to grow with each passing day, each new book, each "building block of the perfect congregation," or each edict from the national office. And when the cost goes up, so can the cognitive dissonance—higher expectations not matched by increased outcomes. Clearly, paying a higher cost for significance—a form of "trying too hard"—does not necessarily result in greater significance, except for the lucky few who already are charismatic, hardworking, and able to make magic bullets into programs.

"Redeemed" seems to be the right word here. Other ways to describe redemption are "buying back," "giving and receiving equal value," or "paying something and getting something." Role-redemption doesn't happen by magic; neither did the redemption of the world. In that case the cost was Christ's tortured death on the cross. In the case of "redeeming the role of pastor," the costs are considerably lower. The pastor's role can be redeemed because Jesus already took care of the really important redemption.

The theory of cognitive dissonance has developed considerably since social psychologist Leon Festinger proposed it more than 40 years ago. The theory explains the sociology and psychology of decision making. How does it work? When your expectations are just slightly higher than your outcomes, you are more likely to change. If your expectations are way out of whack with your outcomes—too high or too low—you will be either completely overwhelmed with impossibility or oversatisfied with easy achievement. In either case, you will not be willing to change.

A better idea

The precepts and practices of "ministry in daily life" theology offer another redemptive possibility: equipping members for their own ministries of significance. In other words, pastors give away significance so that others can find their own. Good teachers know how that works—they help people learn without doing much "teaching." Good managers know how to do that—they construct a workplace where workers enjoy doing their work. The price these leaders pay: relinquishing their significance.

◆

I start with the premise that the function of leadership is to produce more leaders, not more followers.

Ralph Nader

Role-redeemed pastors could do that, too, if they refocused their calendars and self-measurement on the relatively simple tasks of equipping their members for daily stewardship, witness, and worship. To what end? So that members could do the work they do so well—God's work—out in the world. Significant pastors could find and develop their members' assets, not always share their own. They could do less "leading" and "discipling" and more leader-development and steward-building. They could learn to know their members as their members know themselves: God's people even when they are outside the walls and words of church-as-institution.

"Giving away" significance so that others can find their own may be a high price to pay. This may be especially true for clergy so starved for importance that the thought of releasing the last shreds of their self-worth could be debilitating. In the end, this is a small price to pay for the good of God's kingdom, God's will for the church, and the Spirit's leveraging of abundant gifts for the sake of the world.

When that price is paid, willingly and consistently, the pastor can find in the seeming release of self-worth a paradox born of God's Holy Spirit: true significance. Pastors can become less "little Christs" and more "little John the Baptists." Their seeming decrease can make possible others' increase. The pastor-giver becomes more and more significant, more and more necessary, and more and more a generator of gifts.

Pastors who think and behave this way do not try too hard, because they are always building the capacities of their members, multiplying and leveraging gifts for the good of God's work in and beyond the congregation. Sustainability? God's paradoxes operate again: The more you give away, the more you receive; the less anxious you are about institutional survival, the less likely the institution will die.

Equipping for what?

The first task of "equipping the saints" is offering the support and sustenance that God's people want and need for their daily-life ministries. Every day they engage in vocations, avocations, relationships, and challenges in which God's will might be accomplished. (See chapter 5.) Every day they encounter Evil and its ugly brood—stupidity, greed, selfishness, exclusion, fear. Every day they give away their lives for God's goodly work.

In their worlds, people need what God wants most to give them: skill and wisdom to live purposeful and meaningful lives. Pastors' primary role is to make that happen, notably through Word and Sacrament ministry.

One related question: Who's minding the store while all these members are out there in the world with their equipping pastor alongside? Who's looking out for the congregation?

Pastors and leaders who equip members for lives of service—and the congregations in which this equipping is offered—will become necessary to their members. Members will reciprocate with generous gifts of time and money. Why? Because there is no other place where forgiveness is so well proclaimed and practiced, no other place where God's wisdom is so well taught and preached, no other place where loneliness and guilt are so thoroughly displaced.

The Value of Word and Sacrament Ministry

Sometimes pastors and leaders look around at "successful congregations" and see only their outer surfaces. At the surface, they find razzmatazz programs, charismatic personalities, flashy facilities, and catchy slogans, and they think that these qualities typify the congregations. On closer examination, though, the "successful" inner core of these congregations can be described as "authentic Word and Sacrament ministry."

The recent study of 600 "excellent congregations" across the country by religion scholar and researcher Paul Wilkes (*Excellent Protestant Congregations* and *Excellent Catholic Parishes*) describes a variety of practices and guidelines that characterize high-quality congregations. But at the heart of these congregations, says Wilkes, is the beginning of excellence: a faithful relationship with God. Alongside are other factors: trust in one another and imagination applied to the congregation's life. Where might those factors have originated? My best guess: the Word and Sacrament ministry of faithful, trustworthy, trusting, and imaginative pastors.

Word and Sacrament ministry adds value to members' life and work as it:

- Unites them with God, sometimes in transcendent ways.

- Makes forgiveness as tangible as sin, and more powerful.

- Makes sense of a world difficult to understand, one in which ministry is difficult.

- Allays fear of death—the primal fear that may drive all other fears.

- Names and motivates meaningful existence.

- Assures people that they have an ultimate destiny already available through Jesus' death and resurrection.

- Draws them together with other believers in mutual understanding, love, and work.

If you're a pastor, remember: Because of your calling, your training, and your skills, you get to be God's designated Word-giver!

Getting down to metaphoric brass tacks

"Equipping" is a wonderful metaphor to use in describing pastors' work. Paul started the idea in Ephesians 4—"equipping the saints for their ministries"—and thus legitimated a hopeful and possible view of the pastoral role.

What might you see if you were to meet "an equipping pastor" wandering around in your congregation? Let's ask the question, "What is an equipping pastor like?" and look for answer-starters that begin, "An equipping pastor is like . . . ." This could be fun!

THE EQUIPPING PASTOR:

Coach • Seer • Translator • Prophet • Steward • Composer
Humorist • Wholesale Dealer • Waiter • Florist
Well-digger • Accountant

"An equipping pastor is like the number announcer at a Bingo game." The players place the numbers on the cards they have been given. All the number caller does is to draw and announce random numbers. The number caller isn't as important as the numbers.

"An equipping pastor is like an expedition outfitter." If you are given the wrong stuff, your expedition or adventure goes sour. You get the right equipment, and you're ready for whatever happens. The key: The outfitter knows about the expedition because she has already experienced it.

"An equipping pastor is like a supply sergeant." Keeping the army fed, clothed, and housed requires a nimble (and sometimes nimble-fingered) person. Resourceful and shrewd, the supply sergeant can "find you anything you need." You'll rarely see the sergeant at the front lines, but without him, the rest of the troops wouldn't be able to do their jobs.

"An equipping pastor is like an auto-parts dealer." Your car won't run without the right part, and the auto-parts dealer knows how your car is constructed, down to its most finite detail. And the nice thing about this store: All parts are always in stock!

"An equipping pastor is like a Tai Chi instructor." The instructor's moves may be slow and graceful, but their intent is sure: to show you an exercise that doubles as self-defense. An added benefit: The instructor is a good example of controlled wisdom and powerful movements.

"An equipping pastor is like a musical director." The script is written; the actors, sets, and costumes are in place. But it's the director who helps everything come together. The director isn't an actor in the play, and so is able to watch how the actors bring the script to life.

"An equipping pastor is like a personal fitness trainer." All the equipment in the world doesn't do your body a bit of good until you know how to use it. Carefully, slowly, you learn from a patient instructor.

"An equipping pastor is like 'that look' that only your Mother can give." When you're thinking that everything is just about

◆

Wherever we find the Word of God surely preached and heard, and the Sacraments administered according to the institution of Christ, there, it is not to be doubted, is a church of God.

John Calvin

WHAT MAKES METAPHORS FUN

Metaphor-building is one of the brain's favorite activities. That's why ad agencies, politicians, rhetoricians, philosophers, poets, teachers, and clever writers of books about "trying too hard" use metaphors in their work. Early in the history of brain theory—back when the "information revolution" was also hatching—some researchers were describing the brain's activities as "mapmaking," and others were promoting the maxim "Whoever owns the metaphors owns the world." Their thought: Because an information glut threatened to overload the brain's capacities for data storage and sorting, metaphor-making (a kind of mapping activity) could organize and summarize large amounts of data in conveniently recalled constructs.

"Meaning-making" occurs not only because things and actions are defined in precise terms, but also because metaphors call for imagination and playfulness. Nutrients and electrochemical energy sizzle through brain circuits as old and new thoughts are quickly assembled and new neuronal connections are made. The brain is aroused from its background ready-state to tackle a promising activity: making new meaning.

"What is an equipping pastor like?" invites your brain to search its experiences, emotional history, and imagined futures to construct word-pictures. As they are being constructed, these images pulse inside more sections of your brain than are involved in definition-recall activities. The richness of language, affect, and memory are joined and enjoyed by your brain when you make metaphors.

Although they may be constructed in an almost playful way, metaphors are important elements of your memory. Metaphors call forth imagination, but they also serve as a quick shorthand for categorizing what is important or valuable. One recent example of this activity is the suggestion (in *Classroom Leadership*, Feb. 2001, published by the Association for Supervision and Curriculum Development) that metaphors can be used as tools for evaluating the beliefs and practices of educators. Metaphors bring out hidden descriptions of roles, help analyze the motivations for certain behaviors, and aid in the decision-making process. So, for example, an "instructional leader" metaphor might call for a different set of assumptions about teaching than the metaphor of "manager," "coach," or "general contractor."

right (but you know you're faking it), "Mom's look" both provides comfort and requires honesty about how things really are with you.

"An equipping pastor is like an anticipatory thesaurus." Just the right word for the right occasion—that's what you get from a thesaurus that already knows your need for language that will express what's inside you.

"An equipping pastor is like clowns in a circus car." About the time you think nothing more can come from something small, out pops another clown. Fun and surprising, this clown-crowded car!

"An equipping pastor is like a medieval armorer." The hard and meshed metal is fitted to your body alone, enabling you to be both protected and agile.

"An equipping pastor is like Curious George." You learn about the joys and sorrows of inquisitiveness by watching the fun and foibles of this delightful character.

"An equipping pastor is like a pig farmer." The smell may bother other folk, but the farmer knows that the pigs are smarter than some people. Understanding the meaning of squeals and oinks, the farmer also knows the difference between the commitment of chickens and the sacrifice of pigs to the enterprise of "breakfast."

Because no metaphor is ever exact, and because each brain constructs meaning slightly differently, metaphor-making is always a little "sloppy" in its application. But its value is profound: Your whole brain is engaged in finding its own answers to its own questions, answers it will most likely be willing to act upon.

A little more precision, perhaps?

If you're feeling like a brass tack lost in a seat-cushion factory—if this soft metaphor-imagining makes you feel out of place—try some of the following behavioral descriptions of "equipping pastor." If "workers" are God's people at work in the world, doing what God wants to have done, then an equipping pastor:

Shrewd wordsmiths will note that I use neither the word "empower" nor any of its shirttail relatives to describe the work of a pastor. Why not? God is the only real "empowerer." That work starts with the Holy Spirit. For some of us, it happens in baptism; for others it's the moment of "accepting Christ." If I say that I'm "empowering you," I imply that you lack power. That insults you and an empowering God. What word family do I use instead? "Ennoble," because it names what already exists (nobility) or calls out of you what you most want to do or be.

❑ Provides tools and supplies for willing workers.

❑ Shows tool-users how to make the most out of what they know or have.

❑ Helps people make and find their own tools and supplies.

❑ Prepares workers for what they'll face.

❑ Repairs and renews workers' sense of purpose.

❑ Helps analyze the quality and quantity of the work being done.

❑ Keeps the church-as-training-center up-to-date, efficient, and low-maintenance.

❑ Leads and teaches more from experience than from theory.

❑ Helps workers find inspiration, motivation, courage, joy, and satisfaction.

❑ Brokers meaningful work for every worker, not just the most obvious, most talented, or most active.

❑ Never does the workers' work for them.

❑ Helps workers find meaning within seeming confusion.

❑ Understands that "work well done, with good results" is reward enough for willing workers.

❑ Visits workers on the job, to watch and understand the importance of their work.

❑ Stays agile and alert in changing work conditions.

❑ Protects workers from danger, sometimes even from each other.

❑ Sees both the larger picture and the details.

❑ Avoids futile flight/fight responses to difficulties.

❑ Connects present-day workers with their ancestors, especially their faith forbears.

❑ Helps workers find spiritual significance in their work.

❑ Assures workers of God's presence and joy in their lives.

❑ Announces and lives out forgiveness when workers sin.

❑ Accepts forgiveness of workers when "equipping" is inadequate or self-absorbed.

❑ Understands and practices "authority" and "power" as something derived from personal relationships with workers.

❑ Spends considerable time in prayer and study of Scripture, seeking God's power for this exciting, difficult role.

"Equipping" is not "trying too hard"

Perhaps you have a better picture now, whether in word pictures or in task-descriptions, of how "an equipping pastor" acts. You may also have some ideas why "an equipping pastor" is a hardworking leader, but not overexerted. Just to be sure, though, let me explain the difference in these ways:

◆

I pray hard,
I work hard, and
leave the rest to God.

Florence Griffith Joyner

❑ "Equipping" can usually be seen in measurable behavior, especially in the abilities of the equipped worker. Because it is measurable, equipping has starting and ending points.

❑ Responsibility shifts to the worker, not the equipper.

❑ Equipping is best measured by changes in the lives of individuals, not in the management of systems or programs.

❑ "Intangibles" (conversations, relationships, trust, inspiration) are as valuable in the equipping process as are tangible things (resources, buildings, meetings).

❑ Because power, influence, knowledge, and the right to initiate work are all shared, the equipper's load is lightened.

❑ The equipper doesn't need to be the source of all knowledge, skill, or volition. "Knowing where to find out" becomes as valuable as "knowing." Information overload is thus reduced.

❑ Because it is directed at others' capabilities, equipping is less likely to meet resistance or grudging compliance. Focused on others, equipping tasks are always tuned to workers' most cherished hopes. This fact virtually guarantees excitement and energy for the tasks that workers will accomplish.

❑ Because equipping tasks require agility and awareness, the equipper is always faced with brain-exciting newness. Thus an equipper is kept fresh and vibrantly alive in this work.

"EQUIPPING" OUTSIDE THE CHURCH

Because congregations are human enterprises that operate within the basic principles of any human enterprise, it is instructive—and comforting—to find in business-management philosophy and literature the elements of an "equipping pastor" way of thinking. For me, the best continuing examples come from the work of Peter Block. An organizational development consultant, personal advisor to corporate leaders, philosopher, and author (*The Empowered Manager, Flawless Consulting,* and *Stewardship*), Block has insisted for years that enlightened and effective management philosophies can be based on a kind of "reverse flow" of imagined power and energy. In the usual top-down management styles, "the boss in the corner office" is ultimately responsible for handing down wisdom, edicts, decisions, energy and motivation for action.

Block's view: This style makes no sense, especially when you understand how vulnerable such a system might be

to quickly changing conditions in the business world, the well-being of the CEO, and fragile workplace relationships. A business that operates with that mind-set will always be at risk, and will always be working too hard to maintain its competitive edge, its profits, and high morale among its employees.

In *Stewardship: Choosing Service Over Self-Interest,* Block states the issue as a maxim: The task of leaders is to add value to the work of core workers for the benefit of the customers. The maxim makes sense: If all the value in an organization gets concentrated in one spot—presumably at the top of an imagined pyramid of power—then that value is not as widely available. Robbed or cheated of value, or at least having to fight for their share, workers are scarcely motivated to do their best work. By inverting the pyramid, sending value toward the workers, the leaders increase value throughout the enterprise, and enhance the likelihood that

the customers will benefit from their exchange with this company. The basic question: What is "value," and how do you add it to workers?

Writing in *The Empowered Manager: Positive Political Skills at Work,* Block comments on the benefit of an "entrepreneurial spirit" in organizations. Responsibility for innovation, profit, success, or efficiency is given to all workers, and these entrepreneurs share in the rewards as well. The wealth of human creativity permeates this kind of workplace, managed by leaders instead of initiated only by them. Every worker behaves as though he or she owned the company.

Block also offers specific suggestions about fostering trust, negotiating with adversaries, and understanding different motivations for various types of workers. He opens the window to allow into business enterprises an almost spiritual view of the workplace and its interactions.

Equipping who's here

Let's try out some specific ideas for how you can be an equipping pastor—or help your pastor be one. Let's start with a simple assumption: You equip the people who are here. You don't wait until your congregation:

❑ Gets a few more "professionals" as members.

❑ Asks the present leaders to fish or cut bait—or however you say that in your neck of the woods.

❑ Reorganizes in the newest way. (When we've finally saved the whales, I'm betting on "pods.")

❑ Allows you a real "day off."

❑ Stops dying, getting sick, and experiencing so many personal problems.

❑ Solves a few of its financial uncertainties.

❑ Gets rid of the professional snipers and whiners.

You start with "who's here" because those are the folk whom God has given you. (This approach is also fundamental to the asset-based approach we'll play with in chapter 8.) If you wait for "just the right circumstances," you'll never get started on this equipping thing.

Good! Now that you're completely convinced of the wisdom of this approach—I'd have been satisfied with continuing curiosity—let's look at some specific actions that you can begin anywhere, with anyone, at any time.

Prepare your sermons with members

You know a lot about Scripture and theology; laypeople know a lot about life. As you wrestle texts to the exegetical ground together, you'll teach each other. They'll learn how God loves their lives; you'll learn how life loves theology.

Start the process somewhere other than the church facilities; include food and conversation. Don't call this "a meeting." Instead invite people for a "get-together," "text-talking," or "dessert." Include some oddballs in the group; change the group every month. Keep notes.

Ask about "adding value"

Instead of imagining the value you add to members' working for God, ask them! Invite groups of members for breakfast or dessert—in place of a meeting—to talk about their answers to this question, "How could I—or how could this congregation—add value to your life and work?" Press for more than "Sunday-school answers." Gather the groups by occupational similarity, age cohorts, or life situations (e.g., parents of young children, retired folk). Listen for patterns and themes.

Give "awards"

Use note cards, simple "prizes," or personal mementos to "reward" noteworthy accomplishments or developments in members' lives. Don't start with birthdays or anniversaries—too easy, too ordinary. Instead, ferret out times and places where members are noticed by their peers, their accomplishments celebrated, their paid or volunteer work rewarded. Include a note. Write something personal and ask a question that might start a conversation. (For example, "How did you get started in this line of work?" "What's next after this?" "What'd you do to deserve this?")

Visit, visit, visit

Don't visit just at hospitals, mortuaries, and sickbeds. (There are other places where members gather!) Try workplaces, ball fields, late-night watering holes, company picnics, or school events. Avoid the "ceremonial presence" trap, when you notice conversational tones and volume shifting as you enter the room. Peek at what's happening behind "the Wizard's curtain" of members' almost magical abilities. Talk to bosses, workers, strangers, and friends. Go for a walk, work out, sit quietly in the park—anywhere that people might be willing to talk about their lives with you.

The mention of "Sunday-school answers" calls up this new urban myth (the story used to be about a squirrel): A teacher asks the "boys and girls" in the class if they know who wears a lab coat, works with atom-smashing machines, and loves even the smallest particles. The brilliant students, knowing that the teacher is describing a nuclear scientist *and* knowing that in Sunday school you're supposed to answer in a different way, reply, "Jesus?" As they grow and "mature," adults can let that kind of religiosurreality creep into their thinking, answering the way they think they're supposed to when they're talking to the pastor.

Dr. Billy Poobah's
SUBTLE EQUIPPING PASTOR CHECKLIST

Directions: Read each of the items below, checking those that apply to you or your congregation.

❑ Our pastor knows what occupies my time during the week.

❑ Things I hear during a sermon usually follow me into the week—in conversations, prayer, and my thinking.

❑ I appreciate how our pastor sees the world differently.

❑ I don't worry about making mistakes in this congregation.

❑ The pastor is always asking me, "How work's going?"

❑ I've often heard the pastor talking with other members about their work.

❑ Sometimes during worship, I feel that God's right there with me, ready to come into the next week with me.

❑ This church helps me outdo evil and survive dangerous situations in my life.

❑ I feel alive and energetic about my life because of this congregation.

❑ I could argue with our pastor about almost anything; that's how we both learn from each other.

❑ Without this place, these people, this pastor—I'd be pretty much alone out there in the world.

Scoring: If you checked fewer than three items, you're probably just a nice person and you like pastors in general. If you checked as many as six, pay attention to your pastor's equipping skills. If the number of checked boxes approached nine, you need to write a thank-you note to your pastor before you read another word!

Renew your teaching skills

Sometimes "equipping" is "teaching." If your teaching style tends toward "present and discuss," or if you are uncomfortable with your level of skills as a teacher, ask a few professional educators in your congregation to help you learn—perhaps in guided practice sessions—how to use a variety of teaching styles. In that way you'll be able to equip people who learn in a variety of ways.

Spend time with the movers and shakers

Frequently ignored in the presumptions of neediness that govern many congregations, members who are "movers and shakers" in your locale also need God's wisdom and presence in their lives. Meet, eat, and talk with them, in the full assurance that you are neither less important nor more important than they are. Learn from them, but over time be willing to ask hard questions. Answer theirs as well. Make the visits a time of spiritual enrichment; praying with them is a way to start.

Reconfigure some tasks

Some tasks you undertake regularly might turn into "equipping times" if you adjust or "repurpose" them. For example, how can you help equip a terminally ill person for the last ministry in life: helping teach others how to die? Or how could counseling sessions be oriented less toward problem-solving and more toward "equipping for what comes next"? Or how might a caring ministry (such as Befrienders or Stephen Ministry) be repurposed toward other life-equipping ministries in the congregation? Perhaps the easiest example: How could a portion of every meeting be redirected toward "getting ready for tomorrow's tasks in the world"?

Analyze (or change) your communication style

In chapter 4 you read about communication styles. Because you probably equip folk through your words, continue to analyze your speaking or writing. Change the patterns that have rendered you less than capable of authentic conversation or communication. If you can't pull yourself up by your verbal bootstraps, ask a trusted friend in the congregation to walk alongside you for a while, keeping track of how and what you communicate. Start with an English or speech teacher. Trade them something valuable—your review of their writing?—for their periodic coaching.

Write a new newsletter column

For a few months, reframe your regular "column" in the congregation's newsletter. Think of it as a time to help members "make sense" of what happens in your community or neighborhood. Refrain from partisan puffery, meandering musings, and stuffy sophistry. (Also delete all alliterative constructs such as these.) Get to the point, which is not what *you* think about whatever. You're equipping people to face their daily realities from a viewpoint that has "God" splashed all over it. Keep your writing short and off the front page!

> What all of these "equipping"s tasks have in common is that they honor other people. Whether you're asking, listening, conversing, teaching, or offering opinions, think how that task brings honor—affirmation, nobility, deep gratitude—to the people you equip. That's how you'll know the difference between "equipping" and everything else.

Starting at the beginning

Before you finish this chapter, take time to recall the reasons you might want to start or continue "equipping who's here." Rewind to the start of the mental videotapes that contain the emotions and logic that have motivated your leadership. When you're back at the beginning, "watch" the tapes again, remembering how and why you got into this line of work. Recall how God grabbed you and wouldn't let go, how you wanted to make a difference in the lives of other people. Think back to the transcendent moments when you "just knew" that something great and wonderful had been added to the lives of others around you, because of God's power working through your actions or words.

Now look at what you've recalled, seen again, felt again. Do you see the pattern? It's there, and it's called "giving yourself away so that the people you serve will be a blessing to others" (who, in turn, will be a blessing to others). Your life's purpose is a legacy you received, one that you wouldn't want to wear so thin or distort so badly that you couldn't pass it on. The measure of your legacy: the number of people who are equipped for lives of service because you handed to them what you had received from some "equipping person" in your own life.

PARSING THIS CHAPTER

Use these questions and activities as a way to construct from the ideas in this chapter a useful learning tool. Think and talk about any of the following items:

1. Where did you see yourself in the descriptions of "clericalism" or "anticlericalism"? How much of yourself did you see?

2. When it comes to "being a pastor," what makes you angry? What are you afraid of? (Answer the same questions, but substitute the words "being a layperson.")

3. Think together about whom you could bring together to start an equipping process. Make "fun to work with" a qualification.

4. As pastors think about their role, where do you think they "try too hard"? What causes that behavior?

5. Make a list of all the people in your congregation who "equip" as part of their work. (Think of managers, teachers, counselors, coaches, teens, and retired people who are mentors.) How could you learn about "equipping" from them?

6. How do you experience power in this congregation? How do you feel about that?

7. Who are the most egoless people you know? What good happens because of their lives?

8. Decide how you will change the prayers during worship into "equipping prayers." Start by studying the equipping implied in the Lord's Prayer.

7

LEAVING A LEGACY

One of the most powerful emotional drives you possess is the urge to "leave a legacy." Partly because of social biology (your urge to pass on these genes) and partly because of spirituality (your call to pass on this faith), this strong force grows in intensity as you age and wonder whether the effects of your life-work will die with you. This desire to leave something good behind also affects your assumptions about being a leader, your deeper sense of who you really are. Very personal stuff, this legacy talk. But "personal" is where we're going in this chapter, to connect "trying too hard" and "sustainability" to what might be happening inside you.

In the following pages we'll focus on you, individually, as a servant of God getting personal about:

❑ How things can't keep going like this.

❑ The shape of your legacy.

❑ What keeps shortchanging your legacy.

❑ How you might think and act to ensure a legacy.

Things can't keep going like this

If you're like me—and I know that I am—you may have approached this book with a feeling described by these words, "Things just can't keep going like this!" The feeling persists like a sullen *basso ostinato*—a repeating musical theme which both melody and harmony must follow—and you find yourself wanting to get away from:

❑ "Required" leadership responsibilities you know are not all that important or mission-fulfilling.

❑ Whirling activities that seem always to draw you downward emotionally and spiritually.

❑ Insidious blaming processes that start and end with you.

❑ The negative—and perhaps the positive—consequences of all that happens around you.

❑ The realization that this congregation depends on you.

Some congregational leaders have described this quiet despair as a thin mist that covers everything they do. Because "fight or flight" also describes your reaction to "things can't keep going this way," you may feel trapped in existential danger or anxiety. The trap may be immediate—"We're not going to be able to pay these bills if we keep operating this way"—or have a delayed, distant feeling: "When all these generous givers die, who's going to replace them?" In either case, the feeling is probably the same: "Eventually all this is going to get me."

IF YOU'RE LIKE ME (and I know that I am) . . .

Humorist and Chicago television host Aaron Freeman uses a subtle non sequitur to check on his audiences' attention: "If they chuckle, they're awake." I have used this piece of whimsy here to comment on the obvious: How deeply we all wish that others could understand us. Or, perhaps more accurately, how deeply we want to be understood by others as we understand ourselves.

This statement is not what it first seems: an invitation to bolster the speaker's ego. There is little vanity in wanting to be understood, especially by those whom you presume to lead. Unless you are well understood, your words fall empty and your mission stalls in its lonely tracks. (To say this another way: "Lacking followers, you are not a leader.")

The seemingly silly statement also connects to another important matter: how you perceive what's real and what's important. Medical doctor and brain researcher John J. Ratey (*A User's Guide to the Brain*) says that the primary question for therapists—and perhaps leaders—is not "How do you feel?" but "How do you know the world?" Because perception determines emotion (and emotion determines action), "How do you know the world?" has to be answered first. The answer implied in the ear-tickling statement that started this sidebar: I know that my perceptions about the world are true because you think or feel the same way.

Perhaps this phrase isn't such nonsense after all? Perhaps you want to try this little audience-monitoring trick the next time you're leading a group? Perhaps you *are* like me?

Are you really satisfied?

Be honest. Are you really satisfied with the way things are going in your congregation? If yes, you are a blessed minority, and you have great cause to thank God for your ministry. If no, you are a blessed majority and have great cause to thank God for your ministry. You "no" folks may have a harder time being thankful if:

❑ You're constantly bombarded with expectations about your ministry that don't match your outcomes.

❑ Your ability to roll every rock up every hill seems to be the primary ingredient required for most canned solutions and programs.

❑ There seems to be no connection between your efforts and their results.

❑ You can't lower your expectations—that would be denying the passion for ministry that got you started. Worse, lowered expectations would denigrate or squelch your gifts for this work.

❑ You can't find anyone else like you out there. (When you go to judicatory or national meetings, most of what you hear is others' exemplary successes.)

❑ You know what happens to "carping, whining, sniveling weaklings." (You hear the cynical answer inside you: "They end up in places like this.")

Perhaps worst of all: You take your dissatisfaction as a sign of spiritual emptiness, a measure of weakened faith, and a personal insufficiency whose fault is only your own. Now guilt piles on the other feelings like the late-hit tackle of a 300-pound defensive halfback.

Another view of "dissatisfaction"

Perhaps your discontent—"things can't keep going like this!"—is reasonable, acceptable, perhaps even faithful. Your dissatisfaction may even be an asset. Here's how that might be true.

We'll talk more about fear as primary motivator later in this chapter, but here let me briefly spotlight "anxiety," a continuing, nonspecific fear. In his captivating book about fear, science writer Rush W. Dozier (*Fear Itself: The Origin and Nature of the Powerful Emotion That Shapes Our Lives and Our World*) says that anxiety is uniquely human because of our capability to imagine and describe possible futures. Our brains use the etched memories of past events to predict inherently uncertain futures. Because "danger relief" is a first-choice activity of brains, we may choose anxiety as a first-choice attitude about most facets of life.

First, you may dislike your present conditions because your perceptive analyses are true. Because you see what others do not see, you may feel dismay about eventualities that you recognize because you are more than a garden-variety prophet.

Second, if you center your discontent on large-scale questions about sustainability and manageability, you're not going to get caught in inconsequential trivialities that can trap mere malcontents.

Third, you're probably not easily fooled. (My own experience with many supposedly discontented pastors and leaders is that they're actually very skilled at separating snake oil from medicine.) You can see through the too-good-to-be-true promises and invitations of denominational or parachurch programs.

Finally, your dissatisfaction can be a powerful motivation for change. (Remember Festinger's "cognitive dissonance" from chapter 6?) You probably carry hope tucked into a pocket of your dissatisfaction. You know that being dissatisfied does not necessarily mean that you're a pessimist. You see God in the changes you think are required. (More about "change" in chapter 8.)

In summary, your "being dissatisfied" may be a sign that there's nothing wrong with your spirit, and that you're ready for what comes next.

Looking at the horizon

Perhaps it might help soften your dissatisfaction and frustration if you looked at the horizon to see what's heading into the ecclesiological sunset. That metaphor may be complex, but the idea is simple:

❑ You need to hear some good news: You may have already stopped trying too hard to prop up tired or unworkable ideas.

❑ If what's bothering you is that you're not "keeping up with current trends," here is another kind of good news: Some of these popular ideas may no longer be "current" or "trends." You can stop working too hard to chase "what's new."

❑ You might find on the horizon new developments that give you hope.

In this section we'll take a look at some elements of present-day church life that I think may be slowly declining in importance or influence. In each case I've included a few reasons for my opinions. I readily admit that there's more intuition here than science. I see hope at the edge of each of these horizons.

Magic bullets

I've used the term before to describe "one-size-fits-all, easy, quick fixes" promoted almost everywhere in Christendom. (You get the same mail I do.) As we saw earlier in the book, most "good ideas that are guaranteed to get results" have about a one-generation life span. The present generation of magic bullets—new and recycled—is about 20 years old. Some other reasons I think contemporary magic bullets may not be around much longer: "magic" for one kind of congregation may be "poison" for most congregations. Many sure-fire solutions are too big, too complicated, or too unforgiving of mistakes. They may require of you what you have least: energy and time.

A hopeful sign on your horizon: If you've avoided the temptation to rescue your congregation or your personal fulfillment with canned programs, you may also have dodged the hidden overexertion they can bring with them.

One major indicator of waning popularity is the tone of the marketing techniques used to promote a product, service, or idea. "SALE!!" may be a signal for leftover or dated stuff no one else bought. "New lower price" can mean excess inventory, less product in the same package, or "No one thought it was worth the higher price." The appeals to your emotions increase because the seller is anxious. When I see increased marketing efforts for magic-bullet goods or services within denominational, parachurch, or metachurch enterprises, I wonder what this promotion means about the lasting value of this product or program.

Nostalgia

Nostalgia is a mixed blessing. At first blush it would seem to be a good motivator for congregations; on closer scrutiny, it turns out to be a motivation-robbing force. "Nostalgia" is not the same as "remembering fondly." Its etymology leads back to the home-return (*nostos*) sickness (*algia*) of Swiss mercenary troops in the 14th century. Their yearning for what was not present incapacitated them for soldiering. That's why nostalgia is more about energy-robbing memories than it is about fond recall. One way to recognize nostalgia: People are stuck in the past or unwilling to treat the present or future other than with distrust, distress, or lack of interest. You could call nostalgia a kind of "arrested emotional adolescence."

The golden years of the modern American church were the 1950s through the mid-1960s. That means that today there are fewer members and leaders whose fond memories of those days are still driving their hopes for the future. Even those who are still trying to complete the work they started in the 1970s will be supplanted by the generation that follows them. The emergence of "postmodern" thoughts and actions also signals the slow disappearance of nostalgia as a motivating force for congregations.

A hopeful sign on your horizon: If you've led your congregation away from nostalgia, you've kept "the way things used to be" from overwhelming "the way things could be." If, at the same time, you've instilled appreciation of your congregation's history, you've avoided the overexertion of reinventing wheels and the vehicles they are attached to.

The nature of theology

The content and method of theology are moving slowly toward a horizon difficult to describe. (The previous sentence was hard for me to write because my theological heritage honors the value of unchanging doctrinal content and unchanging methods of theological inquiry.) It is apparent that the foundations of theology are currently undergoing large-scale change. Hermeneuticians, linguists, archaeologists, sociologists of religion, systematicians, and practical theologians are working together to unravel and reassemble theological questions whose answers we thought we'd settled long ago. They are using new tools for approaching the Scriptures and other theological content. Complexity/chaos theory, genetics, and neuroscience also contribute to theological questions and answers.

A hopeful sign on your horizon: If you have wrangled with new theological questions, you've probably avoided the more difficult job of holding in fragile balance a theological house of cards.

 # NEUROTHEOLOGY

Experimental evidence about the biological validity of spiritual experience has been around for more than a decade. The idea of "neurotheology" broke into public scrutiny January 2001, when *Newsweek* summarized the book *Why God Won't Go Away: Brain Science and the Biology of Belief*, by Andrew Newberg, Eugene D'Aquili, and Vince Rause.

The experimental conclusions of brain scientists have come from their use of brain-imaging technologies. Both simple and sophisticated, these techniques involve watching the brains of individuals engaged in "spiritual" activities such as prayer or deep meditation. Some of the earliest conclusions are interesting:

● Feelings of spiritual transcendence are located in the brain's temporal lobe.

● Mystical or spiritual feelings can be produced in nonreligious subjects by stimulating this area of the brain with a small electrical charge.

● Spiritual experiences such as praying integrate many parts of the brain and body.

● The brain may be "hardwired" to experience a variety of feelings that bring subjects into "unity with God and with all that exists."

● There may be a correlation between spiritual practices and improved physical and mental health.

● Religious thoughts and actions can derail fear-based brain mechanisms because they redirect the brain away from fear.

● The visions and mystical experiences of epileptics—including famous mystics and spiritual thinkers in history—can be explained as identifiable brain processes.

Most of this material may seem "interesting-but-not-yet-important." But Newberg and D'Aquili also hint at theologically significant matters such as these:

● The human brain has the ability to create reality-explaining myths—literally, "words with authority." (Does the brain "invent" spiritual explanations for imponderables?)

● Mystic thoughts and actions may have important neurological connections. "Oneness with God" and disappearance of self—the authors call it "self-softening"—are explained as the elemental basis for all spirituality. (Do transcendent, emotional experiences of God generate "faith" more than language-oriented teaching methods?)

● "Universal beliefs" can be explained biologically. The general biological descriptions of spiritual experiences are remarkably similar across religious cultures. (Do biologically based mythology and mysticism suggest that "faith" and "god" are nonparticular?)

● Ritual can be explained in neurobiological terms. Rites involving music and repetitive movements seem particularly effective in establishing belief. (How do we best "train" or "initiate" new members so that their spirituality will not readily disappear?)

(continued)

- The neural pathways involved in transcendent spiritual experiences are the same as those involved in mating and sexual experience. (Could this explain the continuing plague of clergy sexual misconduct?)

- Over time, natural selection may favor "religious brains" because of the positive correlations of mystical experience to mental health. (What could paleontology teach us about "religion"?)

- Spiritual experience is not rooted in either "faulty logic" or "mental instability," as explained by conventional psychology or sociology. (What else about faith has been misinterpreted by these two branches of science?)

- Even though the proclivity for mystical experiences is hardwired in the brain, it does not necessarily follow that humans invented God. (How do we ensure caution about the application of brain science to theology?)

By the time you read this book, neurotheology will have grown more certain about its experimental evidence, and more insistent in asking questions. In any case, this newly described merging of theology and biology may yield more answers to the questions we have explored in this book. Perhaps those answers will add to what we already know about the neurobiology of trying too hard.

Church as "center for caring"

Within a decade the generation of Vietnam-era pastors and leaders will relinquish its caring leadership of congregations to another generation. And with that generational shift will come the slow de-emphasis of "caring" as the central feature of Christian enterprise.

This metaphor for the church's major identity or purpose may be dear to you. That's why it may be hard to put into practice what visionaries and systems thinkers (Edwin Friedman, Peter Steinke, Loren Mead) have said for years: Congregations that operate as "hospitals" for needy people cannot sustain that effort much longer. Significance-seeking pastors, deeply loving Christians, highly motivated leaders like yourself—all have been enculturated to believe that "needs-filling" best characterizes what God's people can do together. Why this metaphor is disappearing: The generational cohort that created it—pastors and leader trained in Vietnam-era thinking—is gradually moving out of church leadership. Most organized caring systems require more effort than most congregations can assemble or sustain. (See the "Caring Case Study" elsewhere in this chapter.) Newer approaches and identities—such as asset-based planning or small-group ministries—supplant "caring" metaphors for congregations' structuring.

A hopeful sign on your horizon: You're in good shape about "caring ministries" if you have found and value the sometimes-invisible but extensive caring that members do as part of the greater society—in their neighborhoods, vocations, volunteer activity, or friendships.

Intended consequences

It used to be true that you could reasonably anticipate the consequences of planned actions. That notion seems to be quickly heading for the horizon. You can see this development in several places. From applied complexity theory—explanations of how social systems and human enterprise work—you can see that unintended consequences are sometimes more important, and more certain, than those you expect or plan. From experimental science you can learn that, unless all factors are controlled, the results of an experimental action cannot be attributed to a single cause. From genetics and brain science we learn that there may be biological "predispositions" for certain behaviors or characteristics. But no one can predict with certainty how or when genes or brain chemicals will behave, given the essentially unpredictable and uncontrollable nature of environment, timing, and context.

This means that your careful work to bring about a specific outcome in your congregation is as likely to fail as to succeed. Your plan is as likely to bring with it unintended consequences as to produce those you intend.

A hopeful sign on your horizon: Perhaps you've already given up trying to "manage" and "plan" all that happens in your congregation, and thus have avoided one kind of Sisyphean futility.

THE REVENGE OF UNINTENDED CONSEQUENCES

One of the most frustrating surprises of our technology-driven culture is "unintended consequences." If you like big words, you could call them "illogically multiplied effects of logically derived decisions, seen only with hindsight." If you like colloquial expressions, you might call them the "Whoops!" experiences in life.

In a delightful romp through several contemporary technologies, scientist and journalist Edward Tenner (*Why Things Bite Back: Technology and the Revenge of Unintended Consequences*) shows how our best intentions are dismantled by consequences we could never have imagined. (For Tenner, "technologies" are any modifications we humans make to our biological or physical environments.) Two examples will suffice:

Alarm systems

Valuing safety, we install home and car alarm systems. Unintended consequences: The number of drivers locked out of cars has doubled and tripled over the past 20 years, at a cost of about $400 million per year. In a three-year period in Philadelphia, only about 2 percent of the 157,000 alarm-system calls were real. The proliferation of alarms results in an equivalent time loss equaling the full-time service of 58 police officers, presumably detracting from their other crime-fighting duties.

The paperless society

We value efficiency, and so use machines that communicate instantly, electronically eliminating the need for paper. Unintended consequences: Paper use has skyrocketed since the advent of paper-free technologies. From 1940 to 1980, annual paper consumption per capita tripled in the U.S.—from 200 to 600 pounds. But in only the next 10 years—during which time "paperless offices" were supposed to emerge—paper consumption tripled again, to an astounding 1,800 pounds of paper per year per person.

Edward Tenner groups revenge effects in four categories:

Rearranging effects. Shifting the problem only makes it worse. (Think of air-conditioned buildings without windows; now think of them as self-contained breeding grounds for colds and flu; and now imagine their occupants suffering through power outages caused, in part, by the buildings' own enormous appetite for electricity. In a church, think about rotating the same 15 loyal and committed people through the same five committees.)

Repeating effects. A single action is beneficial; repeating it produces unintended effects. (Think of carpal tunnel syndrome among computer users, or "labor-saving devices" that expend, rather than save time. In a church, think of the effects of continued use of the same sermon style or offering-envelope system week after week.)

Recomplicating effects. The problem is broken into smaller parts; each part grows into its own problem. (Think of suppressing "pests" and watching them scatter or evolve into new problems.)

Recongesting effects. Our good ideas crowd physical space and time. (Think of the 30,000-70,000 pieces of debris littering. In a church, think how cluttered are your closets, offices, hallways, and limited storage spaces because of the detritus of past events.)

Tenner shows how unintended effects occur primarily when things, ideas, events, or actions are joined into systems. Systems have "bugs"; individual pieces are only "broken." He also suggests a "theory of insult accumulation": Any sickness or dysfunction in a system is hazardous to its long-term health.

His description of "intensification"—our improving technologies require more human vigilance—helps explain what happens when we don't monitor our technologies carefully. The more we are critically dependent on our machines, the more "increased vigilance" becomes necessary. That extra wariness or anxiety is an unintended consequence of this technological age.

The results for congregational leaders? The more you depend on "technologies," the more you must watch them, the more you can expect to be surprised by consequences you did not anticipate, and the more time you can expect to spend solving problems instead of enjoying solutions. In a phrase, the more you can expect to be trying too hard!

CASE STUDY: CARING MINISTRY

"Things can't keep going like this," "unintended consequences," and "trying too hard" can be best illustrated in an imaginary case study.

A little over two years ago, Faith Congregation decided to adopt the proven program "Living and Loving," a caring system with the following characteristics:

- Based on psychotherapeutic models of caring

- Centered on the pastor's role and capabilities as trained counselor and caregiver

- Dependent on systematized referrals, terminology, recruitment and support of volunteers, and eligibility of members in need

- Tightly organized ("The system must be followed exactly, or it will not be effective.")

- Trained key leaders

- History of satisfied congregations using the system

Faith first sought the "Living and Loving" system because its leaders wanted to relieve Pastor Kristen's psyche and calendar by lightening her heavy load of caring for members in difficult circumstances. The planned consequences: She would be freed for other, important elements of congregational leadership, and members in need would receive more immediate care from their fellow believers.

It has been about a year since Pastor Kristen and two key leaders were trained at the Living and Loving headquarters. Recently the system has started to exhibit its own "revenge of unintended consequences," including these:

- Because of Pastor Kristen's presumed central role in the system, she approves all referrals for help and matches all volunteers with members in need.

- After they have been trained in caregiving, volunteers in the Living and Loving program have had to learn the behaviors and record-keeping that keep the system working. People who wanted most "to care for others in the church" have also been asked to help the Living and Loving system run smoothly.

- To keep the system alive and well, leaders and congregational volunteers meet biweekly for consultations, support, and further training. More meetings have meant more work.

- Volunteers who know or are skilled in newer philosophies or models of caring have found it difficult to add their insights to the tightly interwoven Living and Loving model. They wonder how up to date the system really is.

- When there have been more member volunteers than members in need, Pastor Kristen has had to work harder to find needy ones who can be matched with the special gifts of each caregiver.

- When there were more members in need than caregivers, the volunteers had to take on more cases, or the leaders had to increase recruitment efforts.

- After a while, the trained leaders and Pastor Kristen found themselves spending more time than they imagined maintaining the Living and Loving program. They have responsibilities for keeping accurate records, conducting meetings, and sharpening evaluative skills. As minor or major difficulties have emerged, some of the leaders blame themselves for not managing the Living and Loving system correctly.

- In cases where there have been deep psychological needs among the members in need, these individuals were referred to—you guessed it—Pastor Kristen.

Looking back at their work so far, the leaders have realized that that the volunteers have cared for about the same number of people Pastor Kristen might have visited. One difference: This system requires increased vigilance because of leaders' anxiety about "caring in the wrong way." And no matter how hard Pastor Kristen and the leaders try, the Living and Loving system has not changed members' long-held expectations about their pastor's caring presence.

In the past two weeks, some of the leaders have come to the realization that "things can't go on like this." Two volunteers and one key leader have resolved their frustration by leaving the program.

The final, ironic unintended consequence? Pastor Kristen has been left holding the Living and Loving program in her hands. She has also been left alone with her own plaintive question: "How did we end up here?"

"Bad chaos"

If you're like me—and wouldn't that be odd?—you grew up in a Cartesian world, where logic ruled emotion, order always trumped disorder, and clean desks were the sign of a well-ordered mind. It was a good world, well portrayed in the superaccurate television programs of your adolescence. (I am, of course, talking about *Leave It To Beaver* or its equivalent in your generation.) It was easier back then to name order as "good" and chaos as "bad." That dichotomy doesn't work very well any more.

> "Plastic" characterizes the brain's capability to use neuronal clusters and pathways in a variety of ways. Your brain does not consist of singularly dedicated cells, each waiting for the right stimulus to "do its thing." Instead, bundles of billions of cells have the capacity for double and triple duty, depending on their connections-of-the-moment with other cell bundles. The brain retains its capacity for plasticity—some say "learning," and others say "rewiring"—throughout life. While still "ordered," the brain's plasticity also exemplifies the complexity/chaos that exists in the rest of the world.

Because of the insights of complexity theory, you may be coming to see that "chaos" is neither bad nor good, any more than "order" is preferable or not. (God's *second* creative act was to order the previously created mess. Go ahead, I'll wait while you check out Genesis 1:2.)

The brain God created in you is another example. While your brain always creates a perception of order, the firing of neurons also can be described as random. Because the brain is "plastic," lightning-quick decisions are made; neurons arrange and rearrange themselves in changing webs; and the brain searches for new patterns.

A hopeful sign on your horizon: If you've come to the point where you can accept seeming disorder in your congregation, you're ready to let go of obsessive order-seeking that might prohibit you from legacy-building.

Understanding the complexities

If you're well educated, you've been trained to believe and act as though you could understand most of what you encounter. Not true anymore! The world is moving too fast, too many systems are too well connected, information is increasing at exponential rates, and "what's true" may be contradictory at best. So the idea that you can somehow "get your head around" matters X, Y, and Z is illusory at best.

In *Faster: The Acceleration of Almost Everything*, science writer James Gleick suggests that complexity-encounters operate as a cycle: Complex ideas (or ideals?) beget choices. Choices inspire technological products. These products require ordering into systems. The systems become complex. The new complexities lead you to new choices. The cycle continues.

A hopeful sign on your horizon: If your discomfort with "the way things are going" has led you to a quiet acceptance of your own necessary and healthy ignorance about most things, you've escaped a contemporary version of Satan's first temptation: to want to be God.

Tight connections

One of the vaguely accepted axioms of "the well-planned organization" is that the system should be well integrated. The presumed value? Closely related, or "tightly coupled," systems respond quickly and efficiently to change. This idea works in an ordered world, where expected consequences are likely.

But in a world that is much more complex, chaotic, and filled with unexpected consequences, loosely connected systems probably work better. Loosely coupled systems can incorporate the shocks, failures, and pressures of change without becoming destabilized.

A hopeful sign on your horizon: If you've already given up on finding "the perfect way to reorganize our congregation's structure," you're moving in the right direction.

Back to your spirit

In each of these examples of horizon-hugging phenomena, your discernment about "the way things are" may have seemed to others evidence that you were either hopelessly outdated or perpetually disgruntled. But let me say it again: It may be that your discernment has led you beyond quick fixes, retrofitted "newnesses," retrograde theologies, and false notions about your managerial prowess. If so, you've avoided putting effort into systems, attitudes, and knowledge that have already run their course. Good for you!

Before we go on, though, let's get back to your spirit, those inner feelings you carry with you that "things just can't keep going this way." It may be good news that you've avoided solutions that are slipping into their own sunsets, but that doesn't put the zip back into your voice or the bounce back into your step. We need to talk some more, this time about how you care for your sense of vocation, how you fulfill your calling to leadership in a way that satisfies you deeply. One way to name that: leaving a legacy. That's where we go next.

In *Faster*, James Gleick credits Charles Perron (*Normal Accidents: Living With High-Risk Technologies*) with the "tightly coupled, loosely coupled" metaphor. It illustrates the danger of working too hard to harden or tighten the connections within a system. Another way to understand this matter: Wood-frame houses withstand earthquakes better than brick houses, primarily because they can rattle and roll with the earthquake's rolling punch. Another: in Tai Chi, many of the body moves are designed to deflect force rather than resist it. A derived question: Is "the best-organized" congregation loosely organized?

The shape of your legacy

If you're like me—and wish I'd stop depending on the same phrase to open all new sections—you've probably considered this "legacy" matter more than once. You've asked yourself questions such as these:

❑ What will this congregation remember about me?

❑ What of my work will last?

❑ Which people will name me as an important gift to their lives?

❑ How will my work continue to generate or legitimate new thoughts, programs, or activities?

❑ By what standards will my work be measured in the future?

❑ What artifacts will remain after I leave?

None of these questions is selfish—in the sense of excluding God or other people—and each can serve as a powerful motivation for your choices and actions. I also believe that "legacy-leaving" can be a strong tool to move you from dissatisfaction with your ministry toward a deeper contentment about the impact of your life in this place. Let's see how that might work for you.

I often ask other Stephen Covey aficionados what they remember most or believe most strongly about what they've learned. Invariably, the same answer pops up: Covey's imaging exercise. (You place yourself at your own gravesite, listening to what your loved ones say about the importance of your life.) From this exercise Cover devotees construct a mission statement and rededicate themselves to "what's important." How easy it is to translate that graveside image into the language of "legacy"!

What is a legacy?

Absent from the Bible—the term wasn't coined until the late Middle Ages, when it described the enforcement of the church's canon law—"legacy" refers to anything that is inherited (the recipient's legacy) or passed to the next generation (the benefactor's legacy). So there are legacies you receive, legacies you steward, and legacies you pass on. Each carries with it emotional freight and responsibility. People who understand "legacy's requirements" usually understand "stewardship" as well.

Some quick observations might help you think about the legacies you have received, stewarded, and advanced:

❑ There are good and bad legacies, important and insignificant legacies. We'll think about the good and important ones here.

❑ A legacy is like an inheritance, except that its benefits extend to more than "rightful heirs."

❑ Legacies are wonderfully untidy in their effects on people and systems.

❑ The overwhelming emotion that gets attached to legacies is gratitude. Right after that: joy!

❑ Most legacies are grace-filled; no one deserves a legacy.

❑ Unlike "gifts," legacies are known not by their having been received or given, but by their usefulness.

❑ Legacy receivers become legacy stewards so that they can eventually be legacy givers.

❑ The size and nature of the legacy you leave is more important than the size and nature of the legacy you receive.

❑ Legacy-building is enjoyable work.

❑ Legacy-giving involves your imagination, as you consider what possible good may continue into the future.

What's really important?

If you're like me—we share over 98 percent of the same gene pool with each other and with chimps—you've come to the "What's important, really?" question a thousand times. Perhaps each time you come up with the same set of answers. For example, you know that what lasts is more important than what disappears quickly; that people are more important than things; that integrity is more important than success; that what you do proves what you believe. You don't have that much trouble listing what's important about your life.

What may be more difficult for you is making sense of your priorities. What you're trying to avoid: letting "urgent" crowd out "important" in your schedule. What you're

Robert Sylwester, an educator, philosopher, and expert in applied brain science (*Celebration of Neurons* and *A Biological Brain in a Cultural Classroom: Applying Biological Research to Classroom Management*), describes part of the brain's work as a "search for the points that dichotomies separate." Early in life you learn about opportunity/danger, space/time, true/false, fair/unfair, and beautiful/ugly. You spend the rest of your life deciding the exact point, occasion, circumstance, or context at which one side of a dichotomy ceases to be itself and turns into the other. (For example, in reading this book you have worked to decide the exact point of separation between "interesting" and "useful.")

hoping: that "trivial" doesn't describe your days. You may try to manage your time, but find that dutiful list-making still leaves you tired and behind schedule. (It's beyond the scope of this book to suggest how you can find a better way to manage time—I'd suggest "What Matters Most" systems from the Franklin Covey folks—but you need to work at this matter to ensure that the legacy you pass on will be a greatly enriched version of the one you received.)

Here are some Coveyesque observations that have helped me identify "what's important" in my own ministry:

❑ If you don't know where you're going with your life, you're bound to get there fairly easily. (You've heard that one already, yes?)

❑ The more you're overloaded with information, the more you'll label that information "urgent," and the more you'll try to deal with most of it.

❑ "Important" seldom requires speed; "urgent" always does.

❑ A fast-paced life is less likely to allow time for "importance-seeking."

❑ The time you take to write a lively personal mission statement has benefits for your congregation. (If you haven't articulated your personal mission, how can you construct a "mission statement" for your congregation, except by stringing together a set of negotiated platitudes?)

❑ You can say no more easily when you have a passion for the "yeses" in your personal mission.

❑ A place to start your mission-building: What do you want people to say about your importance for them?

❑ Another place to start: What do you remember about the "voice of God" that first called you into this work?

❑ Prayer, meditation, Scripture reading, conversation with spiritual mentors—all these can foster your continued attention to what's important.

❑ Think of time management less as dutiful work and more as a joyful dance. ("This is how I get to move around God's world today!")

◆

Insanity: doing the same thing over and over again, and expecting different results.

Albert Einstein

How legacy-building satisfies

If you're like me—and starting to think that I may be right—you might conceive of yourself as a "legacy builder" and find these satisfying outcomes:

❏ You live in perpetual gratitude. Thankfulness to God is a joyful brain activity that overwhelms fear and anger, opens the window to love/loving, and helps keep your self-image in perspective.

❏ You become a long-term "giver," knowing that what you do now will be judged by coming generations. Your generosity may move from duty into life-work.

❏ Your imagination extends past the present moment. By definition, "imagination" always takes you past the moment. In legacy-building you move into a preferred future. More parts of your brain get to join in the fun, too!

❏ You start and end your daily activities with the assurance of grace. You have deserved nothing, yet have received wonderful legacies. (Grace!) You have been given the personal gifts and assets to steward your legacy. (Grace!) You will work this day to build and prepare a legacy for new generations of equally undeserving people. (Grace!)

❏ Legacy-building does not mean that you ignore the reality of the moment. Instead, legacy-builders put this moment and its activity into perspective. "Finding perspective" is another way to slow down to sort the chaos.

❏ Having a greater purpose in life helps you adjust to life's circumstances. You are not easily tempted to consider "immediate gratification" as the primary goal of your life.

❏ Because "legacies" often result in tangible artifacts—we're talking about more than the "Rev. Dr. Drexel Memorial Parish Hall Addition" here—your work results in what you can see, touch, feel, or measure. (Think of booklets, marriages, sculptures, videotapes, worship space, musical instruments, or new staff members as examples of "artifacts.")

❏ At the same time, you can chortle over how some of the legacies that you extend into people's lives are wonderfully

I once watched a pastor, disillusioned with his ministry's direction, suddenly become excited as he considered incorporating into his shared ministry his gift as a sculptor. What especially excited him: involving others as cooperating artisans, passing on his skill to young members, and adding beauty to his congregation's physical surroundings. Not a bad legacy!

invisible. Because of you, people will know how to forgive; they will know their place in God's heart; they will give their own lives away as legacies.

❑ "Sustainability" is an automatic accompaniment to legacy-building. By definition, when you work at building a legacy, you're working at developing a godly enterprise—this congregation—that stays lively and useful.

So legacy-building adds value to your ministry as a leader and extends your sense of "important life-work" into the future lives of those you dearly love and those whom you will never meet.

◆

Stop doubting and have faith.

Jesus

What might shortchange your legacy

Your intent to build a legacy is a good first step in redeeming the dissatisfactions that may sap your energy for ministry. You need to take another step: identifying the things that might shortchange the possible rewards of legacy-building. We'll do that together in the next few pages. As I list the things that have thwarted my own sense of being a legacy-builder, you may find other possibilities.

Fear itself

We've visited and revisited this emotional circuit breaker several times. The reason: fear is so powerful and pervasive that if you leave it hidden or unnamed, it can operate as an invisible "emotional emperor," issuing orders and offering opinions without challenge. Let me summarize some of the work of science writer Rush Dozier, Jr. (*Fear Itself: The Origin and Nature of the Powerful Emotion That Shapes Our Lives and Our World*) that characterizes fear. This material might help you see how fear affects you and your congregation.

Fear is a helpful emotion, necessary for your survival in the face of danger. Your genes want to live forever, and fear helps protect you from anything that would decrease your natural desire for living. The processes of fear arousal and response are among the quickest in the brain. The amygdala attaches emotional tags to incoming information. The brain quickly decides "good" or "bad" and takes appropriate action.

There is no time for discussion when "bad" might mean great harm or even death. You trust these processes implicitly and intuitively, if not immediately.

Biologically, fear is a self-correcting emotion. That means that fear motivates you to take action to eliminate the source of stress. When the danger is gone and your fighting or fleeing is complete, fear diminishes, and your brain returns to its pleasant background activities. (Hunger operates in the same way, except for the fighting and fleeing.)

Fear is contagious, not dependent on language for quick transferral from one person to another, and thus it enables a group to protect its members. Anger (aggression) is connected to fear, sometimes alternating with fear as a preferred response to danger. When fear has passed or been reduced, opiatelike neurochemicals flood the brain, and we feel pleasure.

Fear can become a problem for you because of your capacities for thinking and verbalizing:

❏ You can imagine hundreds of things to fear, well beyond our biological ancestors' simple lists. Adam and Eve's first fear (Gen. 3:10) seems simple by comparison to the list of psychologically certified fears now available for your consideration. For example, you can fear men (androphobia), closed spaces (claustrophobia) or speaking in public (glossophobia). Because of imagination and language, you can also fear clowns (coulrophobia), bicycles (cyclophobia), and otters (lutraphobia). When fear begins to control more and more of your brain's working mechanisms, the stimulating cause of fear might be as unlikely as clothing (vestiphobia), the color white (leukophobia), or anything new (neophobia). The wag in me also wants to warn you about homilophobia (fear of sermons) and ecclesiophobia (fear of church).

❏ Fear for yourself extends to include your fears for others, or your fears on their behalf. Oddly enough, loving something—or someone—increases fear.

❏ You not only can remember what caused fear, but also can imagine similar causes into the future. (This is called "anxiety," whose Greek etymology suggests "strangling.")

❏ No matter how well you work to ensure safety, health and pleasurable living, your primary fear is probably about dying.

◆

The thought of being punished is what makes us afraid. It shows that we have not really learned to love.

St. John

❏ When they connect to other neural patterns and go out of control, fears assemble into anxiety disorders. These maladies afflict over 25 million people in the United States, and are ranked among the primary health problems we face.

❏ In either its primitive or language-using manifestations, fear tends to be inflexible, fixating on the cause of fear to the exclusion of everything else. Fear mechanisms in your brain do not easily diminish in response to logic or language.

❏ You can easily be tempted to make important decisions during times of fear-based stress. (Remember the emotional intelligence epigram from chapter 1: "Stress makes you stupid.")

How fear might work in congregations

Fear operates in congregations just as it works in individual members. So in your congregation you might find:

❏ Fear of institutional death.

❏ Unreasonable fears.

❏ Quickly spreading hysteria or panic.

❏ Stubbornly persistent fears that are not changed by persuasive logic or brilliant sermons.

Think, for example, how fears about the devil (satanophobia), the pope (papaphobia), alcohol (methyphobia), homosexuality (homophobia), saints and holy things (hagiophobia), or Jews (Judeophobia) have tarnished the history of congregations and denominations, and how they have led to ill-considered and fear-propagating decisions.

❏ Anger and aggression toward leaders.

❏ A wide variety of fear-stimulating sources.

❏ Obsessive behaviors that exclude other possible explanations, solutions, or emotions.

❏ A sense of institutional helplessness.

❏ Cultish leaders who promote fear-based reliance on themselves.

❏ Other leaders who use fear-inducing techniques to control other people or their decision-making.

The same fear mechanisms that propel individual brains to actions and reactions operate within the brains of a gathered congregation. Perhaps the saddest commentary on fear in congregations: We may make many of our important decisions within the framework of fear's stressful stupidity!

Unintended consequences

Unintended consequences may short-circuit your attempts to organize your ministry and self-image around the idea of "legacy-builder:"

❑ You may try to eliminate all unintended consequences, an oxymoronic activity whose consequences include obsessive fascination with "urgent" matters.

❑ You may fear unintended results, and so hesitate to take risks, flirt with failure, or engage in any activity that might increase your work load.

❑ Because "legacy-building" deals with the future, it's possible that you could imagine yourself as the cause of generations of unintended consequences. You might worry that you will be blamed for problems that, with the hindsight of those future times, "could have been foreseen earlier." Again, this fear may compel you to draw back from legacy-building.

Unintended consequences will invariably extend into several generations, like mutating genetic conditions. Because this outcome is inevitable in a complex and interrelated world, you can either worry about it and live fearful and hesitant about legacy-building, or you can make prudent-as-possible decisions and not be fearful.

Nostalgia

Earlier, we treated nostalgia briefly, as a feature of contemporary life that may be disappearing. But as long as nostalgia remains a part of the human condition, it can delimit your capacity to build a legacy that will be a blessing for the people you serve. Here's how that might work:

❑ Nostalgia—your own or that of your congregation—freezes you into an imaginary pleasurable past, usually at the time of the memory-maker's adolescence or early adulthood. Thus it may preclude more mature or thoughtful approaches to the past or the future.

❑ Nostalgia carries with it a kind of fear of the future, and so can undermine a hopeful approach to legacy-building. Nostalgic people may misunderstand and perhaps even misrepresent the legacy that has come to you and your congregation.

❑ Because memory recall is pleasurable for the brain, "false memories" seem helpful at first. This may be why it is difficult to displace nostalgic memories with "accurate" recollections. Your working memory—the memory you need to accomplish tasks right now—is susceptible to suggestions, especially those that speed the tasks that the memory is supposed to aid. Nostalgia is, by definition, heavily endowed with memories of this sort.

♦

A great memory is never made synonymous with wisdom any more than a dictionary can be called a treatise.

John Henry Cardinal Newman

The "wrong" questions

"Ask the wrong question, and you get the wrong answer." Consultants, planners, and social researchers use this simple sentence to characterize the importance of the starting place in any process. Certainly, "no question is wrong, except the one you don't ask," but there are times when ill-considered questions—for example, starting points, beginning premises, first moves, baseline assumptions—might short-circuit your attempts to be a legacy-builder.

If you start with the "wrong question," you may end up with the "wrong results"—for example, ending places, solutions, goals, outcomes, or conclusions. Starting-place questions may end up "wrong" when they:

❑ Encourage fearful or angry answers. (Questions that invite defensive answers are included here.)

❑ Limit possible choices for decisions or directions.

❑ Consistently require immediate or reactive answers.

❑ Take as their source inaccurate or incomplete facts.

❑ Require only logical or linear responses.

❑ Encourage or legitimate simplistic thinking.

As you construct planning processes or attempt to change your attitude about your ministries, consider the places you begin, the first questions that come to mind, or the specific goals you hope to reach. These "questions" will determine where you end up.

How would legacy-builders construct their questions? These observations might help you:

❑ Unless otherwise necessary, consider the possible long-term effects.

❑ As specifically as possible, name what values, principles, and universal goods you hope will endure.

❑ Ask who will be the most likely carriers of the legacy.

❑ Construct questions that call for imagination, creativity, positive approaches, and risk-taking.

❑ Ask about "what has been true" to get a sense of "what might be true."

So, here we are, near the end of this chapter. You've looked at your feelings about "things not going on this way for much longer." You've peeked at possible elements of contemporary church life whose sun may be setting. You've seen how "legacy-builder" might be a way for you to imagine yourself. And you've examined what might get in the way of that possibility. It's time for the last step: deciding what to do next.

◆

The one who asks a question is a fool for five minutes; the one who does not ask a question remains a fool forever.

Chinese proverb

Thinking and acting to ensure a legacy

If you're like me—and this is the last time I'll consider that possibility—you're saying to yourself, "Bob, what's next? What should I think, what should I do that might ensure my role as legacy-builder?" (Amazingly, you and I ask perfectly positioned transition questions, although they're just a little too long and a little too formal.) In these last pages of this chapter I'll try to answer with a few ideas that might get you started in that direction.

Cast out fear

If fear is a major problem for your ministry, start your legacy-building with any activity that diminishes fear. (Remember, fear should not and cannot be completely eliminated, because it is necessary for survival, and your brain is hardwired to protect the rest of your body.) In both his works, journalist and researcher Daniel Goleman (*Emotional Intelligence* and *Working with Emotional Intelligence*) underscores consistently the possibility that people with low EQs (emotional intelligence), especially people with a high propensity toward anger, can learn new habits of emotional response that diminish "emotional hijackings" of the brain—kneejerk reactions of anger or fear. He also spotlights a variety of successful programs and approaches in American education and enterprise. You can read and adapt any of these techniques to combat your tendency to make fear-based decisions.

You may also want to start closer to home. Religion or spirituality can combat fear. Consider the considerable resources of spiritually gifted people in your congregation. Look for evidence of these hopeful signs:

◆

Where there is love there is life.

Mohandas K. Gandhi

❑ Biologically, "perfect love"—or its imperfect equivalents—can diminish fear. St. John's memorable assurance, "Perfect love casts out fear," has a neurological description: In the presence of perceived love, the left frontal lobe—through the left orbitofrontal cortex—suppresses the negative emotions of the primitive fear system. Fear is thus controlled, extinguished, muted, or suppressed. Neurotransmitters for optimism, happiness, and well-being flood the limbic system and a "euphoria of love" overwhelms fear (summarized from chapter 9, "Diseases of Fear," in Rush Dozier, Jr., *Fear Itself*).

❑ In calm conversation and physical contact, the limbic (feeling) system is quieted. Because touch is the first sense to develop, we may trust it more implicitly. The sound of the human voice—not necessarily the content of the words—is also capable of diminishing fear. Churches can be places where loving touch and spiritual conversation—heartening stories, caring interchanges, inspiring witness—help alleviate the effects of fear.

❑ Our religious beliefs directly address the power of God over death, the certainty of our eternal futures, and the temporary nature of pain.

❏ In communities of faith, life purpose and meaning are formed and supported. Congregations can diminish fear with the simple message: Your life makes (and will continue to make) a difference.

❏ Congregational leaders exemplify fearless behavior. (Edwin Friedman's "nonanxious presence" comes to mind here, too.)

❏ Congregations working from asset- or gifts-based approaches minimize helplessness and vulnerability, two major stimuli of fear and anger.

❏ Congregations can provide reasons and occasions for humor and laughter, which are quickly effective in quieting fear.

❏ If fear is a habitual response to imagined danger, actions that decrease fear can also become habits. A congregation's ritualized behaviors—worshiping, learning together, praying, or caring for each other—can help in the formation of habitually courageous attitudes and behaviors.

❏ The opportunity for transcendent experiences—such as feelings of nearly inexpressible unity with God, self-emptying, and oneness with others—is available during worship, meditation, and fellowship. These states of mind may be hardwired into the brain (see the "Neurotheology" reading earlier in this chapter), and readily displace primitive fear and anger.

Laughter's effects on healing are well substantiated. Biologically, laughter is a "whole-brain" activity, replacing pain and serving as a gateway to such emotions as hope, love, faith, will to live, purpose, and confidence. Even the simple movement of smiling has been shown to change the mood of the newly smiling person! Note for leaders in humor-impaired denominational families: coffee seems to have some of the same effects (from *Fear Itself* and *The User's Guide to the Brain*).

Work toward the long haul

Legacy-building presumes your attention to and patience about the future. But if your attention is always drawn to the flood of urgent information that requires your immediate attention, you may behave like a person who suffers from attention-deficit disorder. Planning, memory, and concentration may suffer. You may experience "leadership shutdown" as you try to avoid more work, more responsibility, or more information.

The solution? Control the amount of information that comes in, using the filter named "important in the long haul," to judge which information is ultimately valuable and which is ultimately "noise." (You might want to revisit chapter 3 for a quick review of how to reduce information overload.)

John Ratey (*The User's Guide to the Brain*) describes attention-deficit hyperactivity disorders as an "addiction to the present." People afflicted with ADHD are flooded with stimuli, lack the neurochemical capacity for sorting or inhibiting the stimuli, and so "shut down" to avoid the horrific "noise" that keeps them trapped in the moment. Memory, concentration, and planning are difficult when the flood of information overwhelms the brain's capacity for sorting.

A personal mission statement also helps you focus on the long-range goals for your life. So do prayer, meditation, and Bible reading. My favorite activity for keeping "the long haul" in mind: conversations with elderly people.

Assess your personal integrity

Personal integrity—how your actions consistently fit your avowed principles—can be difficult for experienced leaders to sustain. Over your years as a leader, you may have learned less-than-authentic forms of decision-making, persuasion, negotiation, personal conversation, or truth-telling. "Speaking the truth in love" may have included more imagined love and less actual truth. One way to renew your personal integrity is through the eyes of a trusted confidant, mentor, or coach. "Spiritual directors" seem especially valuable to many pastors and congregational leaders.

In conversation, or with formal instruments, assess how you communicate, how you listen, how you preach, how you deal with conflict, how you say no, or how you steward time and money.

One example: A standard activity for stewardship consultants is to ask participants to take out their calendars—now resident in hand-held digital organizers—and their checkbooks. The consultant walks participants through a series of simple exercises that help them see how their stewardship of time and money—life's most precious commodities—matches their avowed principles. You might try this activity with your spouse or an honest and plain-spoken friend.

Being "authentic" (true to yourself at all times) is part of personal integrity and correlates with effective legacy-building. Over time, inauthenticity reveals itself. The quality of your relationships, the truth of your words, and the character of the artifacts you produce—these accumulate over time to form a fairly accurate picture of your legacy.

Find your personal power

We've covered this topic in chapter 6, in which "the equipping pastor" was seen as a powerful person. Here let me phrase this matter just a little differently: Don't doubt God's power in you. "Powerful" transcends any personality type, leadership style, or preferred method of learning. As you discover your personal power, you will find its highest manifestation in giving away power to others.

How does that connect with being a "legacy builder"? In an almost physical sense, a legacy is evidence of the power of the legacy-giver. Legacies are less about interesting information—"Grandma Kristen used to have braces on her teeth"—and more about passed-on power that is now available to the legacy-receiver: "Grandma Kristen's smile could make people feel good about themselves in an instant."

As you develop your sense of God-given personal power, you'll also find yourself planning ways to give it away to others, including coming generations.

Strengthen your imagination and volition

As you work toward a powerful role as "legacy-builder," strengthen your ability for action, as well as the imagination that compels you to action.

You strengthen your capacity to take action by taking action. (Remember "acting your way into thinking" from chapter 2?) Although no one earns salvation or any other form of God's favor by righteous deeds, it is also the case that congregations lose identity, positive feelings, fearless behaviors, and a will to action when they delay decisions by protracted planning or evaluation.

You can strengthen your will to act (volition) by keeping your imagination (or vision) strong. Imagination is developed in times of quiet, among people with energy and creativity, in situations free of fear or anger, and within your sense of personal power.

WHAT IF . . .?

Six Quick Tips to Foster Imagination

1. *Calculate the worth of others' attention.* What if you had to pay for your members' attention over the next month, at the rate of the minimum hourly wage? What would a two-hour meeting be worth, or a 30-minute sermon? Plan how you could thank people for "the gift of their attention."

2. *Think of your congregation as a model.* What if *you* were the model congregation all others wanted to know about? What would you do to help them discover the hidden excellences in your congregation? Now go tell a few other leaders what you've imagined.

3. *Imagine away old bromides.* What if the bromidic solutions you rely on are composed of old "facts?" For example, what if the idea that "we use only 10 percent of our brains" was biological nonsense? Talk about "old facts" or "old remedies" you might discard. (By the way, the view that we use only "10 percent of our brains" has been quietly exposed as an urban myth.)

4. *Think "no!"* What if "no!" were accepted as a legitimate, helpful, and godly answer to questions about possible programs, "good ideas," invitations, or offers? What would happen if the overloaded "yes!" people said "no!" joyfully? (By the way, did you know that the term "workaholic" was coined in 1968 by pastoral counselor Wayne E. Oates, to describe the behavior of pastors addicted to their calling?) Imagine yourself with a free night, empowered by "no!"

5. *Write a mental musical.* What if you imagined the plotline, characters, and ending of a musical about your congregation? What songs would you sing? What kind of music would describe your way of being? Now go ahead and start constructing an actual musical!

6. *Imagine tragedy or good fortune.* What if your congregation were divested of its resources? Or imagine the opposite: a time when nearly overwhelming good fortune appeared. Which would be easier to deal with? What would be your new priorities in each case? Now reconstruct your priorities as though each eventuality actually has occurred!

Parsing This Chapter

The following items may be helpful to you for purposes of review—or even as a quick way to pretend you've read the entire chapter! Try any of the following questions or actions with other leaders:

1. What emotions well up inside you when you think about the legacies you have received? What emotions come to mind as you think about passing on those legacies? How are the emotions different or the same?

2. With your pastor or another leader, try this activity: Pick one especially helpful section of this chapter and share your answers to the question, "Where do you find yourself in this section?" Ask follow-up or clarifying questions of each other. Pray about what you've shared.

3. Where do you find similar phenomena in the world outside the church? (For example, how does "legacy" operate in businesses or the government?)

4. For devotions, ask each member of a task group or team to briefly characterize, in writing, the spiritual legacy they have received. After sharing and posting each written evidence of God's grace, pray together. (*Note:* Some people have come to faith with limited legacies. As you are sensitive to that fact—not everyone is a dyed-in-the-wool Christian—also be sensitive to the extraordinary stories of conversion or revelation that have come into the lives of new believers. By grace!)

5. Where in this chapter did you find an especially hopeful gem or touchstone that you could carry with you awhile? What did that discovery make you want to do next?

6. What might your leadership group do together to spark your imagination or strengthen your willingness to act?

Part 3

WHAT'S POSSIBLE?

Trying too hard" is not a terminal disease of congregational leaders, nor is it a permanent condition of your life. These last chapters are filled with the expectation that you will be able to change, in small ways at first, the behaviors that may have turned you into a modern-day Sisyphus. Because hope is always stronger than despair, these chapters invite you to a realistic hope. Because actions compel thoughts, and those thoughts compel further action, these chapters will include gentle nudgings and elbow-tuggings toward small changes.

This final section brings you full circle, back to the hesitant hope that caused you to pick up this book in the first place. Chapter 8 ("Playing with Substance") lays the groundwork—you'll look at "change" and "planning"—and chapter 9 ("Getting to Start") sends you back to the starting line: how to be an effective leader without trying too hard.

8

PLAYING WITH SUBSTANCE

Joseph P. Kennedy may have etched truth into many souls when he uttered his famous epigram, "When the going gets tough, the tough get going." But written under that up-by-the-bootstraps view of adversity should be the color-splotched graffito: "And when the tough get going, they start playing." *Playing* is another way of describing purposeful, enjoyable movement. When you move, your brain engages its surroundings and adapts to what it encounters. Whether you're a child or an adult, you solve problems best by moving. To state matters differently, adult humans don't approach problems like adult sea squirts, which can't solve their problems because they can't move. Human adults, you see, are mobile, problem-solving organisms.

In this chapter, we will examine and play with two major areas of congregational life:

❏ What needs to change.

❏ How to plan for change.

The chapter is both substantive and playful, because I want to engage more than the usual parts of your brain. The substantive material is concerned with change theory and asset-based planning. The playful part—how you turn these theories into actions—is scattered amid the substantive material. By "playing with substance," you'll get to do what your brain's various mechanisms like to do: work together.

And since "working together with you" is what my brain likes to do, we'll get started with some basic questions about change. And we'll begin the chapter by considering how an older view of "change" might cause you to try too hard. Let's look at these topics:

From your classes in Ocean Biology 101 ("Our Animal Friends in the Sea"), you will remember the distinguishing feature of sea squirt development: When the larvae find a suitable location, they attach to that place with their suckers, eat their own rudimentary brains, and never move from that spot again. Thus sea squirts provide a whimsical metaphor for "congregations that don't do anything but sit around" (after they've eaten their metaphorical brains?), as you will recall from your classes in Church Biology 101 ("Our Animal Friends in the Church").

❑ How most folk think of "change"

❑ Why that doesn't work anymore

❑ How change has changed

❑ How change occurs

❑ "Leading" change

❑ How change theory affects congregations

How most folk think of "change"

If you're like most pastors or congregational leaders, you assume that you are called to be a "change agent." You based your view of that role on two seemingly self-evident truths, "Change is inevitable" and "Effective change is managed by effective leaders." As you live out this role, you:

1. Gather evidence about the areas of congregational life that need to be changed.

2. Set up processes—usually persuasive, sometimes "collegial"—by which the necessary changes will be understood, embraced, and enacted.

3. Start with the first and most logical step, and carry out all the remaining steps. (You "plan your work and work your plan.")

If you're working from this classic view of change, you will probably proceed with the following principles in mind:

❑ The nature of change remains constant—that is, change is a measured difference between a previous and present state, or between present and future states.

❑ Change obeys the laws of cause and effect.

❑ Changes are more likely to succeed if they are based on facts. You are doubly assured of success if you understand the systems in which the desired changes take place.

❑ Change is predictable, or at least can be understood.

❑ Logic and rational processes enhance change.

❑ Change can be "managed" or directed, using varieties of "social engineering."

❑ Changes in behavior begin with changes in ideas or ideals.

❑ The better—or more persuasive—the techniques by which change is engineered, the more pervasive and lasting the change.

❑ Resistance to change comes from people who are unwilling or unable to change. (Sometimes these imagined "problem children" include "middle managers" or those who have the most to lose if a change takes place.)

❑ The purpose of change is to bring order, solve problems, or reach some kind of equilibrium.

❑ The larger the need for change, the more comprehensive the plan for change needs to be.

In *Surfing the Edge of Chaos: The Laws of Nature and the New Laws of Business*, consultants Richard T. Pascale, Mark Millemann, and Linda Gioja characterize social engineering as a classic—but obsolete and unworkable—framework for change. If you practice social engineering, you act as though the leader is the head (and the organization is the body). You believe that primary, secondary, and tertiary levels of change can be predicted. You are fairly certain that initiative cascades down from the "change agent" to the rest of the enterprise, sometimes with a veneer of collegiality.

Why that view doesn't work any more

If you are operating with a classic view of change, you may be working toward an unreachable goal that has been framed by untenable premises. Here's what business management consultants and change theorists are saying about the classical view of change, and how those ideas might be seen in your congregation.

The rate of change has increased. The blurred speed and directions of change have exceeded the coping capabilities of most leaders. (Think of the many changes in your congregation's confirmation programs or Sunday school curricula over the past 10 years.)

Change may now be toxic. When the rate and content of change increase, so do the costs in financial and human capital. U.S. businesses are now spending between $30 and $50 billion per year for the cost of change consultants. About 70 percent of those efforts at change fail. Corporate restructurings—usually "downsizings"—have displaced tens of millions of workers. But the supposed financial streamlining has also been costly as corporate worth has declined in many of those "re-engineered" corporations (from *Surfing the Edge of Chaos*, by Pascale et al.). (What do continuing upgrades in office equipment cost your congregation, including the cost of retraining staff to use new hardware or software?)

Changes have become more complex. Because we live in an interconnected world, the effects of one decision ripple through the networks of influence that exist in every organization. Because of the complexity, those ripples cannot be completely known or predicted anymore. (Think about the complex answers to the simple question, "Why aren't there enough pastors?")

"New change" requires new leadership styles. Leadership styles based on classic views of change may keep leaders from expanding their vision about their roles. One example: an overexertive notion about "cooperation" or "collegiality." (If your consistent reaction to your congregation is "How will I change them?" then you also believe that your role is "to improve things around here." Besides its inherent arrogance, this parochial presumption may limit you to one style of leadership.)

There are fewer authorities. As businesses move toward employee-oriented decision-making, they make information more accessible. Thus, reliance on classically defined "authorities" decreases. (Our society's disregard for leaders of any kind now includes stereotypical distrust of religious leaders as well. The trend may extend into your congregation.)

"Success" is hard to duplicate. It is difficult (or unwise) to emulate "successful change." Rapidly changing conditions virtually eliminate the ideal of learning from best-practice organizations. In 1982, Tom Peters and Bob Waterman (*In Search of Excellence*) listed qualities they believed contributed to the success of 43 high-quality enterprises. Pascale et al. (*Surfing the Edge of Chaos*) note that while the traits were beyond reproach (e.g., clear vision, strong values), within five years half of the highlighted companies were in trouble. (This point leads to the question, "How many exemplary congregations will still be models of excellence five years from now?")

◆

Only the wisest and stupidest of men never change.

Confucius

IN HIS FIRST ATTEMPT AT "SHARED LEADERSHIP,"
PASTOR ARGYLE FOUND HIMSELF TRYING
JUST A LITTLE TOO HARD.

DEBUNKING SOME MYTHS ABOUT CHANGE

Social scientists have examined closely some cherished ideals about change and found that they lacked substance. Consider these few examples of debunked "facts":

● People will change if they are rewarded extrinsically. In fact, most reward systems aimed at accelerating or motivating change deteriorate into grievances, game-playing, conflict, or shortsightedness. Rewards motivate people to get rewards.

● *Change* is happening everywhere. *Rapid change* often means only "technological change." Some areas of life—for example, the divorce rate, individualism, generosity—have remained fairly stable over a long period of time.

● Most people do not want to change. On closer examination, social scientists have found that what workers and volunteers resist are the ways in which change is foisted on them, including top-down methods masquerading as cooperative decision making.

● The rate of change can only increase. Although they be only a glimmer on the horizon, "end of change" philosophers express hope for the possibility of "stable organizations."

● "Survival of the fittest" is a driving force in organizational development. This term (coined not by Charles Darwin but by sociologist Herbert Spencer) does not represent completely what is true in nature or in corporations. "Social Darwinism" may more accurately describe altruistic or cooperative behaviors in nature and organizations.

● Human organizations can be described in deterministic terms, and measured by sociometrics. In fact, human organizations may behave more like living organisms, and many forms of data measure only the outcomes of change, not its causes.

(From *Surfing the Edge of Chaos,* by Richard T. Pascale et al., and *The End of Change: How Your Company Can Sustain Growth and Innovation While Avoiding Change Fatigue*, by Peter Scott-Morgan et al.)

Basic assumptions about change may not be true. Social scientists have examined more closely the underpinnings of classic change theory and found that they are simply not true. (You may have wondered how many long-held assumptions about "excellent congregations" have actually been supported by reliable research.)

How change has changed

The change processes you experience in this postmodern world are now based on a different set of assumptions. Whether you recognize them in your congregation or not, these assumptions about change are increasingly important for leaders in commerce, government, and the social-service sector. You might want to talk to congregation members whose work keeps them current with societal trends and ask them how the following propositions work in their settings.

Change is chaotic. Change is now is described as a complex process, not a series of events along a cause-and-effect time line. "Organic" is another way to describe complex processes. Complexity science and its derivatives best characterize social systems. This science has taken its place alongside psychology, social psychology, brain science, and sociology as a theoretical basis for change.

Change happens in a blur. The speed of change can be described as a blur, or as nearly instantaneous. ("Five minutes ago" describes something that falsely presents itself as "new." This derisive phrase now has its own derisive detractors as well.)

Interrelated changes defy manageability. Because "everything is connected to everything," many descriptions of "facts" or "systems" are dated and incomplete as soon as they are framed. If you lack accurate information, you cannot "manage" or "direct" change with any certainty. Because there are fewer certainties, the best bases for your decisions may be only best guesses.

Controlled change rarely yields its desired outcomes. For example, even when "participative management techniques" are employed, over three-quarters of these attempts fail because they are still a form of social engineering.

◆

Without me you can do nothing.

Jesus

"New" commodities have emerged. A primary example is "attention," which is now considered a commodity that can be bought and sold. In a world of information overload and stressful, speeded-up lifestyles, the momentary or focused attention of individuals or groups is a precious thing (from *The Attention Economy: Understanding the New Currency of Business,* by Thomas H. Davenport and John C. Beck).

Small details are the key. Because "the big picture" is getting bigger and more difficult to describe, change may be most clearly seen in the smallest shifts in circumstance or direction. Descriptions of "whole group change" are most likely couched in terms of almost imperceptible changes in individuals. "Fractals"—patterned structures nested inside larger structures that show the same pattern (for example, a fern leaf)—are both metaphor and description of this reality. One example: "microenterprise" has become a preferred method for economic renewal. Another example: individual entrepreneurs make up the fastest-growing segment of the economy.

"Microenterprise" is a term that describes small-scale business development in Third World countries and in places where economic renewal is desired. Typically, small low-interest loans are granted individuals through their participation in a cooperative venture. The result: self-employed and self-reliant citizens of villages and inner cities.

You may have reached some limits. You may be running out of hours in the day, words, venture capital ("Hey, buddy, wanna buy a dot.com?"), bandwidth, or sleep.

You've already read about the brain's capacity to filter out information—and some of the changes it carries. This "filtering" may suggest that the brain isn't paying attention. The brain's supposed inattention can be described in several ways, such as that of John L. Ratey, M.D. in his book, *The User's Guide to the Brain*:

❏ "Competitive inhibition," in which a second signal to the brain lessens the effect of the previous signal

❏ "Salience," which describes the fact that the brain pays attention to specific images in its visual field—similar to what occurs with hearing and touch

❏ "Attentional specificity," a way of describing how the brain ignores everything except what it craves

Resistance to change may be increasing. Some businesses now value "change resister" employees for their help in slowing change to manageable levels. In his model of caring consultancy, Peter Block (*Flawless Consulting: A Guide to Getting Your Expertise Used*) demonstrates how resistance to change is predictable, natural, and necessary. He names a variety of "faces of resistance"—some even rather pleasant—and suggests that each is rooted in legitimate emotional reactions to change.

Change has a technological heart. In the world outside the church, technology enables change and change focuses on technology. New and emerging technologies have driven the forces of market capitalism, as well as the reinvention of the "new economy."

During the months this book was being shaped, the manageability and sustainability of a technologically dependent economy was being called into serious question. "Dot.coms" were folding as venture capitalists escaped unprofitable enterprises. The technology side of the stock market continued to slide. Down- or dumbsizing of companies continued, mostly in technology-based markets. By the time you read this book, a basic question may have been voiced: What will happen to change if the rate of technologies' change slows? Are we living at the dawn of a newly stable era?

Change may be values-driven. Your machines mirror your values, and values can always be described in metaphysical terms. So the changes you see around you may be more "spiritual" that they seem at first. Some theologians have wondered, for example, if our inventing new and better technologies doesn't mirror the Babel story in Genesis 11. Spiritual changes—e.g., a return to "godly living"—may drive the marketplace in the future.

Change happens at the edge. In *Surfing the Edge of Chaos*, Pascale et al. remind readers that if you're in the middle of something it's hard to tell in what direction the thing might be moving. Further, they recall how our brains look for edges to distinguish figure from background, and what's dangerous from what's safe. Finally, they note that it is at the edges where nature's mutations are most prolific.

How change occurs

According to complexity science, change happens in organizations because of self-organization, strange attractors, and emergence. Pascale et al. *(Surfing the Edge of Chaos)* summarize the matter somewhat metaphorically:

❑ "Self-organization" is the tendency of some systems to shift to a new shape, state, or function when their constituent elements generate unlikely combinations.

❑ Self-organization occurs when strange attractors attract elements into an emergent relationship. (Here the metaphor includes an invisible magnetic field—the strange attractor—and iron filings that line up along lines of magnetic force.)

❑ The result of the self-organization is either new routes (ways around barriers or solutions to adversity) or new destinations (results never before seen).

Another way to describe the matter is the minor doctrinal formulation, *solvitur ambulando*, suggested in Paul's recounting of heritage (legacy) in 2 Timothy. This Latin phrase— "The thing will reveal itself as it moves along"— describes not only the matter of self-organized change, but also a theologically tinged reality: God reveals wisdom as it becomes necessary.

The best example of "self-organized change" is the termite mound. Apparently without benefit of plans or hierarchical mechanisms, termites build their exquisitely sophisticated mounds by individual termites' seemingly random acts of piling dirt.

In *Imaginization: The Art of Creative Management*, Canadian business school professor and change consultant Gareth Morgan delights the reader by describing termite mounds as ideal examples of self-organizing systems.

Organized around the basic structure of the arch, the mounds' hallways, spiral staircases, storage rooms, and living areas make them miniature cities capable of housing millions of termites. The mounds are kept at ideal temperatures and humidity, and their ventilation systems feature opening and closing vents.

Apparently without a central coordinating plan, these insects still are able to construct and maintain 12-foot-high

◆

Nobody sees a flower really; it is so small. We haven't time, and to see takes time—like to have a friend takes time.

Georgia O'Keefe

mounds of mud equivalent to human-size buildings a mile high! How does it happen? The plan emerges as the dirt is piled. (Perhaps this could be a useful motto for new churches.)

"Leading" change

One of the most fundamental precepts of change theory is that it can somehow be "led." You've probably already guessed from the previous pages that I am not quite so sure about the idea that "causing change" can be laid at the feet of leaders. At the same time, you *are* a leader, and change *does* happen as a part of your leadership. The following ideas from current change theory might help your find your place in the process of change.

Change starts with behaviors, not ideas. Because you "act your way into thinking," changed behaviors may be the first step in a process of change, instead of the last step. If you persuade people to accept a new idea, you are not engaged in a lasting change process. Or worse, if you persuade members of your congregation to use the language of the new idea, you may watch, frustrated, as they now use new language to describe what they've always done!

Change is about emotion. As you deal with change, you're always dealing with emotions. Dealing with the emotions associated with a change is a necessary component in seeking lasting change. For example, how will you diminish "fear" or the perception of danger implicit in an imagined change? Approaching change only as a logical matter is not approaching change logically.

Change occurs in small steps. Whether they happen all at once or over a period of time, changes—even the largest—are composed of small steps, each of which makes another step possible. When you recognize each small step as a part of an eventually larger change, you can find satisfaction in what has been (and what will be) accomplished. (We'll explore the "small-step approach" to change in the last chapter of this book.)

Changes happen within individuals. The changes you might seek in groups, such as your congregation, are always

Humming along at a 40-Hz level of electrical energy, brains are always working, always ready to initiate action. The same circuits that are used to order, sequence, and time a physical act are used to order, sequence, and time a mental act. Thus, the brain can imagine itself into action, and increase its imagination by acting. Movement becomes crucial for every other brain function, including memory, emotion, language, and learning (from *A User's Guide to the Brain*, by John J. Ratey).

Change Agency, Not Change Agent

In classic change theory, the role of the "change agent" is key. In that way of thinking, this person's behaviors—and the wisdom and skill that support those actions—are the core ingredients for successful or lasting change. The idea has significant problems for congregations:

● Congregational changes instituted or "motivated" by charismatic leaders frequently disappear when that leader's energy is no longer used to maintain the change. (The leader can move to another passion or another pastorate.)

● The etymology of the word *change*—from the Greek *agein*, "to drive or lead animals"—hardly suggests a mindful or intelligent role for those who are supposedly motivated by the "change agent." (In previous chapters, we looked at similar problems with "teacher/disciples" and "shepherd/sheep.") If you think of your task as "pushing or shoving lesser beings to do what they would not otherwise do," you will always be trying too hard, if only because people get tired of being led that way, and start to ignore that kind of "change leader."

● Significant and lasting changes emerge from within the group, not from a single individual, especially a pastor or professional worker. Codependencies can easily become institutionalized, and eventually rob energy and initiative from both partners in the relationship.

● God's agency is the primary cause for change. (Here "agency" means capacity, condition, or state of acting or of exerting power.) God is the only empowering force.

Better metaphors and "job titles" for "change agent" include coach, instrument, lawyer, advocate, transformer, mediator, provocateur, truth-teller, consultant, evoker, and change insurgent.

These metaphors describe leaders who are less anxious. They suggest leaders whose success is measured in the long-term changes that come from the people they serve. They also characterize leaders who move a bit more slowly, who are more reflective, highly capable of self-differentiation, and willing to face difficulty with their personal integrity.

What do these leaders do about change? Their tasks are to help constituents or partners through change. They sort information and make sense out of sensory or emotional overload. They are skilled in conversational methods of decision making. They carry a deep curiosity about life and are capable of insistent, gentle questioning. They have a minimal stake in the potential changes; instead, they cherish the yearnings and hopes of those for whom the change is most important.

the sum of collective changes in individuals. Change happens one person at a time. That's why "a majority vote" doesn't always signal change, and why "consensus" usually does.

The idea of "change agent" may be a delusion. Although a small percentage of leaders can seemingly effect change, the great majority of changes emerge from within groups without the directed control of a charismatic leader. Strapping on the imagined responsibility of the primary cause for change is certainly a Sisyphean behavior, and over-exertion a certain result.

How change theory affects congregations

As collections of human beings, congregations share many characteristics with other enterprises. So change theory can be instructive as you try to decide how your congregation might conduct its business.

Common-sense change. For all its seeming complexity, change theory is at its heart fairly pragmatic. You may already be following intuitively some of the guidelines of change theory. "Common sense" can be a rarely trusted commodity in congregations. In *The Power of Simplicity: A Management Guide to Cutting Through the Nonsense and Doing Things Right*, marketing consultant Jack Trout tweaks the noses of leaders who intuitively make things more complex for others. He encourages readers to ignore insults—"You're being simplistic," "You're just lazy," or "You just don't understand"—and seek simplicity as a preferred solution.

Diminished embarrassment. Change theory helps take away some of the guilt and shame you might feel about your congregation's straggly structure. (You remember how exquisite order can be embedded in seeming chaos.) If you know how your "disorganized" structure accomplishes its mission, you don't worry how it looks.

Invisibly powerful change agents. If you know the people in your congregation who are the strange attractors—"Sylvia and Leroy, the vision people"—you can focus your ministry on strengthening theirs. You can name and affirm the people whose quiet influence helps shape decisions, spirit, or mission.

Another way to look at adversity. Because complex adaptive systems change, grow stronger, or multiply under adversity, you don't have to work so hard—or think so sadly—when your congregation faces real or imagined calamities. You know that something different—and perhaps better—will emerge from this negative circumstance; you just don't know quite yet how it will look.

> Adversity can be the source for amazing adaptive mechanisms that ensure sustainability. In the natural world, think of the tenacious liveliness of bacteria, fire ants, or coyotes. In your congregation, think of the tenacious liveliness of longtime members who can be amazingly adaptive in their strong desire to "keep this church alive."

The emergence of order. Understanding "emergent simplicities" helps you to be patient for the unfolding or unraveling of what seems to be complex. You look for recurring patterns that reveal those simple ideas, and the "ordinary members" who possess considerable skill in bringing order out of chaos. Understanding how self-organized change emerges from large, diverse groups of people working together, you can more easily trust planning or visioning processes that at first seem cumbersome, messy or time-consuming.

Applied fractals. If you understand the significance of fractals, you will see their application: "The solution to the problem may lie within the problem itself." (A variation: "The solution to the problem lies very close to the problem.") This idea helps you refrain from depending too quickly on outside consultants, or panicking about the seeming absence of solutions. ("Trying too hard" automatically accompanies both of those reactions.) You can remember the times when "impossible problems" were solved by a simple solution right under your nose. Or more significantly, perhaps, your soul can be grateful that God's amazing grace "saved a wretch like me."

Staying at the edge. Because you know that change occurs at the edge of complexity, you can always be aware of the "edge people," or "edge situations," where changes might already be starting. (For example: What are the "inactives" accomplishing in their lives instead of "doing church"?) You understand how the middle will always follow one or more of the edges. This makes you more patient about change, and about the contrarians among your congregation members.

The beauty of small changes. If you know and accept the importance of small changes—some "small changes" are actually strange attractors—you will always remain aware of the beautiful intricacies of seemingly insignificant details and live in constant appreciation of "small-but-important things." For example, think how you could approach each Sunday's worship if you adjusted your tone of voice, sermon, or words of welcome to the reality that weather (air pressure, temperature, humidity) affects the moods of worshipers.

Decreasing control behaviors. Your need to control—and all its accompanying hard work—will start to diminish if you understand its near-toxicity in bringing about change. You will exchange your metaphorical cat-herding for dog-walking. (See the matter of "unintended consequences" in the previous chapter as well.)

"Failures" forgiven. Change theory allows you to be more forgiving (of yourself?) when "failure" occurs. You understand failures as learning opportunities, or part of a larger, yet-to-emerge pattern. So you don't try too hard or too quickly to hide, blame, or fix failures. Instead, you look for the larger patterns, adapt to the consequences, learn how to behave differently, and keep moving.

Holding everything together. Change and complexity theory relieve you of the overwhelming burden of trying to hold everything together, or trying to keep everything in a state of equilibrium. Because you know that in nature equilibrium shortly precedes death, you can thank God for all the untidy growing edges you see in yourself, other members of the congregation, and the congregation itself.

Shared change agency. If you accept the fact that you are not the major "change agent" in this congregation—a role overloaded with responsibilities and pressures—you can try the roles of "coach" or "consultant," assisting others with the changes they want to undertake.

These examples help you see how complexity and change theories give you a new mental map from which to construct some of your attitudes and actions for ministry. From my own experience as a congregational leader, the intertwined corollaries of these two theories offer a calming, reassuring approach to what could be debilitatingly difficult. At times, I've even felt that I've heard God's voice in all this.

In his *Learning to Read the Signs: Reclaiming Pragmatism in Business*, advertising agency CEO F. Byron Nahser helps readers gain skills for seeing "what's really going on." One of his important techniques: guided conversation, loosely akin to the caring conversation that can characterize your leadership style.

Peter Block (*Flawless Consulting: A Guide to Getting Your Expertise Used*) describes the consultant's work as authentic conversation between friends, or helping people with their imagined ineffectiveness. The effective consultant has an almost spiritual capacity to bring out what has previously been unspeakable. Specific consultant skills and techniques are necessary complements to the basic equipment you carry in your heart: compassion, sympathy, groundedness, self-confidence, emotional intelligence, and humility.

The Poobah Letters, Part CCCVII:
ON COMPLEXITY AND COMMESSITY

(Author's note: Before his early retirement, Dr. Billy ["William"] Poobah, noted Christian expert and host of the weekly radio show "Focus on Billy," penned "The Poobah Letters," in which he offered to a local pastor his observations on most of life's deeper questions. Here I reproduce, from ~~Napkin~~ Letter 307, his observations on the differences and similarities between "complexity" and "commessity," a term Poobah coined for no apparent reason.)

Dear Reverent Matthew,

You asked how, in your pastoring, you could tell the difference between wonderfully expectant complexity and "commessity," a term which I coined for no apparent reason. Let me try to help you with these examples:

1. It's complexity when you ask your congregation's children to "color the Palm Sunday bulletins." It's commessity when they also color the Palm Sunday pew cushions.
2. You can expect the wonderful results of self-organizing complexity any time there's a pot-luck supper. Commessity occurs if you try to control the amounts of Jello and tuna.
3. Complexity would be possible if [unintelligible green splotch] at the church picnic. You'd be seeing commessity if the beanbags were filled with [slight tear in napkin] instead.
4. "Let's pray for each other" is a complex strange attractor at a meeting. "Let's pray aloud for ourselves" might turn into "silent commessity."
5. Commessity describes the last rehearsal before the Christmas pageant; complexity describes the actual event.
6. You can expect complex answers to the question, "How is our church kitchen a part of our mission?" and commessious answers to the question, "Should we let the Boy Scout troop use the kitchen for their cooking merit badges?"
7. You can find the joys of complexity in deciding your annual plan for mission funding, and the sadness of commessity in deciding how to appropriate the remaining $35.86 from the Snively Memorial Elm Grove Trimming Fund.
8. Want to find complexity? Ask your youth what they're good at doing. Want to find commessity? Ask them how they clean their rooms at home.
9. You're into personal complexity when you start keeping a journal. You're inviting commessity if you write it on paper tablecloths in ethnic restaurants.
10. You can see God's hand in complexity when you start preparing any sermon; you can see God's hand in commessity when you've finished preaching it.

I hope this helps you understand that God works through every seemingly complex set of circumstances to bring beauty and purpose to what you do. As for commessity, God has a hand in that, too!

Your friend until [unreadable mauve smear]

Billy

How to plan for change

The title of this segment of the chapter matches the titles on entire shelves in bookstores. "How to" is the grabber in the title, and "change" is the "vexing agent." But true to my word at the start of this chapter, the title of this section is just another way of playing with you: I have no intention of telling you "how to plan for change." Instead, now that I have your attention, it's time to vex you about planning the usual way.

Planning the way we usually do it

Most planning is needs-based—and thus an arduous task that rarely effects lasting change. Add in the questionable oxymoron "long-range," and you have a mighty tall mountain for that big rock of yours, Sisyphus. What makes "needs-based planning" a tall mountain? There are more needs than you'll ever fill. In addition, the better you are at finding the "true needs of these people," the higher Mount Overexertion will get.

"Long-range" means that the single mountain is part of an entire herd of mountains, all stacked next to each other like—um, well, like a long range! Just in case you get that infernal rock pushed to the top of the first mountain, the other mountains assure you that your job will never be done, long into the future.

The substance I'm playing with includes the following truths:

❏ Because it adds to information overload, fosters a negative view of God's world, and invites you to exaggerate your life mission, needs-based planning and thinking can engage you for the rest of your life in "trying too hard."

❏ "Long-range" adds the delusion that you can achieve long-term understanding and control of change. This is not possible unless you want to spend down all your personal assets for what may be nothing more than a well-meaning gamble about an imagined future.

Needs-based planning persists as a feature of most congregations' ways of doing business, however, even though it doesn't work all that well any more.

You guessed it: "Change provocateur" is my favorite metaphor to describe how to operate in a changing world. It's also a good way to say "troublemaker" in a nice way. In my working with senior congregation members, I always get a rise out of about half the group when I ask to sit with "the troublemakers." Strangely, the perkiest twinkly-eyed ones immediately want to be known that way. What does this mean? That well into our later years, some of us understand the excitement and energy that come from this odd word, "trouble." That something about "getting old" helps us accept and lead change. And what might that mean for your congregation?

PLANNING WITH DR. POOBAH

Directions: You need to check the Yes and No boxes to reflect your likely behaviors or attitudes.

Yes	No	Item
☐	☐	1. I use "need to" to describe what I want other people to do.
☐	☐	2. I'd rather help you than have you help me.
☐	☐	3. At church, I think of myself as a "problem solver."
☐	☐	4. I think of my volunteering as "helping our pastor."
☐	☐	5. We build our budget on what we need to do, and we ask for contributions to meet our budget needs.
☐	☐	6. I see or hear the word "need" a lot at our congregation.
☐	☐	7. God needs me to do God's work.

Scoring: If you checked less than one box, you already know about the trap of "needs-based planning." If you checked more, you might ~~need~~ want to read this section carefully.

The alternative: asset-based planning

You have another choice for effective planning. Its starting point is not the needs of people, but the unique collection of assets already resident in your congregation.

This alternative way of thinking and planning—asset-based planning—has benefits that needs-oriented planning cannot offer. Think what it would be like for you to experience "doing church" with:

❑ Positive and hopeful thinking.

❑ Energy, enthusiasm, and emotional satisfaction.

❑ Less likelihood of "failure."

❑ Quicker, more efficient agreement on outcomes.

❑ Quicker, more efficient ways to get work done.

❑ Authentic reasons to say, "No, I won't do that."

❑ Opportunities for a higher percentage of members to use a higher percentage of their personal assets for God's work.

❑ Feelings of solidarity, appreciation, and purpose.

This way of work is called "asset-based" because both its thinking and acting components are based on assets, not needs. You can tell that asset-based thinking and planning offer you the chance to break out of the cycles of ecclesiastical overexertion I've described in this book.

The business-management sources I've used in this book picture planning and consultancy in this way. The best examples are any of Peter Block's writings. (For beginners: *The Empowered Manager* or *Stewardship*. For those of you who want to jump into techniques right away: *Flawless Consulting*.)

How "asset-based planning" works

First, asset-based planning works! The approach I'll describe here has been successful in overseas agricultural and community development for over 20 years. Rural communities in this country regularly use asset-based approaches to renew their sense of possibility. Many social-service agencies approach large-scale change with asset-based planning and implementation methods. Most consultants and business gurus talk about some variety of asset-based work in their various systems or methods.

Let me outline an asset-based planning process that is based on the continuing work of the Asset-Based Community Development Institute, part of the Institute for Policy Research of Northwestern University in Evanston, Illinois. You can probably find local sources by talking to almost any community development organization or agency. The process of planning develops according to the these general steps:

1. You start with the people who have some emotional motivation for the general task you have in mind together. (The important word here is "general," because you haven't started planning yet.) They are the first asset.

2. You come together in a place where you can spread out— open space on walls, tables, or floors is important. You briefly characterize the idea of asset-based planning and review the general task or goal that brought you together.

3. Using the questions, "What are you good at?" and "What do you like to do?" each participant describes or characterizes each "asset" he or she brings to this general task, listing each one on a separate piece of paper.

4. When all participants' assets have been listed, together you construct a "map" of the assets, grouping them into categories. When it is completed, this map becomes visual proof of your giftedness as a planning group, and of your willingness to use your assets for a purpose.

5. With the map in front of you—on the wall, tables, or floor—you try to discover what specific tasks you might work on together, aiming at the outcomes that brought you together. One guideline to follow: "We will do only what we're good at and what we like to do."

6. Having decided what to do next together, you quickly agree on specific responsibilities, a time line and the next time you'll come together.

The case study that follows is an amalgam of my personal experiences, and illustrates how each of these steps was played out in the case of "The Surprising Stewardship Program."

Case Study:
The Surprising Stewardship Program

The stewardship crew at Faith Church had a good idea: "Let's 'fund God's mission' instead of 'funding the budget.'" Two other good ideas were attached: "Let's have a dinner," and "Let's have some fun!" (Assets: a desire for a better approach to "stewardship" and hope for a positive experience.)

A broad-yet-personal invitation was extended to anyone in the congregation "who wants to help plan and work on a congregational stewardship dinner." Attendance at two planning dinners would be required, with the congregation's budget providing the meals. (Assets: The enthusiasm of the inviter and the congregation's stewardship budget line.)

Over 30 people attended the first planning meeting, which encouraged Pastor George immensely. "Encouraged," that is, until he looked around and noticed that about half the eager planners were children under the age of 13. On closer examination, he also noticed that some of the adults were part of the "wild and crazy" bunch at church. And these people were going to be entrusted with gathering the pledges for financial commitments to fund God's mission at Faith for an entire year? (Assets: More than 30 people, about half under age 13; members of the "wild and crazy" bunch; and a pastor's willingness to trust the leaders and the people of the congregation.)

After a quick supper the group took to its first task: in smaller groups, listing every possible asset anyone could imagine that might, in any way, contribute to the success of some kind of stewardship dinner. The questions: What are you good at? What do you like to do? (Assets: food, big tables, markers, slips of paper, plenty of time, and easy questions for creative people to answer about themselves.)

The planning dinner concluded with each table group looking for preliminary answers to another question, "When you look at all the assets of the people at this table, what patterns do you see?" Groups reported out their ideas, which were displayed on newsprint. (Assets: newsprint, markers, analytical thinking skills.)

The second planning dinner drew about the same number of people. This time the process centered on a large group discussion of the question, "Knowing what we know about ourselves—our assets—what kind of stewardship dinner could we do?" After a few hesitant responses, one child said, "I'd

Some "assets" this group did not overlook:

- Things we own or can get
- People who owe us favors
- Community members who really like this church
- People we know, and who know us
- Generous movers and shakers in this town
- Children
- Past skills and experiences ("I used to play the clarinet.")
- Time
- Quiet

like to act and sing." That was the spark. One of the wild-and-crazies gave the child's idea a name: "dinner theater." And then the ideas jumped out of the groups like clowns out of their clown car. Newsprint sheets were soon crowded with possibilities. A rough outline emerged, and big chunks of work broke into little chunks. Adults and kids volunteered to take logical first steps. A next meeting was scheduled for several weeks later. (Assets: the right question, the "spark moment," and the group's respect for a child's courage to speak up.)

Two months later, "Faith Revue" was offered for the entire congregation, graced by the work of more than 60 members of the congregation. They danced, sang, told jokes, performed a homemade drama, showed a deeply moving slide show about the congregation's people, and talked about the things they would do together as God's people in the next year. Financial commitments were collected, whose aggregate total was a full 13 percent above the previous year's. (Assets: 30 additional participants, each with her or his own assets, a delighted stewardship team, and Pastor George, whose sermons and letters added to the spiritual core of the annual stewardship response program.)

For the next two years, that same group, now augmented with other children and wild-and-crazies, offered a dinner theater night at Faith Church. Although it wasn't connected with mission funding, the event helped draw together the congregation in fellowship and fun. (Asset: the enthusiasm of people who had experienced the thrill of an asset-based planning approach.)

What else you might want to know

Asset-based planning is a way of behaving that, over time, yields a way of thinking. At the same time, this way of work requires changes in your way of thinking. I offer you the following assorted comments to help you explore asset-based thought and behavior.

❏ This approach is not magic, nor does it work everywhere in your congregation. (Some tasks, mostly those required by law, must be done, whether or not someone enjoys doing them.)

❏ Asset-based planning will eventually affect the way you conduct yourselves in every aspect of your life together.

❏ The first steps in the process—carefully listing assets and mapping them—take longer the first time around. Once you have constructed the assets map, subsequent planning consumes less time.

❏ Asset-based planning may result in your eliminating some goals, some work. You may not have the assets to accomplish everything you want to do. "Trying too hard" often comes from wanting to do what you lack the capacity to do.

❏ If you keep at this asset-based approach, though, you will find assets multiplying. Assets develop inside individuals; assets are attracted to your congregation; and assets emerge from unexpected places. Where needs-based planning keeps sucking capacity out of you, asset-based planning keeps adding to good things God has plopped down onto your congregation like second helpings at a Thanksgiving dinner!

❏ Because they build capacity, asset-based approaches sustain liveliness in your congregation.

❏ Because it is positive, forward-looking, and realistic, the asset-based approach can gradually displace the burdensome emotions that you may drag along behind you like a trash-filled wagon with square wheels.

❏ Although you can start thinking this way easily enough, learning the skills of asset-based planning requires some training. Your best source for help: a local community-development organization.

❏ Asset-based planning takes care of two invisible "action stoppers" in congregations: lack of volition (will to work) and capacity (ability to work). Because you work at what you want to do and are good at doing, these necessary pre-requisites for excellence are virtually guaranteed.

Where asset-based planning will flounder

Because this approach is not magical, it can fail just like any method of planning. Watch for these "asset-stoppers":

❏ Members whose humility or low self-regard shows itself in their overuse of the words "just" or "only," as in "Pastor, I'm just an ordinary housewife"

What We Never Talk About at Meetings

You've gone to enough meetings to know how this chain of inactivity can happen:

1. Well-meaning but tired people approach a necessary decision.

2. At surface level the group appears thoughtful and wise, but below the surface two questions lurk like monsters under a three-year-old's bed:

    ●   If we decide, who can do the work?
    ●   When we decide, who will do the work?

3. Deep in the brain of almost every person in the room is an answer, suggested by overload, perceived danger, or stress: "I hope it's not me."

4. As the time for decision-making draws perceptibly closer, the group seems less able or willing to make the decision, which skitters into a corner like a scared kitten.

5. Eventually the person responsible for the meeting pushes hard, and a decision is made.

6. Now what has been invisible shows itself. As the group tries to figure out how the decision will be implemented, participants wrestle with the prospect of more work. Eventually, responsible participants attach to necessary tasks as cats attach to a leash (which is to say, with tenacious reluctance).

7. The meeting ends with a feeling of muted expectancy among those who did not take on more work, and a feeling of reluctant dutifulness among those who have now assumed additional responsibilities.

You can describe the invisible forces in the room quite simply: These folks lacked both sufficient volition (a will to act) and capacity (the ability to accomplish their tasks) to get the work done in an effective or excellent way.

The group may also have lacked the courage or experience to confront the matter with these questions:

●   Does anyone here really want to do this?
●   Is anyone here really good at doing this?

Unasked and unanswered, these two questions deprive that group of what it needs the most: some assurance that it will succeed. Because the group never talks about these feelings, participants may go about their business with quiet despair. Even though the tasks will eventually be accomplished, excellence and excitement may have been beaten yet once more by the low trump cards of "duty" and "loyalty."

❑ Supersophisticated, sure-fire asset-based planning systems that require advanced degrees in sociology

❑ Control freaks and other egotists

❑ Mean-spirited and evil members who have the audacity to disagree with you about anything

❑ A pastor whose first name is either Mildred, Chauncey, or Bob

❑ Members still caught in the 1970s, who keep hearing "acid" every time you say "asset"

If by now you have not caught my teasing tone, let me say this another way: There are few reasons not to try asset-based planning or thinking. And even if there are, you have the capacity to traverse any barriers that you see.

The entrepreneurial spirit

One of the most consistent elements of current business management thinking is the idea of "the entrepreneurial spirit."

This attitude is especially important in businesses where rapid change necessitates flexibility, innovation, or immediacy. These enterprises stay ahead of competition and meet their customers' requirements because each employee in the company is encouraged to behave and think as though "the company belonged to you." In teams or individually, employees make decisions about products, services, and operations. Managers open lines of communication throughout the company structure, and provide easy access to the company's information streams. In some cases, the big decisions are made using large-group change processes. Encouraged by this way of doing business, workers respond with enthusiasm for possibilities and energy for their work. They benefit individually because the entire company benefits. They respond positively because they are affirmed, trusted and challenged.

The Change Handbook: Group Methods for Shaping the Future is a good source for these whole-group methods. In this useful reference manual, consultants Peggy Holman and Tom DeVane have summarized more than 15 specific large-scale change processes, most of which could work quite well in congregations (for example,

While asset-based planning requires group process skills, be cautious of overblown systems that require more work than this simple idea really requires. Especially beware of any program written or otherwise generated by Dr. Billy ("William") Poobah.

◆

If I didn't start painting, I would have raised chickens.

Grandma Moses

"Appreciative Inquiry," "Open Space Technology," and "Future Search" methods). Ask business leaders in your congregation to describe their experiences in these methods. See which you might purchase or adapt for whole-congregation decision-making about important matters.

Developing an entrepreneurial spirit

You may wish for this kind of spirit in your congregation—that programs, ideas, events, and processes would emerge from members' passions. This atmosphere would likely ensure enthusiasm and ownership. You can begin that process by taking actions such as these:

❑ On a sheet of paper, list every congregational activity, program, or ministry. Try to recall who initiated each item on the list. Analyze the names on the list and see what patterns emerge. (For example, how many different names appear, how many names are listed repeatedly, how often the only name is the pastor's.)

❑ Ask, "How do good ideas get started in this congregation?" Probe the answers to see how you feel about the process of generating good ideas.

❑ Think together how "permission-giving" works in your congregation. How many layers of approval are there? Where does your pastor fit? Who "has to know" about everything that happens before it happens? Who are the real gatekeepers?

❑ Share your honest feelings about how good ideas are squelched or discouraged. Who are the naysayers or disapprovers? Whose careful conservation of the congregation's resources limits new ideas? Who's afraid of whom?

Entrepreneurial stewards

If you start with the questions or activities above, you may find a spark of entrepreneurial spirit. You can steward that bit of fire and turn it into a bright and steady flame with activities such as these:

❑ Establish a "new mission ideas" fund that any congregational group can tap into, with "grants" capped at about $250 per new idea—no questions asked, no long approval process required. Consider the exciting ministries that might be seeded by this money. After a year, collect "new mission" stories and tell them to each other.

❑ Schedule quarterly "What if?" meals, where leaders and pastor come together to imagine preferred futures of whatever size and scope. *Hint 1:* Don't make these into "meetings." *Hint 2:* Don't "decide" anything.

❑ Pick any area of congregational life—for example, the way this church looks to outsiders—and challenge the entire congregation to conceive of improvements or changes they are willing to work on. Ask one individual—not the pastor—to serve as a coordinator or traffic director.

I saved this metaphor for "change agent" until now because it works best here. As a "traffic director" you move active people along, but don't control much more than their speed. Your real concern is that they reach their destination safely. Your work: watching the big picture, communicating with everyone, and perhaps waving your arms a lot!

❑ Find just a few people in the congregation who are idea generators or can-do types. Bring them together—you guessed it, with a meal involved!—and ask them to be an ecclesiastical "skunk works" (that is, an "idea hatchery") for six months. Their task: to tackle some important or invisible vexation in the congregation's life. (For example, they might work on the "we're an unfriendly bunch of toads" problem, the "worship wars" question, or the "untie our pastor from an impossible profession" issue.) Assure them of free rein, provide them with a small budget, require periodic check-ins, and turn them loose!

As you develop an entrepreneurial spirit among members, you will notice the "trying too hard" spirit diminishing. You will also be assured of a sustainable congregation. Why? More than a few people "own" this place, and tasks are begun and finished with energy!

Playing it out

We've come to the end of this chapter, in which we looked at how "change" might work in your congregation and with your leadership. We've also touched on "asset-based planning" and its possible benefits for your congregation.

In the final chapter, I will introduce you to pigs named Pneumos, describe my ideas about world domination, and summarize this entire book. I will also stop playing with you and spend the time on a simple subject: how to start on a new path.

Parsing This Chapter

To use this chapter as a shared learning experience, play around with some of these substantive questions or activities:

1. What's the best way to approach change in your congregation? How do you know?

2. What sparks your personal or collective imagination?

3. Tell about a time when you "started with nothing and made something of it." What stories like these could be told about your congregation?

4. Argue together—then laugh together—about this proposition: "We have everything we need here to do whatever we want together." What would you "argue" about? What would make you laugh?

5. Pick any one of the replacement metaphors for "change agent" (e.g., "coach"). Answer this question for the one you choose: If you were a (*new metaphor*), how would you help people in this congregation work at their own changes?

6. Have fun finishing this comparison: "A church that doesn't ever change is like . . . ."

7. A trick question you can figure out together: Where (with whom) does "real change" start?

8. See what you think about this statement: "The young and the very old are most likely ready and willing to change; it's the rest of us who have problems with change."

9
GETTING TO START

Before you close this book, you have this one chapter to consider, a final invitation to think about how your leadership will help your congregation last. In these pages you'll look at "getting to start," a process like the check-off list cross-country runners complete as they prepare for the start of a meet:

❑ Limber up muscles.

❑ Stretch ligaments and tendons gently.

❑ Focus imagination and concentration.

❑ Review physical features of the course.

❑ Rehearse strategies.

❑ Size up (or "psyche out") opponents.

❑ Analyze coaches' instructions.

❑ Double-check condition of running spikes.

❑ Assay wind and temperature conditions.

In this chapter you'll engage in the same kinds of start preparations, actions you can take before you head out across the landscape that is your congregation's future. Let me invite you to:

❑ Stretch your conceptual frameworks. (You'll learn about how thoughts spread.)

❑ See how a long-distance race might be run. (You'll read about how "tipping points" occur.)

❑ Imagine a new strategy. (You'll practice the "small steps" approach.)

❑ Review "the course" found in this book. (You'll review what's basic.)

❑ Listen to some last coaching thoughts. (You'll decide what to pay attention to during the race *after* you've put down this book.)

When you've completed the chapter, you will find yourself at "start," the place for which you've been getting ready. Once ready, you'll be ready to run the course of leadership you've chosen to take. Enjoy your preparations!

Getting to start

In *Stewardship: Choosing Service Over Self-Interest,* philosopher and consultant Peter Block says that "How?" is an important question that can prevent you from taking action on new beliefs. "How?" can be an excuse for inaction, as in "Honey, how does this vacuum cleaner work?" "How can I get started [on this change]?" might also deny the freedom you have, or denigrate your capabilities.

In this chapter I show you possibilities for your own "Yes!" to every "How?" and assure you again of your capacity to build the future you most hope for your leadership in this congregation. In these pages you'll get ready for the race in which you will soon engage. I'll stick with you up to the starting line. Your "Yes!" will then propel you to work toward the future that God's hands have shaped for you.

Block writes: "If we took responsibility for our freedom, committed ourselves to service, and had faith that our security lay within ourselves, we could stop asking the question, 'How?' We would see that we have the answer. In every case the answer to the question 'How?' is 'Yes.' It places the location of the solution in the right place. With the questioner" (*Stewardship,* p. 235).

How thoughts spread

In chapters 1 and 2, I briefly referred to "thought contagion theory" and suggested that it connects to the general direction of this book. Let's examine those connections now, so that you can see how this biological explanation for change might be helpful in a change process.

This theoretical model of change suggests that ideas can propagate like epidemics. According to this way of thinking, your first approaches to "trying less hard" might be more successful if you relied on the idea of infectious plagues. Let's see how that might work.

The basic premises

You can understand the simple metaphor, "Ideas may spread in the same way epidemics spread." The metaphor advances several basic premises:

❑ Memes—rhymes with "teams"—are the basic unit of thought contagion, chunks of ideation that combine to form full-scale ideals.

❑ Like viruses or bacteria, memes proliferate by effectively programming for their own retransmission. Some memes carry the seeds of their own liveliness and thus are more likely to continue over time, generating other connected contagions. For example, think how the meme of paper-oriented communication methods led to file folders (places to store paper), Post-It Notes (sticky-backed paper that puts information close to your eyes), or desktop paper-shredders (sensitive-document eliminators). Or think how lively ideas or ideals in your congregation—such as fellowship groups for age cohorts—continue for generations. (Distilled from the book *Thought Contagion: How Belief Spreads Through Society*, by Aaron Lynch.)

How thoughts spread like diseases

You might approach the starting line—what you'll do after you close this book—with greater anticipation if you knew that the race was not going to be another Sisyphean task. "Thoughts that spread like disease" suggests that you can take advantage of natural biological processes to lessen your rate of exertion. Let's see how the process might work.

The methods by which memes (chunks of basic ideas) spread include the following, each of which requires a carrier and a host population. (I have included Lynch's terminology for your reference.)

❑ **Making more offspring (quantity parental).** The early growth and spread of immigrant-based Christian denominations in the United States was caused largely by the birthrate among those families.

❑ **Separating out offspring to propagate (efficiency parental).** Congregations begin other, like-minded congregations or send missionaries to other locations in the world.

❑ **Spreading the contagion beyond one's offspring (proselytic).** The fastest method of thought contagion, this mode depends on emotion and evangelistic fervor. The evangelism efforts of some congregations are an example of this method.

❑ **Convincing hosts to remain hosts over a long period (preservational).** A slow-growth proposition, this method relies on the host's long-lived nurture and protection. By avoiding conflict over their ideals, congregations can continue to be lively, or at least can avoid death for a longer period of time.

❑ **Sabotaging competitive contagion (adversative).** This method is best exemplified by the varieties of Christianity in which other viewpoints are considered de facto competition. Thought contagion occurs because the competition encourages fitness for survival.

❑ **Seeming to make sense to the host (cognitive).** An idea or ideal propagates itself because it fits into a system of other ideas, and thus is nurtured and sustained by the system. "Professionalized clergy" is an example.

❑ **Bringing advantage to the hosts (motivational).** The meme adds value to the hosts, and so is given strong support. A strong youth program—and its presumed benefits to parents of adolescents—might be a good example.

Like diseases, memes propagate better when several methods are linked. (Lynch suggests that the Reorganized Latter Day Saints have grown rapidly because they use multiple methods of thought contagion.)

New approaches and new cautions

As you approach the point where you will begin a new, less-taxing way of sustaining your congregation and its ideals, the theory of memes might suggest new approaches and new cautions such as the following:

❑ Because the proselytizing method yields the quickest growth, ideas with high emotional content (or context) will spread most quickly. (This may be why a "congregational dinner" method for collecting financial commitments could be a more easily transmissible idea than "every-member visits.")

❑ Memes that live longer help sustain long-lived hosts that, in turn, sustain the memes. (Congregations that provide more emotionally fulfilling cultures grow because they retain members for a longer period of time.) Here the contagion is slow and sure, and aimed at the long haul. If you choose this method, you might spend time on the meme of "incorporating new members," or work hard to sustain the emotional fulfillment of empty-nesters.

❑ Some memes are already self-propagating by their nature. (This may be why it is difficult to disregard "piety," a strongly active meme in your congregation. Acts of devotion to God engender strong emotions of satisfaction, unity with God, and transcendence. In turn, these emotions make pious attitudes and actions more attractive and possible. Among people of faith, ideas probably propagate more easily when their connections to deep piety are easily made.)

❑ Just as disease agents can defeat themselves—for example, a cancer that cuts off its own supply of blood—each of these methods of meme propagation can shorten its own life span or that of its host. This part of the theory suggests that you consider how an idea might defeat itself if carried to its logical extreme, or is applied too widely for too long. (For example, cognitive propagation may be too slow in a congregation dying rapidly; adversative propagation requires a ready supply of "enemies"; and motivational propagation can easily lapse into self-congratulatory rhetoric.)

Lynch spends considerable time on the application of thought-contagion theory to churches. (The chapter is curiously titled "Successful Cults: Western Religion by Natural Selection.") He credits contagious worth to soul-satisfying elements such as symbols (for example, religious art, music, fellowship) and small rites (prayer before meals, the wearing of crosses).

THEIR NEST NOW EMPTY, JOSÉ-MIGUEL AND SYLVIA QUIETLY DETACH FROM THE CONGREGATION.

❑ Some modes of thought contagion—preservational and adversative—also immunize against other memes. (In some communities of faith, exclusivity and intolerance become their own rewards. Faithful adherents are protected against presumably dangerous memes and remain "safe" inside their own beliefs.) This method might set people against each other, or otherwise separate them from each other's influence.

❑ Parental propagation is attractive but limited. (Starting a congregation on church-growth techniques is an attractive meme—for example, joy and pride in developing like-minded disciples—but it may be limiting if the primary parent is a cleric.) This helps explain why some new congregations last only one generation, the length of service of the congregation's organizing pastor. This may also suggest that it is wise to develop new leaders as "carriers" of each new idea.

❑ Thought contagion that relies on more than one method of propagation will be most effective over the long term. (As you consider the ideals that you hope will take root and spread in your congregation so that it is sustainable as a living organism, you might consider how those ideals can take advantage of several methods of propagation.)

❑ Thought-contagion theory requires you to examine the basic core—the meme—of each idea, program, or event. Asking "What's at the heart of this?" helps you understand the ideal you hope will grow and spread. You can be calmer about extraneous or superficial matters when you know what's really important.

❑ Thought contagion may likely occur without your initiation, planning, or effort. In the kind of congregation we've been imagining together in all these pages, "good ideas" can arise anywhere. Thus you need to be ready to recognize and deal with an "idea epidemic" when you see it happening.

❑ You're right to wonder whether some contagious thoughts can be toxic for the congregation. In those cases, the metaphor of "epidemic" matches reality very closely, and your quick reactions might include immunizing, inoculating, or quarantining to limit the spread of what may be harmful.

Lynch notes that "among the most attentive to church growth, at least in modern times, are the ministers and leaders of slow-growing and dwindling movements. With their jobs and careers at stake, they often go looking for a success formula in a thriving congregation and try to replicate it in their own flocks. This can further spread ideas of biblical literalism, easy salvation and so forth." He suggests that proselytizing methods of thought contagion eventually run their course because of the narrow cultural niche from which adherents can be drawn. He describes this as "running out of customers" and "proselytic saturation." (*Thought Contagion*, pp. 121-122)

THE MEMES OF EARLY CHRISTIANITY

One of the most fascinating books I've read in recent memory is Rodney Stark's *The Rise of Christianity: How the Obscure, Marginal Jesus Movement Became the Dominant Religious Force in the Western World in a Few Centuries.* Stark, a sociologist of religion, retrofits standard sociological analysis onto the behaviors of Christians in the early centuries of the faith, and draws conclusions that make sense in the light of thought contagion theory:

Lifestyle, then message. The faith spread first because of the lifestyle of the Christians, and later because of the message. For example, Roman officials, merchants, and members of the upper class were attracted to the fulfilling, moral lifestyles of Christian women. They married these women, and then converted to their beliefs and ways of living.

Higher status for women. The role of women was a critical factor in the growth of the church. In the early centuries of preinstitutionalized Christianity, women had higher status in Christian communities than they did in the general society. Christian women steadfastly decried the practice of infanticide, especially of female babies. Fertility rates among Christian families were higher, and infant mortality was lower. The status of Christian women attracted other women to the faith.

Influential believers. The early Christian communities of faith were more likely to draw the "movers and shakers" than the downtrodden. Much of the growth occurred in the major cities of the Roman Empire, where members of the upper class were more likely to live.

Simple ideas with profound results. The simplest acts of Christian living had profound effects. For example, the ritual cleanliness of Christians (many of them converted Jews) meant that fewer of them succumbed to the plagues of the years 165 and 251 A.D. Further, Christians cared for their sick and were thus more likely to survive both epidemics and ordinary infections.

Slow growth at first. The rates of growth began slowly and then became exponential. Stark provides credible proof that the post-Pentecost Church was actually quite limited in numbers across the entire Roman Empire. He also shows how the percentage of Christians in the realm was so great by the time of Constantine that his "conversion" may have been more political necessity than the beginning point for the institutional church.

Several times, Stark notes how the growth of Christianity in the first three centuries parallels the growth of Mormonism in our times. His conclusions about the early Christian church shed light not only on those early days of faith; they may also be instructive about our own approaches to "evangelism" or "discipleship."

How "tipping points" occur

The idea of "the tipping point" is another useful construct for understanding how you can approach next steps in your congregation. This delightful metaphor, drawn from both complexity theory and thought contagion theory, suggests that there are times in any organization (and in the general society) when conditions are nearly perfect for a large change to occur. With only a little effort—for example, the nudge of an elbow, a slight increase in the emotional temperature, or one more person working on the project—an entire way of thinking, system, or enterprise can switch directions, take on a new identity, or gain importance. Another way to characterize "tipping-point change" is the familiar phrase, "the straw that broke the camel's back." Tipping points can occur in almost any setting, because in almost any setting there is an ebb and flow of energy that fuels change.

In a book filled with fascinating anecdotes, science reporter and writer Malcolm Gladwell (*The Tipping Point: How Little Things Can Make a Big Difference*) provides plentiful examples of this phenomenon, including these:

❑ The much-maligned "Band-Aid solution" actually allows for the substantive healing abilities of the body to take place effectively. This simple protection tips a wound toward recovery.

❑ The "broken-window theory" of New York's mayor and police officials—fix every broken window, clean every graffiti-scarred wall, beautify every trash-strewn lot as soon as possible, arrest every subway fare-cheater—hastened the blossoming of a wider public determination to eliminate other forms of crime. Thus the overall crime rate was lowered.

❑ The re-emergence of Hush Puppies as fashionable footwear has been traced back to a few individuals in New York who retrieved and wore shoes from thrift shops.

You can probably think of examples in your own setting, times, and places in which a sudden change occurred. With some careful scrutiny you were able to determine the single moment or factor that "caused" the change.

THE TIPPING POINT IN A LARGE NUTSHELL

In *The Tipping Point,* Malcolm Gladwell characterizes the phenomenon of "tipping points" by describing its requisite conditions and agents. Social epidemics (his term for "thought contagion") start when these three elements are:

- *The law of the few.* The actions of a few individuals can effect a change.
- *"Stickiness."* An idea remains alive, and attaches itself to people, events, or other ideas, even in the face of obstacles. "Stickiness" is characterized by people's attention and understanding, and the quality and duration of their involvement with the idea.
- *The power of context.* When people are sensitive to small changes in the contexts surrounding them, change is more likely to occur.

In assembling his stories about tipping points in the general society, Gladwell found that for the small changes to turn into larger movements of change, three kinds of people needed to interact:

- *Connectors*—people well-situated to reach varieties of other people;
- *Mavens*—people who collect, organize, and store large quantities of useful knowledge: information brokers, teachers, or "human data banks"; and
- *Salespeople*—those people whose enthusiasm, charm, optimism, and relational skills enable them to be persuasive.

Gladwell's research also led him to the conclusion that conversation is the social context in which tipping-point persuasion takes place, and that real or momentary "peer groups" are the most powerful context for decisions about change.

What makes "tipping points" work

The basis for tipping-point change is emotional contagion. Connectors, mavens, and salespeople—the agents of social epidemics—are effective because their emotions are easily read and understood by others. Connectors genuinely value those whom they know intimately; mavens project an aura of authority and power; and salespeople communicate their appreciation and love for others as they persuade.

As you have seen in previous chapters, emotions predispose people to possible changes in attitude and action. The value of "emotional agents"—those who send and receive emotionally laden content—is therefore high. Those whose social intelligence, or "people skill," is high, have a correspondingly powerful influence in decision making.

The content of the message does not guarantee its "stickiness." If you want to ensure an idea's sustainability, pay attention to the subtle changes in audience behavior and adjust your method of presentation to fit the audience. Hence, the kind of music used in worship may be less important than the perceived excellence of its execution, which may be attributed to the emotional maturity of the musicians or their ability to synchronize their emotions with those of worshipers.

You can be more fully assured that tipping-point changes will take place if you understand how a peer group can influence decision making. Emotional contagion in groups has sometimes been described as "electricity"; its tangibility can be evident in the sudden willingness of a group to reach consensus.

Groups engage in change especially well when "transactional memory"—or group memory—is well formed and universally known. Group memory is composed not only of facts but also the individual transactions in which those facts are shared. Group memory is based on members' knowledge of each other, and their ability to communicate intuitively about each other. People know each other for their abilities, not just for their personalities. Group memory comes as a result of shared activities that foster trust and admiration over a period of time. (This may be why an asset-based planning approach works well; it maps and formalizes the positive aspects of group memory.)

Tipping points are volatile, unpredictable, and difficult to plan. They are composed of literally thousands of small, interconnected decisions—"small steps," whose importance we will explore later in this chapter—and are wonderfully complex in their structure. At the moment of "tipping," though, a quick glance backward in time can reveal the now-visible patterns of those decisions and their inexorable movement toward the change now occurring.

> Elaine Hatfield, John Capioppo, and Richard Rapson (*Emotional Contagion*) suggest that you are infected by others' emotions through mimicry: Because you are a social being, you mimic or repeat what you perceive to be acceptable; thus emotionally supported ideas spread.

"Tipping points" in your congregation

The concept of tipping points may have bearing on how you approach the next steps you take in your congregation. You probably have started to imagine possibilities such as those that follow.

Planning with tipping points. Because, like memes, tipping points are essentially not amenable to most planning processes, they can't be assembled into a formal way of "doing church." You can, however, create an environment for decision-making

> Methodism's founder, John Wesley—named by Gladwell as a primary example of a "connector"—may have instinctively understood the dynamics of tipping-point change. He traveled thousands of miles on horseback to help "religious societies" understand and adhere to the groups' beliefs and codes of behavior. By his work he connected groups of believers, not individuals, thus assuring the epidemic growth of Methodism.

that is likely to produce tipping-point changes. Trust, authenticity, collegiality, flexibility—these attributes might characterize a congregation (and its leaders) capable of taking advantage of tipping points.

Naming tipping-point elements. At the same time, this construct gives you another way of naming what occurs in your congregation as changes take place. For example, you probably already know the "connectors, mavens, and salespeople" in your congregation, and have some inkling of how their personal power affects decision making. Once you've named what's happening, you are less likely to overstress yourself about what you believe is not happening. For example, even if an important decision is being made slowly, you might notice that ideas are becoming "sticky"—more and more people are talking about the subject—and so you can be patient while connectivity builds between people and the ideas that underlie a coming decision.

◆

That's the way things come clear. All of a sudden. And then you realize how obvious they've been all along.

Madeleine L'Engle

Affirming visible and invisible leaders. The theory of tipping-point change allows you to affirm connectors, mavens, and salespeople—even those not formally responsible for leadership—for their powerful roles in change. They will be thrilled when you name and affirm their fairly well-developed picture of their relationships with others, including their personal power. The simple act of acknowledging emotional agents can increase the bonds between you and these sometimes quietly powerful leaders.

Waiting for teachable moments. Because you understand that tipping points will regularly occur in your congregation, you wait for "teachable moments" and are ready to seize opportunities as they occur. Clearsighted and flexible, you take advantage of near-tipping-point moments and emotions. You are poised and ready, not anxious about creating or controlling change.

Trying less hard. Understanding tipping points keeps you from trying too hard. Most of what this metaphor describes seems natural, easily recognized in any group, and easily harnessed for decision making. You don't make people into connectors, mavens, or salespeople. Instead, you identify them, and equip them to grow in those capacities. You take what exists and make good use of it for the congregation's benefit. For example, in your decision-making processes, you look for what's about to tip instead of trying of manufacture all the right conditions for the tipping-point change.

Seeking sufficiency. You are satisfied with what happens and excited about what might yet occur. Tipping-point theory also encourages you to hold a hopeful, positive view of every person and every moment you experience. Although you may be humbled by your inability to control or cause change, you can be deeply satisfied in knowing that because of your ministry a future tipping point is assured.

Practicing the small-steps approach

At several points in this book you've seen the obvious hints about an obvious truth that this book echoes: significant changes happen in small steps. In this section let's look together at how small steps can make your ways of work less difficult. We'll start with a quick review of the small-steps approach and then examine its application to sustainability and "trying too hard."

The "small steps" approach summarized

You can summarize this way of considering and affecting change in these few points:

❑ Small steps are, well, "small." Their size and shape and complexity are easily seen, described, or circumscribed by small numbers, small verbs, and small words.

❑ Small steps are easily taken.

❑ The footprint of a small step may be shallow or deep.

❑ There are few requirements or preconditions for taking small steps.

❑ Very little prohibits or inhibits small steps.

❑ Therefore, small steps can be taken by almost anyone, at any time, and under any conditions.

Dr. Poobah's
TEST FOR TIPPING-POINTERS

Directions: To measure your readiness for tipping-point leadership, check the box that most accurately describes your responses to the following questions.

YES　**NO**

❏　❏　1. I know the difference between "tipping points" and "tipping cows."

❏　❏　2. I am comfortable with not controlling who or what tips where or when.

❏　❏　3. I have experienced tipping points in groups of which I am a part.

❏　❏　4. I am a "connector," "maven," or "salesperson" or know someone who is.

❏　❏　5. I think I could spot a tipping point when it happened, or when it was about to happen.

❏　❏　6. I am generally aware of the emotions of other folk around me.

❏　❏　7. I believe that little changes can make a big difference.

❏　❏　8. When I was a little kid, I used to play on the teeter-totter, and we would pile kids on each side to see how the see-saw would tip, and that's when I first wondered whether this simple metaphor could be applied to social systems like congregations.

Scoring: If you answered yes to more than one item, you are ready to use "tipping-point" theory in your congregation. Congratulations!

❑ When combined, small steps become a journey or result in a thoroughly trampled space.

❑ When combined with the efforts of others, small steps can become a movement, a revolution, or some other kind of historical force.

❑ God's movement in history has included millions of small steps, as well as sudden, large-scale activity.

Putting small steps to work in your congregation

If you want to sustain your congregation into the next generation, you can trust and use a small-step approach in these ways:

Evaluation questions. Include in every evaluation process a question like "What small activity or condition did you notice, that everyone else may have missed?" Record the answers to that question as carefully as you track other evaluative items.

Devotional times. Use devotional times to highlight how God's large-scale activity is embedded in small things. This idea is standard fare in printed devotions, and can be strengthened by asking participants to name their thoughts as small-step change.

Sermons. Feature small-step stories in sermons, and include small-step stories from the Scriptures. For example, the boy with the loaves and fishes, Jesus' "small step" of forgiving the man with palsy, or multitudes of "small-step advice" in the Proverbs.

Small affirmations. In thank-you notes or conversations, always include affirmation for a significant action, gift, or attitude that may have seemed small at first.

First steps. As you engage in any planning, agree on a series of "small steps" as your first action, even before the plan is fully developed. For example, keep "the stewardship program for the fall" as a developing goal, and take as your first small step, "finding some fun people to work with."

◆

*A good beginning
makes a good end.*

English proverb

Historical recollection. If you are approaching a significant congregational anniversary or the preparation of a "congregational profile" (prior to calling a pastor or other staff member), collect stories of how large changes, programs, or events began with small steps.

Public acknowledgment. Periodically name—in small group times, in public forums, or in newsletters—all the people in the congregation who regularly engage in small tasks whose aggregate significance is overwhelming. For example, use prayer times in meetings to thank God for the "invisible" work of members whose lives inside and outside the church contribute to the fulfillment of God's will for the world. (Recall the emphases of chapter 5, "Finding What's Good.")

Reassuring maps. If you're having a leader's bad-hair day, quickly jot down all the small steps you've undertaken so far this day. Around each, write words and phrases that describe the possible significance of what seems "small," or the possible outcomes or next steps that will emerge from these tiny events. Look at the resulting information and see a "map" of what God might be doing during your day!

Prayers. In your daily prayers, include one or more individuals whose "small-step lives" you deeply admire. If possible, let them know that you pray for them by name.

Recording small changes. Start keeping a file, folder, or diary of "letters" to your successor. (Because you're working at sustaining this congregation, someone will undoubtedly follow you in this work!) Tell this future leader what you notice, what you appreciate, what you thank God for.

Sabbath rest. To sustain leaders in this congregation, build "sabbaticals" into every agreement for service. For example, after two years of service, give new leaders three months' time away from their tasks, and encourage them to engage in some interesting or enriching pursuit.

Meeting locations. Change the culture of meetings by conducting these gatherings in the homes of members. After six months compare the quality of decisions and interactions with the "always at church" meeting format.

Small steps toward less exertion

Because you trust the small-step approach—implicitly it requires a nonexertive approach to congregational life—you can use this way of thinking to begin lightening your load. Take some of these small steps to move in that direction:

Shadowed work. Ask another leader to "shadow" your work as a congregational leader. Ask that person to assess how and where you seem to be trying too hard.

Limited yeses. For three months, every time you say yes to some task or role, eliminate one current yes or role.

Expanded no's. What? Saying no is a big step for you? Then pare down that task into a first small step such as: Responsibly delay or postpone some task that can wait; practice a "no" conversation with a friend or spouse; or have coffee with a businessperson who's using an effective time-management system.

Relaxed example. Have a heart-to-heart talk with a congregation member whose attitude about life is serene, or whose schedule seems to be relaxed.

Created prayer. Make up your own short "serenity prayer." Carry a touchstone in your pocket or handbag to remind you to pray that prayer often. Or create a prayer you can use as the "Today" tab in your daily planner. Review the elements of the small-step approach, and you'll see that prayer is one of the most effective "small steps" you can take in any situation. If prayer is not a daily discipline you keep, consider adding this activity to quiet moments in your day, such as commuting time, the breakfast table, routine house tasks, time in the shower or bathtub, or exercise time.

Scheduled sabbaths. Schedule or surprise yourself with miniature sabbaticals during each day. For example, a brief time of simple exercise, a phone conversation with a friend, or a nap. Keep the surprises coming for a month.

Disregarded time. Try diminishing the number of time-reminders that surround you. Start with your wristwatch or the most visible wall or desk clock. Leave your digital time-toys in a drawer for a week.

◆

We can do no great things—only small things with great love.

Mother Teresa

Diminished hurry. Crowd out the busy feelings by singing, whistling, or smiling more often. No, you don't need a reason, but remember that "actions beget thoughts."

Admitted failures. Give away several of your present or ongoing "failures": Openly admit to another leader that you've not been "successful," ask for forgiveness, and give away the feelings of guilt and shame that accompany the misjudged hopes or less-effective work that haunts you. If possible, give away the tasks as well, or start on similar tasks that are more achievable. Trust the forgiveness you receive.

Cleaned workspace. Clean out your office or the work space you devote to congregational leadership. Throw away what you haven't used or referred to in a year, and file everything else. If you're worried about maintaining institutional memory or official record-keeping, move your files to the official church file system.

Mapped activities. Make a quick visual map of all the activities in which you're engaged, especially the places where you're pushing Sisyphean rocks up hills. Look at the map and pick one area where you will start diminishing overexertion.

Recalled ideas. Review and try out one of the simplifying suggestions in earlier chapters. (For example, see the suggestions on limiting information overload in chapter 4, "Knowing Too Much.")

In each of these cases remember that a single small step most likely engenders others, that you can expect success in taking these steps, and that they will require you to try less hard!

What's basic?

In this section I'll begin wrapping up what I most hope you will remember about the subjects we've considered. I'll state each "basic idea" as an action you can take, so that you'll come away with more than "good ideas" that add to your information overload. In keeping with the themes of complexity theory, I have included these items in no special order so that you can discover your own patterns.

Build up "social capital"

The bonds and bridges you forge among members—social capital—are a key ingredient of your congregation's health. When you strengthen or broaden the foundations of loving relationships—trust, hope, friendship, mutuality, collegiality, diversity, honesty, integrity, and civility—you are lessening the amount of work you would otherwise have to undertake were these elements weak or missing. By engaging people's souls—the spiritual core that best characterizes the meaning of their lives—you engage their skills and willingness to initiate action. Building up social capital is necessary and fruitful.

This may be a good place to scribble in the margins your reactions to these actions. These thoughts might serve as "idea-ore" that you can mine and refine into a de facto action plan.

Management consultants Roger Lewin and Birute Regine (*The Soul at Work*) reflect: "To engage the soul is to see people as people. . . . It is to assume an intention of goodwill on their part, and that it is better to err in trusting too much than not enough. It is recognizing a job well done . . . with genuine appreciation. It is to remember that people are inventive. It is to believe in them, not just the numbers" (p. 27).

Avoid situations where you feel helpless

When you operate from an asset-based approach, helplessness and vulnerability are not important. When you work at your strengths, you work less hard. When you lose the traces of neediness, you gain sinews of sustainability. When you recognize the power of forgiveness and the richness of the gifts God spreads throughout your life, your congregation moves past "Whoa!" and heads toward "Wow!"

Disperse your fears

Because fears help protect you from danger and death, you can never eliminate them completely. But when fears and anxieties characterize the deepest emotional state of your congregation, or when you make most decisions anticipating danger, you will most likely be damaging your congregation's potential. Since stupidity accompanies stress, and because stress is a natural outcome of fear, you must continue to displace fear, as well as continue to name and dismantle its effects in your life and that of your congregation. Fear and its family of ugly relatives can only make you try too hard, and thus severely limit the sustainability of your congregation or your leadership.

Stimulate other emotions

In the chapters on "legacy" and "asset-based planning," you learned how other emotions—for example, trust, excitement, creativity, gratitude, and love—might displace fear. You saw how they become powerful motivations for change. Because emotional contexts determine how change will take place, the least difficult road to travel is one on which these positive emotions are fellow-travelers.

Stop chasing "solutions"

"Solution-seeking" presumes that your leadership is focused on problem-solving. You will always be trying too hard when you ignore your own intuitive abilities and instead take on the ill-fitting quick-fixes of others. You will always be risking institutional death if you allow cowbirdlike "solutions" to crowd out the natural-born instincts and assets already present in your nest!

Cherish simplicity

◆

My only concern was to get home after a hard day's work.

Rosa Parks

Usually the simplest way is the less exertive way. As long as you keep cherishing simplicity as an ideal, as long as you require it of yourself, and as long as you hold accountable those who make complicated what could easily be simple, you will be able to avoid the overwork of trying to understand and analyze an overload of information and possibilities.

Straight-talking consultant Jack Trout (*The Power of Simplicity: A Management Guide to Cutting Through the Nonsense and Doing Things Right*) explains the problem that simplicity-seeking solves: "Our general education and most management training teach us to deal with every variable, seek out every option, and analyze every angle. This leads to maddening complexity. And the most clever among us produce the most complex proposals and recommendations."

Live with complexity

Complexity—in this book distinguished from "complication" or "confusion"—cannot be avoided in this technologically driven culture. In these chapters you have come to understand that complexity, or "chaos," is a temporary state in which endless variety emerges from simple truths, and simple truths emerge from endless variety. You have learned that by accepting the reality of complexity you free yourself from the false notion (and the resulting hard work) that "control" or "complete understanding" is possible. You have learned to trust the emergence of order amid chaos, and to be patient while it takes place. You have breathed easier, forgiven yourself and your congregation, and welcomed the beautiful liveliness of systems moving back and forth between complexity and simplicity.

Creatures in the natural world illustrate this valuable lesson. For example, all the complex interactions and social systems of ant colonies seem to be derived from these simple rules: "Danger, come quickly," "Food, follow me," and "I am a nest mate, not an alien" (*The Soul at Work*, p. 37).

Trust God's ambling revelation

A simple Latin epigram, *solvitur ambulando* ("the thing will resolve itself as it rolls along") was buried earlier in the book, so let me restate it here. The theology in that phrase invites you to trust in a God whose revelation gradually unfolds as you move. The proof of your trust and the key to God's capability: that you move along. Because you trust God's providence, you also trust that your actions will rearrange your own attitudes. Because you trust God's gradual revelation, you also trust God's forgiveness when you have trod too slowly or too quickly on wrong paths. You can trust God to lead you gently away from self-justifying overexertion. You can trust God to sustain you and your congregation over time.

Plan by improvising

Throughout the book you've seen how complexity and change make "planning" difficult, and "long-range planning" most likely a futile exercise in institutionalized overwork. The alternative, "asset-based planning," works well because you are willing to assemble tactics and strategies in an improvisational way. "We're making this up as we go along" is not necessarily an indictment of your work. By seeking an improvisational style, you avoid the hard work of shaming yourself and other leaders.

Move to the next level

It may be that you get caught in the traps of overexertion and nonsustainability because you have reached a plateau at one stage of your spiritual or emotional development. In this book you have seen several ways to reach for other, more satisfying visions of your role and personal power. Although it may be painful or initially difficult, you might consider this book's message as a call to ride the breath of God's Spirit to another, perhaps more mature stage of meaning and mission.

In *The Critical Journey: Stages in the Life of Faith*, spiritual director and consultant Janet O. Hagberg and seminary professor Robert A. Guelich provide a thorough description of stages in the maturation of Christians' faith lives. Corresponding to Hagberg's earlier description of a cycle of personal power (in *Real Power*), the book combines personal testimony, spiritual insight, and deep philosophical insight. Of special interest are the authors' careful suggestions about how to move past the barriers or cages of one stage to the next stage of faith. (See especially chapter 4, "Stage 2: The Life of Discipleship," for an insightful examination of the benefits and shortcomings of this stage of faith maturation.)

Balance stability and innovation

We have seen throughout this book that congregations are living systems. They do not obey the Second Law of Thermodynamics, and thus are not subject to entropy—the seeking of a state of equilibrium. Living things are "open systems," continually rewinding their clocks, continually recreating themselves, continually adapting to their surroundings.

You will always work too hard (to roll rocks up impossible hills) if you work against the liveliness of God's creation. Because living organizations want to sustain themselves, your efforts to ease their death may require more

◆

One never notices what has been done; one can only see what remains to be done.

Marie Curie

work than your efforts to develop their capacities for lively service to God. Legacy-building, asset development, truth-telling, and change-seeking are examples of the less exertive choice.

Author and business guru Margaret J. Wheatley sums up the matter neatly: "When we see decay as inevitable, or society as going to ruin, or time as the road to inexorable death, we are unintentional celebrants of the Second Law. If we believe that the universe is on a relentless road to death, we can't help but live in fear of change. In a down-hill world, any change exhausts our store of valuable energy and leaves us empty, one step closer to death" (from *Leadership and the New Science: Discovering Order in a Chaotic World*, p. 77).

Stability comes not from resignation to the inevitability of death, but from the sustaining power of innovation. The best innovation comes from the people themselves, derived from the lively Spirit of God's own self.

Use the power of conversation

Throughout the book you have learned about the power of "ordinary conversation" in affecting change, building capacity, bonding people in common purpose, and overcoming debilitating fear. This seemingly effortless activity is a cause, and also an effect, of leadership that understands and seeks sustainability. You have seen how conversation is a basic human ability and need.

Conversation, it turns out, is a "dance" of sorts, hence its delightful character. As you take part in conversation, you engage in "interactional synchrony," in which you and your partner intuitively harmonize and time your exchanges. The volume of speech, the rate of words per minute, and even the unintentional mimicry of the facial movements of others—these all illustrate how you are hardwired to engage pleasurably in the movements, emotions, and information-gathering of face-to-face conversation (from William Condon's "Cultural Microrhythms," in M. Davis, ed., *Interaction Rhythms: Periodicity in Communicative Behavior* [New York: Human Sciences Press, 1982], pp. 53-76, as cited in Malcolm Gladwell, *The Tipping Point*, pp. 80-84.)

As you take advantage of conversation, keep in mind that it is a cherished element of life, not to be

◆

What is a friend? A single soul dwelling in two bodies.

Aristotle

wasted or captured. Value your delightful conversations with other leaders and with congregation members, and remember the power of a God who became Word and lived among us!

Work first on what's manageable

Implicit in this book's many ideas is the axiom that you will work less hard and be reasonably assured of a sustainable congregation if you keep your work focused on what you can actually do. Your overreach may be motivated by good intentions, but you will always work too hard when you cannot accept the principles of "Enough!" and "Don't bite off more than you can chew." All the good ideas and invitations of denominations and members notwithstanding, you can order your daily schedule and name your work "well done" if you are capable of saying no to any request that extends you past reasonable capacities.

You have seen practical alternatives in delimiting suggestions (for example, don't try to know everything) and in capacity-building ideas such as to plan with assets in mind, not neediness.

Recognize and name inauthenticity

Only your real friends will tell you when your face is dirty.

Sicilian proverb

One of the threads I've observed running through almost every soul-revealing business-management book is the idea of authenticity. Many of these business prophets first help their readers name inauthenticity when they spot it. Why the negative approach? Inauthenticity is so easy to fall back into, so easily hidden that the first task in developing authenticity is to root out its opposite.

I encourage you to name your own inauthenticities: tendencies toward being "nice," subtle bendings of spirit or ethics, game-playing, manipulation, or ego-seeking. In the end, each of these activities results in organizational dysfunction or destruction, or in the diminution of your spirit. You end up working harder when inauthenticity characterizes your leadership.

Roger Lewin and Birute Regine (*The Soul at Work*) agree: "Being real rather than trying to look good is a lot simpler, makes life easier, and takes a lot less energy. When being authentic becomes a collective norm, there's a lot less destructive politicking going on and work relationships are a lot simpler and take a lot less energy" (p. 312).

Recall the places in this book where you understood implicitly how easily "trying too hard" can legitimate inauthenticity. As you insist on authenticity in your leadership style, you reverse what may have subtly sapped your energies and will.

Listen to language

This is not a plea for better listening skills. Instead, I'd like to call your attention to a primary element in change, the intricacies of language. As you move toward a less exertive leadership style or assist others in doing so, consider how the smallest memes of language might get in the way. For example, the pervasive presence of passive verbs might reveal someone easily prone to thinking as a victim. Or the frequent use of "just" and "only" might reveal someone painfully aware of shortcomings or inferiorities.

In these pages, you have been encouraged to use new language, especially metaphors, that can reshape attitudes and behaviors that counteract overexertion. You know how to find even better words.

Foster generosity

I've suggested that trying too hard robs your spirit of its capacities over time. Generosity may disappear most quickly. It's hard to be generous when that Sisyphean rock is weighing on your shoulders and you're worried about the imminent death of your congregation.

It may be strange to read about "generosity" in a book whose message seems more about conserving and protecting precious energy and time. But without generosity in your heart, conserving and protecting may become the center of your overexertion. Generosity builds rather than subtracts from capacity, and thus overwhelms the wasteful practices of nonsustainability or overexertion. The essence of generosity is an extravagant capability to give your life away for God's purposes, and so generosity is both cause and effect of the spirit of sustainability.

Lost in the well-organized sheaves of notes for this book is a reference that I dearly want to credit, because the idea is so important. With the true remorse of an author who values minds sharper than his own, I refer you to the language pattern dubbed "overload aphasia," in which hurried and harried individuals, especially of the boomer generation, are suffering from a lessening in their ability to retrieve words. Word-stumblers are not necessarily afflicted with the early onset of senile dementia, but instead are trying to live an overloaded and incessantly overexertive lifestyle. Now if I could only remember the name of that author . . . .

Take risks

Any of the premises and promises in this book may be counterintuitive, and thus may hold behind their back the danger of risk or failure. (You may try too hard *not* to "not try too hard," and thus be doubly cursed!) But taking risks is what you must do to translate the "interesting, important, and useful ideas" of this book into habitual behaviors.

◆

Living at risk is jumping off the cliff and building your wings on the way down.

Ray Bradbury

In the essay "Risk Is Where You Find It," from *Flawless Consulting Fieldbook & Companion: A Guide to Understanding Your Expertise*, philosopher and consultant Peter Block writes about risk: "We need a way to understand risk and people's wish for safety. Ultimately the value of our service will be defined by all of us having the courage to face now what we have so long postponed. There is no safe way to do this. If we try to manage the risk, postpone the risk, treat the risk as a problem in skills or structure or lack of clarity, we are engaging in a pretense about the nature of human existence and organizational life. All growth, change, and optimism come from acts of adventure and risk" (p. 15).

Ask good questions

This book is peppered with questions and question-provoking statements. Their presence has at times needled you, a sign that they're good questions. You can begin moving away from trying too hard by asking good questions. Peter Block (in the essay "Change Is in the Details," in his *Flawless Consulting Fieldbook & Companion*) characterizes "good questions" as having these properties:

❑ A good question is ambiguous, tantalizing respondents to seek clarity in the middle of complexity, and diagnoses instead of right answers.

❑ A good question is personal, inviting people to disclose themselves and integrate new ideas and ideals into their personas.

❑ A good question carries accountability, encouraging respondents to see their responsibilities and capacities for change.

Whether your own good questions meet these criteria, you must never be content with questions whose answers end a matter too quickly. Instead, ask questions whose delightful possibilities are a "small-step approach" by themselves, whose answers require whole-brain work by respondents.

Live thankfully

This is where we first met each other: you, thankful for this congregation you serve, and me, thankful for people like you leading congregations. We met in these pages to accomplish a difficult task together. Whether or not we've succeeded, we have still ended where we began: grateful to God for who we are, who God is for us, and what God calls us to do. There is no better way to live than in gratitude to God.

Thankfulness can also characterize your continuing search for a life of service that doesn't sap your energies or feel futile. Whether you roll rocks up hillsides for the rest of your ministry, collapse at the bottom of the hill with your burdens pinning you to ground, or find in these pages some hints for alternative forms of work, you can be thankful.

Last things

We've come to the end of this matter, at least the writing and reading part of it. But before we part company, I need to fulfill the promises I made at the end of the last chapter: to meet pigs named "Pneumos," to speak of world dominance, and to summarize this book.

Pigs named Pneumos

How fitting that pigs named Pneumos would take us out of these pages. Pigs can provide the best metaphors for who you are, what your life is like, and how you treat other people— metaphors that don't pretty you up, but still honor who you are; word pictures that both startle and delight you.

First let me provide a word of explanation for those of you who are unappreciative of pigs: Forget your negative stereotypes (perhaps born of "unclean cloven-hoofed animals" in the Bible) and consider the facts. This animal's intelligence,

◆

*Think with the wise,
but talk with the
vulgar.*

Greek proverb

cleanliness, and ubiquitous presence around the world might make it a metaphor-of-choice for good and proper activities of humankind. The pig's reputation notwithstanding—the smell, the grunting thing, that nose, the body shape, all the squealing—pigs could even be symbols for possible good in the church.

Still unconvinced that you should consider the worthy image of pigs? ("Honey, did you say that book you've been reading all these weeks is about pigs? Is it time for us to go visit Dr. von Schrinkwrapp again?") Let me try some ideas with you:

❑ In the minds of people outside the church, we Christians may seem like pigs. In their view, we spend a lot of time penned up (staying inside our safe churches), we make loud noises (criticizing everything we see), we have a penchant for garbage (valuing what most people dislike), we smell (giving off distinctive signs of our presence), and we make big messes (creating problems for government or the general culture).

❑ We are ordinary or worse. Some of us—perhaps secretly in our souls—harbor the suspicion that everything we consider important is really nothing more than piggish indifference to reality. We fear that people in the world beyond our grubby existence look at our steepled pens and consider us with pity or contempt.

❑ Still, there is more to us than meets the eye (or ear or nose). Our species has been around for a long time—40 million years by some estimates—and we know how to survive and prosper. Our appearance and surroundings belie our high intelligence and capabilities for cleanliness. By our omnivorous rooting, we redeem what would otherwise be discarded, decaying clutter.

❑ We are useful primarily because we give our lives away completely. In the greater scheme of things, we exist so that others may prosper on our account.

❑ Our generic name may be "pig," "hog," or "boar," but we know ourselves as *Pneumos*, "wind people." First given breath by God's own Spirit, we are carried along through our lives by that same Spirit. Whether despised or mocked, we do not lose the spirit of servanthood that characterizes our lives.

For example, some historic English churches feature carvings of sows suckling piglets. Because pigs represented worldly wealth, the carvings reminded parishioners about the exemplary biblical practice of tithing one's worldly wealth (represented by pigs). (From *The Complete Pig: An Entertaining History of Pigs*, by Sara Rath.)

The Mother Goose rhyme about pigs going to the market is one evidence of a lingering Medievalism in which pigs headline a bestiary of vices. For example, exegetes have dissected the "piggies going to market" rhyme to discover "The Seven Deadly Sins." Thus maligned by a rhyme-writing female goose in the Middle Ages, pigs have not been given a fighting chance to redeem their image (from *The Complete Pig: An Entertaining History of Pigs*).

However you play with this metaphor, you can accept its underlying proposition: You and your congregation are both ordinary and special. Because of this wonderful tension, you can expect to prosper in God's own time. You can expect to prevail as surely as pigs and God's windy Spirit.

Speaking of world dominance

Your life is not your own, nor is your congregation's life its own. Your collective vitality is not a small matter. In your life together, you and these people you serve extend God's creating, redeeming and sanctifying activities to the world. Your goals extend beyond yourselves.

The "differences you make" ripple into the worlds of commerce, industry, government, family, school, and friendship. God's dominion extends from your congregation into the tiniest crevices of God's creation. To use a metaphor from complexity science, you are the butterfly whose fluttering causes a typhoon in another part of the world. As you diminish your overexertive ministry styles, you both calm and energize what surrounds you. God's own calming/energizing presence spreads. God is glorified and the world is blessed.

"Stewardship" says it all

This book is really about stewardship, how you fulfill some part of God's will through your congregational leadership. Your challenge: To use carefully the assets with which God has graced you. Your life has purpose and meaning. Dodging the trap of "trying too hard," you approach the possibility of sustaining yourself and your congregation into coming generations of God's people. You are a steward, and God is pleased.

Parsing This Chapter

You can extend the usefulness of this chapter by bringing its ideas to groups of which you are a member. The questions and action items below might be helpful.

1. Talk about times in recent memory when an idea or ideal "spread like an epidemic." Retrace the spread of the idea to its start. Name its mavens, connectors, or salespeople.

2. If, in recent memory, no idea or ideal in your congregation has spread like a disease, ask yourselves what has prevented that kind of contagion.

3. Which of this chapter's metaphors most grabbed your curiosity or imagination: epidemics of thought, tipping points, pigs, or others? Explain the reasons for your answers.

4. If tipping points occur in organizations, they may also occur within individuals. What "tipping point" are you facing at the present moment? What could nudge you into the imminent change? How could the people in this group help?

5. Review the action items in the "basics" section. Pick the three that you believe your congregation is already doing well. Talk about the reasons for that excellence, and what you might do next together.

6. What have the ideas in this book done for your spirit as a leader?

7. The book summary asserts that the matters of trying too hard and sustainability are really all about stewardship. What else does the word "stewardship" summarize for you?

8. Ask each member of your group to pick one or more of the action items in the "basics" section of the chapter. Rewrite each one as a saying or aphorism that might encourage others. (For example, "Take risks" becomes "A leader who doesn't risk is like a plant that doesn't like thunderstorms.") Share what you have written, and decide what to do with your new wisdom.

WORKSHOP
(Not) Trying Too Hard

This section of the book contains a plan for a weekend retreat for congregational leaders. What you'll find here is a series of workshops that you can string together into a short-weekend retreat, or combine into other leader-training formats. To make the retreat a mountaintop experience, you'll need to add what you're good at doing, what you like to do, and what you know about successful retreats in your setting.

This retreat design comes in three parts:

❑ Outline of the weekend experience

❑ Individual workshop designs

❑ Other activities and notes

The retreat helps participants understand the contents of the book you have just read, *(Not) Trying Too Hard: New Basics for Sustainable Congregations.* The aim of the retreat, however, is not to learn everything about the book, but to strengthen your congregation's capabilities.

As soon as you decide to conduct this retreat, begin asking yourself the two asset-based planning questions: "What are you good at?" and "What do you like to do?" Apply your answers to the general goals you have set. Another question to start thinking about: With what emotions do you want participants to leave the retreat?

Outline of the weekend experience

The following pages outline the weekend experience so that you can see its broad dimensions and decide how you will adapt the workshops and activities here for your own use.

Audience

This retreat benefits leaders of congregations that are willing to examine themselves and the way they operate. I have written this design for a group of eight to 15 leaders to reinvigorate the congregation's shared leadership. The design provides time for honest, critical conversation as you seek God's will for your congregation.

Hoped-for outcomes

The retreat "(Not) Trying Too Hard" benefits you and other leaders because it:

❑ Acquaints you with new information from fields of inquiry outside the usual framework of "church."

❑ Displaces some overexertive ways of approaching leadership.

❑ Heartens participants with new hope and energy for your congregation's future.

❑ Gives you practice in new ways of behaving as leaders.

Brief description

This retreat takes place over one and a half days (with an optional extra half-day), from Friday supper through Saturday evening. Congregational leaders examine their personal struggles with leadership overexertion, and learn about new fields of inquiry that help them think and behave differently. Based on the book *(Not) Trying So Hard: New Basics for Sustainable Congregations,* the retreat provides hope for leaders who want to ensure their congregation's sustainability into the next generation.

Schedule

You can construct a short-weekend retreat—Friday evening through Saturday evening—according to this schedule:

FRIDAY

5:00 P.M.	Arrival
6:00 P.M.	Supper
7:00 P.M.	Session 1, "PUSHING ROCKS UP HILLS"
8:30 P.M.	Devotions
9:00 P.M.	Conversation

SATURDAY

8:00 A.M.	Breakfast
9:00 A.M.	Session 2, "WHAT MAKES SENSE"
10:30 A.M.	Break
11:00 A.M.	Personal Time
NOON	Lunch
1:00 P.M.	Session 3, "A GENEROUS GOD"
2:30 P.M.	Group Experience
4:30 P.M.	Personal Time
6:00 P.M.	Supper
7:00 P.M.	Session 4, "MOVING ON FROM HERE"
8:30 P.M.	Closing Devotions
9:00 P.M.	Departure

SUNDAY *(Optional)*

8:00 A.M.	Breakfast
9:00 A.M.	Session 5, "(NOT) PLANNING TOO HARD"
10:30 A.M.	Eucharist
NOON	Lunch
1:00 P.M.	Departure

"(Not) Planning Too Hard" is an optional series of activities you can use if you want to add some kind of "planning" to the retreat format. Some congregations find that, because it sounds more like "getting down to business," the "p" word can be a motivation for some leaders to attend. The planning suggestions in this design, however, will be consistent with what this book has advocated.

Workshop descriptions

The weekend retreat "(Not) Trying So Hard" consists of four 90-minute workshops, each of which is based on sections of this book. You can also use the workshops individually—in the same sequence as the retreat—over a longer period of time, such as four once-a-week "dinner conversations." The workshops are described in general terms here; longer and more detailed descriptions follow.

Pushing Rocks up Hills. In this workshop participants encounter the basic question, "What does it feel like to be working too hard in our leadership of this congregation?" (chapter 2).

What Makes Sense. Here participants learn some of the "worldly wisdom" that might counteract the overexertion that threatens the sustainability of their congregation (chapter 1, portions of chapters 8 and 9).

A Generous God. Participants in this workshop react to two theological underpinnings of the book, including God's way of work in the world and God's legacy in this congregation (chapters 5 and 7).

Moving On From Here. The final workshop provides participants with a shared experience in taking next steps together (chapters 6 and 8).

Each of the workshops is experiential; each requires participants' active engagement. Each workshop requires moderate group-leadership skills and methods, as well as preparation—for example, collecting materials, reviewing the contents of the book, choosing from among suggested activities.

Individual workshop designs

The following workshop designs are written in their simplest form, so that you can conduct the retreat with a minimum of reading. Use the margins to add your own side notes. This will help you make the workshops fit your leaders and your setting.

Pushing rocks up hills

This workshop is based on the following content from chapter 2:

❑ Elements of the "trying too hard" phenomenon

❑ Possible individual and collective overexertion in this congregation

❑ Possible solutions

To prepare for this workshop, read or review chapter 2 of *(Not) Trying Too Hard,* highlighting points you would like other leaders to consider. Provide a copy of the book for each participant in the workshop. Make copies, one per participant, of "Trying Too Hard: A Checklist for Leaders," p. 51 Gather standard workshop materials—newsprint and easel, felt-tip markers, writing materials for participants—and other materials as indicated in the activity descriptions below.

"Testing and Talking" *(25 minutes)*. Distribute copies of "Trying Too Hard: A Checklist for Leaders," and ask each participant to complete this simple survey. Tally the results by asking participants to indicate their response to each item (1-5) by standing at the corresponding numeral on a numbered line on the floor. Use newsprint to record the number of respondents at each numeral on the "Strongly agree—Strongly disagree" continuum. Use the second item on page 52 to categorize the patterns of participants' responses.

"Sisyphus Unmasked" *(25 minutes)*. Briefly characterize the story of Sisyphus (using materials on pp. 23-24). After brief comments or questions, direct participants to the labeled drawing of Sisyphus on page 24 ("The Sisyphean Church Leader: Sketching a Parable") and the accompanying descriptions of overexertive behavior, (pp. 25-28, ending before the section, "How you can know when it's happening to you"). Ask participants to read or skim those sections quickly. While they are reading, write any or all of the following questions on the newsprint:

To build a "tallying line," apply about 20 feet of masking tape to the floor in a straight line. At five equally spaced points, attach to the floor a piece of paper, each labeled with a number—1, 2, 3, 4, or 5. These pieces of paper will mark the spots where participants gather to indicate their responses to each item on the survey "Trying Too Hard." *Option*: Tape only the numerals to a wall, at equally spaced intervals.

❑ Which of the metaphors for "trying too hard" (pp. 25-26) is closest to your own experience in your daily life?

❑ What is your definition of "trying too hard"? Begin with the phrase "Trying too hard" happens when . . . ."

❑ Can you name an area in this congregation's life where you see people "trying too hard"?

The prompting phrase "'Trying too hard' happens when . . . ." is an example of an "operational definition." This kind of definition moves past difficult—and sometimes rigid—characterizations of ideas. Instead, ideas are described by the actions they generate. Operational definitions approximate metaphors, and they engage the part of your brain that springs into action when you imagine yourself moving.

After five minutes, assemble participants into groups of three or four, where they will discuss one or more of the questions you have written. Inform participants that later they will share with the entire group one insight from this discussion. Tell them about how much time they will have for their conversation.

Save about five minutes at the end of this activity for each group to report one insight that emerged from its discussion.

"Walking and Talking" *(40 minutes)*. Ask participants to form pairs, who will be taking a short "walking talk" with each other in just a few moments. Direct participants to the section, "How you can know when it's happening to you" (pp. 28-32), and give them these directions for their work in pairs:

❑ Read this entire section silently.

❑ Talk together about your own experience of "trying too hard" and its possible causes or motivations.

If conditions do not allow for the "walking" part of this exercise, direct participants to alternate places within the retreat site for their conversations.

Provide about 25 minutes for this activity, which will function as one-on-one confession or "reality-testing" time. Direct participants to possible walking paths or places away from the meeting place. Ask them to return promptly.

When participants have returned, use the remaining 10 minutes for a whole-group discussion based on this question: What causes any of us to "try too hard" in this congregation? Record participant responses on the newsprint.

End this workshop with a time of silent prayer, based on the "bidding prayer" model, in which you suggest prayer prompts—for example, "Let us pray for those whose lives are unnecessarily busy"—and participants construct their own silent prayers in response to your bidding.

What makes sense

This workshop pulls from chapter 1 some of the "worldly wisdom" that may help you understand unnecessary overexertion and how you can begin to diminish its effects in your congregation. The workshop includes discovery activities that help participants learn about several fields.

❑ brain theory/science

❑ organizational development

❑ chaos/complexity theory

❑ asset-based planning

❑ change theory

❑ information-overload science

❑ thought-contagion theory

To prepare for this workshop, read or review chapters 1, 8, and 9 of *(Not) Trying Too Hard*, highlighting sections you would like other leaders to consider. Provide a copy of the book for each participant. Gather standard workshop materials—newsprint and easel, felt-tip markers, writing materials for participants—and materials as indicated in activity descriptions below. Write on newsprint the seven category names listed above, plus the phrase, "Other ideas."

"Idea-Mining" *(40 minutes)*. In this activity, participants will peruse portions of chapter 1 (and others) to discover the places in the world where wisdom about the church might be available.

Divide participants into eight groups of two or three individuals. Assign each group to one category of "worldly wisdom." (If the number of participants is small, assign several categories to each group of two or three.) Characterize their task as follows:

1. Each group will search chapter 1 for explanations of or references to its assigned subject area.
2. The group's task: Write on newsprint a summary of characteristics of this field of human endeavor.

3. Should groups choose, they may examine other chapters for further explanations and examples.

4. One group, designated "the roamers," will have an interesting task: to search other chapters of the book—especially chapters 8 and 9—for other bits and pieces of "worldly wisdom" that lie beyond or are connected to the seven categories on the newsprint.

If you assign the roaming task to an especially sharp group, you might make groups members' tasks just a little more difficult: Challenge them to think of other areas of human endeavor not recounted in the book—perhaps those they encounter in their work or avocations where wisdom about "trying too hard" might be available.

Announce to participants that they have 20 minutes for their tasks. During the time they work together, circulate among the groups, answering questions and encouraging participants to search carefully. (*Hint*: The side notes and sidebar readings are also good sources.) Groups should avoid getting sidetracked, focusing instead on their responsibility to portray their fields of endeavor accurately and succinctly.

Inform groups when only five minutes remain of their allotted time. Then clear wall space to receive the newsprint sheets groups will bring back. Also prepare eight sheets of newsprint, each with the same title: SO WHAT? Save wall space for these sheets as well.

Spend the last 15 minutes of this time segment in small group reporting. After each group affixes its completed newsprint sheet to the wall and reports, post one of the SO WHAT? sheets next to it, without comment.

"Update and Improve" *(15 minutes).* In this activity, participants circulate among the sheets of newsprint, reading more carefully what has been written and adding comments that reflect "updated" information that they possess. (For example, a member of the group may teach high school physics and have a better way of expressing "complexity theory" than was found in the book.) The intent here is to make the information on the sheets as accurate as possible.

"So What?" *(35 minutes).* During the final activity of this workshop, participants work as a large group to answer this question: "So what might that field of human endeavor have to do with 'trying too hard' in our congregation?"

Use about 25 minutes of this segment for this activity, moving from sheet to sheet, asking the entire group to brainstorm possible connections of a particular part of "worldly wisdom" to the matter of congregational overexertion. Distribute your time equally among the eight areas of inquiry, deferring discussions and disagreements until later in the retreat.

End the workshop with a time of "mind-mapped prayer," as follows: Distribute single sheets of blank paper and a pen or pencil to each participant. Direct each participant to write the word "wisdom" in the middle of the page and surround it with a circle. During the next five minutes participants will "pray" by making a mind-map of thoughts that come to mind when they think of "wisdom." The exercise becomes a form of prayer as participants direct those thoughts to God in thanks, need, or acceptance of the gift of wisdom.

Complete the process by adding a closing prayer thought that brings participants' minds back to the whole group.

A Generous God

This workshop helps participants confront some of their fears about this congregation, as they encounter God's action in the world and in their own lives. It provides a devotional/spiritual experience in the middle of the retreat.

This workshop includes the following:

❑ Reflections on God's astounding actions in the world, actions in which participants are also engaged.

❑ The substance of participants' individual and collective legacies.

To prepare for this workshop, read or review chapters 5 and 7 of *(Not) Trying Too Hard*, highlighting points you would like other leaders to consider. Provide a copy of the book for each participant in the workshop. Gather standard workshop materials—newsprint and easel, felt-tip markers, writing materials for participants—and materials as indicated in activity descriptions below. The "legacy artifacts" activity requires some preparation, as listed below.

"Quality Qualia" (30 minutes). In this activity participants use the book to help spark their own faith-thoughts about "the Good News" and "fear."

Divide participants into two groups, one responsible for answers to the question "What is so good about 'The Good News'?" and the other group responsible for answers to the question "What's so fearful about fear?" Refer participants to the descriptions of "Good News" (p. 127) and fear (pp. 208-211). Give each group a large quantity of creative building toys, such as wooden blocks, Lego blocks, modeling clay, or

A "mind map" engages people to begin writing about a subject close to them. The finished product, a map or diagram of all their thoughts about a particular subject, sparks further creativity and also can serve as the beginning point for an outline of the subject. In this workshop, the mind map engenders prayers.

Three suggestions: Whatever comes to mind gets written. Each thought is surrounded by a frame of some kind. And each is connected—with arrows, dotted lines, "highways," or "rivers"— to other ideas.

Tinkertoy construction sets. Each group's task: In 15 minutes, to build a "model" of their answers to the question assigned to their group and present their model to the whole group.

A "model" might be a city, a many-faceted object, a three-dimensional story, a map, or a collection of smaller models. It can be literal or figurative. A model moves an idea off dead center but doesn't explain the whole idea. Simple models work best, but more complex models can be fun to play with. If participants are a little hesitant about building conceptual models from toys, remind them that their work will be symbolic, metaphoric, or even allegorical. The toys might show what some quality "is like"; what animal or plant might symbolize an element of fear, or how a toy might be used to start or end a meaningful story. Another way to start the creative juices flowing: While the group talks about its answers, one participant starts doodling on paper about what he or she "sees" in the conversation.

Remind participants that the main worth of the activity is in its doing, not necessarily in the artistic merit of its product.

At the 10-minute mark, ask each group to complete its model and to take the next five minutes to ready itself for a presentation. When the groups are ready, give the "fear model" group about five minutes to present its model, explaining the model's features or elements. The "Good News" group goes next, using its five minutes for the same task. If time allows, the presenting groups can ask questions of each other.

Use the final five minutes in this activity to talk together about matters such as these:

❑ What connections or disconnections did you notice between the models, of fear and the Good News?

❑ Which answers seemed easier to model?

❑ What parts of each model most clearly match our congregation?

❑ What are the motivations behind fear and "Good News"? Explain how the "Good News" model could overwhelm the "fear" model, and how that might be portrayed. (If time allows and participants are willing, try the "overwhelming" suggestions by doing them!)

❑ When it comes to fear and Good News, what astounds you about God?

"Putting Wisdom to Work" (20 minutes). Refer participants to the book section, "Where is the 'good' in God's 'good world?'" (pp. 131-151). Their individual task in the next 10 minutes will be to find how "God's good wisdom" in one or more places in the world—for example, business, government—could be put to work in some specific area of this congregation's life. (*Hint:* The book provides some starter ideas, "Putting the Wisdom of _____ to Work," for each worldly place.)

After 10 minutes, call the group back together and begin writing participants' findings on newsprint. If possible, list the ideas by categories of congregational life, such as stewardship, youth ministry, or evangelism, for later use by leaders.

"Legacy Artifacts" *(30 minutes).* This workshop requires some preparation: Bring copies of congregational artifacts from the recent and distant past.

❑ Copies of annual reports

❑ Newsletters

❑ Newsletter clippings

❑ Congregational history or profile

❑ Pictorial membership directories

❑ Minutes of specific work groups, teams, or committees

❑ Financial records (budgets, special funding events)

❑ Banners, paraments, or Christmas decorations

❑ Curricula from Sunday school, youth, or adult Bible classes

It is important that you bring a variety of artifacts, that they cover a significant portion of the congregation's history, and that there are enough items to give workshop participants some choices.

The activity begins with your 10-minute summary presentation about the value and place of "legacy" in the matters of "trying too hard" and "sustainability." (Use as starting material the sections from chapter 7, "What is a legacy?," "What's really important?," "How legacy-building satisfies," and "How you might think and act to ensure a legacy." Consider using newsprint to write key concepts (or symbols for those concepts), as a way of keeping participants' attention. (*Hint:* If participants are comfortable writing in their books, they can follow your presentation as you refer to sections of the book, taking notes on the pages you reference.)

When the presentation is completed, give participants this challenge: "Using any of the artifacts, think of words and phrases that characterize the "legacy" that has come to you personally because of this congregation's history." They will have only 10 minutes for this task, and will be asked to share what they have discovered. Direct participants to the tables or wall space where you have displayed the artifacts you have assembled.

At the end of 10 minutes, bring participants together and ask for some words and phrases that describe the legacy that this group of leaders has inherited. List these on a newsprint sheet with the title "What We Have Inherited from Our God."

"Generous God" *(10 minutes)*. Save the last 10 minutes for a devotional experience loosely framed by the idea that your bountiful legacy comes from an equally generous God.

Gather participants in a tight prayer circle, shoulder to shoulder, facing outward. Begin with a prayer about fears, and invite any in the group who wish to add their own spoken prayers on that subject. After about four minutes, ask participants to turn around and face the inside of the circle, still shoulder to shoulder. Now they bind the circle together by joining hands around each other's waists or shoulders, in a kind of "group hug." You begin the second prayer focus, about the legacies that this group has inherited. Again invite participants to add their own spoken petitions on the theme. After another four minutes, end the devotional time with thoughts about God's astounding gifts. After a moment of silence, dismiss the group for the next activity.

Moving on from Here

This workshop helps participants imagine what they might do next, individually and collectively. They learn about these ideas:

You can sharpen participants' discovery skills by reminding them:

◆ That "artifacts" include big things (buildings), news about big events (addition of new staff), and announcements about big ideas (to sponsor a missionary).

◆ That sometimes the smallest artifact might also reveal something important.

◆ That each artifact reflects the actions and attitudes of people like them.

◆ To look "under the obvious" to see what basic traits—e.g., love, compassion, pride, determination—compelled an action or created an artifact.

◆ To look for patterns.

❑ Change and change agency (leadership)

❑ Asset-based planning

❑ Tipping points

To prepare for this workshop, read or review chapters 8 and 9 of *(Not) Trying Too Hard,* highlighting passages you would like other leaders to consider. Provide a copy of the book for each participant in the workshop. Gather standard workshop materials—newsprint and easel, markers, writing materials for participants—and materials as indicated in activity descriptions below.

"Trying too hard to change" *(35 minutes).* In this activity participants examine "older" and "newer" concepts of change, and see how the view of change presented in this book might offer them and their congregations some new hope.

Begin the activity by asking participants to take an oral "test" about change, using the following true/false items. The test should take no more than five minutes.

TRUE OR FALSE

1. Change is predictable, or at least can be understood.
2. Change can be "managed" or directed.
3. Change obeys the laws of cause and effect.
4. Changes are more likely to succeed if they are based on facts, not emotions.
5. The nature of change remains constant.
6. Changes in behavior are usually preceded by changes in ideas or ideals.
7. The better or more persuasive the techniques by which change is engineered, the more lasting the change.
8. Resistance to change comes from people who are unwilling or unable to change.
9. The purpose of change it to bring order, solve problems, or reach some kind of equilibrium.
10. The larger the need for change, the more comprehensive the plan for change needs to be.

Participants can score their own responses, turning to pages 224-225 in the book to review the sources for these items. (The "correct" answer to each item is *false*, because each statement identifies an element of an older view of change.)

The group will undoubtedly have questions, which you should invite but not yet answer. Write each question on newsprint, and when about five minutes has elapsed, move to the next step in this process.

If participants are particularly upset with the "completely false" nature of the "test" statements, you might want to follow that experience with this alternate activity: Ask participants to read most of the chapter. Together answer item 1 or 2 in the end-of-chapter section, "Parsing This Chapter." The question here is about how an older view of change might make leaders try too hard. For example, one of the older views, that "change is always good," can compel a leader to the overexertion of mindless or constant change.

Refer participants to the sections, "Why that view doesn't work any more," "How change has changed," "How change occurs," and "'Leading change'" (pp. 225-235 in chapter 8). Divide into groups of two or four individuals. Members of the groups read one (or two) of the sections, and report to each other what they have read. This method will ensure that each member of the group has some knowledge of the content in these four parts of the chapter. Take about 10 minutes for this activity, which will answer some of the questions that emerged from the true/false test, and prepare participants for the activity that follows. The final 15 minutes of the workshop will be spent in dissecting "case studies" of situations in which change is not understood well.

Describe each of the following situations to the entire group of participants, challenging them to answer the following questions for each case study:

❑ How do the people in this situation view the matter of change?

❑ How might they be trying too hard?

❑ How might a newer view of change help in this situation?

Case Study 1: The Contrarians

Pastor Roberto Ruiz and the other leaders knew that Karla, Elian, and Sofie would be automatically critical of their new idea about teaching children. That's why they kept the three former leaders out of the communications loop. "They're threatened by change," The pastor and the other leaders agreed, "So why bother them—and us—by thinking they'd be willing to change?"

Case Study 2: The Planning Group

Jim Steffens and the long-range planning team presented an exquisite five-year plan for Faith Church. It included demographic projections from the county planners, estimates of future economic growth from the chamber of commerce, trends in home ownership from the board of Realtors, and a statistically valid sampling of congregation members' opinions about the "preferred future" of Faith Church. With proposed mission and vision statements, the five-year plan would be a valuable tool for Faith's leaders as they made decisions in the next five years.

Case Study 3: The "Skunk Works"

The Rev. Wendy Bamesberger knew how to effect change in the congregation: Find two or three really persuasive people who would be "change champions" for her vision of the changes this congregation needed to make. To her pleasant surprise, Pastor Bamesberger found five people willing to spearhead the change process. In their first meeting this new group—a "skunk works," or "idea hatchery"—came up with new ideas and set about selling the ideas to the congregation.

Ask participants to offer comments on the three questions listed previously and to reference sections of chapter 8 in defense of comments about each scenario.

"Being who you want to be" *(20 minutes)*. In this next activity, participants imagine how they would behave as new kinds of "change agents." Ask participants to skim the reading, "Change Agency, Not Change Agent" (p. 234 in chapter 8).

While they are reading, list on newsprint these titles: coach, instrument, lawyer, advocate, transformer, substitute, mediator, provocateur, truth-teller, consultant, evoker, and change insurgent.

When all participants have completed their reading, or after five minutes, divide the group into twos or threes, asking each group to undertake the following task: "Choose one of the replacement metaphors for "change agent" listed on newsprint. If you were (*new metaphor*), how would you help people in this congregation work on their own changes?" Each team member should talk about his or her thoughts. No large group reporting will take place.

Small Steps Diagramming (35 minutes). In this exercise participants see how the small-steps approach works, by applying its techniques to make meetings more enjoyable.

Give participants about five minutes to read the section "Practicing the 'small steps' approach," (pp. 263-268 in chapter 9). Using materials from the section "How 'tipping points' occur" (pp. 259-261, especially the reading "The Tipping Point in a Large Nutshell"), explain the basic concept of "tipping points." Take about five minutes for this task.

> You might illustrate the concept with a simple balance scale, adding slight weights until it tips, or use the clever descriptions of Malcolm Gladwell—for example, connectors, stickiness, etc.—to present a "chalk talk" on the subject.

Now participants apply the small-step approach to one omnipresent feature of most congregations: the meeting. Distribute writing paper and markers to each participant. Here are the tasks, which should take about 10 minutes:

1. Read the two selections, "Your Brain Goes to a Meeting" (pp. 33-34) and "What We Never Talk About at Meetings" (p. 246).
2. From what you have read, identify one small step that could be taken right now, by this group of people, to improve its own meetings.
3. Imagine what might happen (or not happen) if that first step were taken. What other tipping points might occur because of the first step? Using a flowchart or other mapping technique, diagram the spread of this one small step into other small steps.

At the end of 10 minutes, bring the group together, asking willing individuals to share their ideas about improving meetings. Take about 10 minutes for the reporting.

During the final five minutes, wrap up the retreat with a group benediction. Explain that "benediction" literally means "good words," and that all blessings and benedictions start with God. To end the retreat, form a close circle, and ask each participant to say a "good word from God" to the rest of the assembled leaders, a short and meaningful God-wish for these beloved people. End with your own blessing and a short prayer for safe travel.

Other activities and notes

You can use the following suggestions to help make this retreat an enjoyable experience for the leaders with whom you serve.

Preparation for leaders and participants

You can help leaders get ready for the retreat with any of the following "assignments":

❑ Skim the heads and subheads of the book, highlighting those that you want leaders to consider during the retreat.

❑ Read the quotations or cartoons included in the book. Come ready to talk about your favorites during conversation times.

❑ Complete all the "tests" (e.g., checklists, surveys) included in the book. Come to the retreat ready to reflect on what you have discovered about yourself.

❑ During the week before the retreat, pray about the following matters: honesty in revealing yourself, a hopeful spirit about this congregation, clarity in discernment about your leadership.

❑ During preretreat devotional times, read the "letters to the seven churches," as found in Revelation 1:9–3:22. See what patterns emerge, which warning and praise might apply to your congregation, and what comfort you derive from the reading.

❑ Set up an e-mail group of prospective participants in the retreat, asking a few key questions to start a warm-up conversation. For example, "Which tasks do you feel compelled to do as a leader, and which do you feel privileged to do?"

Extra activities

The retreat schedule includes some spaces into which you might insert other activities. In addition, you might want to replace some workshop activities with those described here:

❑ Each "Parsing This Chapter" section includes at least one action-oriented item that includes more than "present-and-discuss" possibilities. Pick content areas important to your congregation.

❑ "Map" some ideas that emerge during the retreat. For example, make a diagram of recent "failures" in the congregation's life, and what good has come from them.

❑ Bring one or two laptop computers, and connect them to the Web. Play with some of the Web-based activities suggested in the book. For example, find search words for Web browsing in the section "Where is the 'good' in God's 'good world'?" in chapter 5 (pp. 131-151).

❑ Turn some of the quotations into discussion starters. Consider using the quotes as starters for an activity, "Make your own epigrams," which can serve as a good review or concluding activity.

❑ Use any of the ideas suggested in the section, "Putting small steps to work in your congregation" (pp. 265-266), as a series of final activities.

❑ Convert chapter content to retreat-based activities. Check a favorite chapter for places in which a possible activity is implied, using those ideas as introduction, discussion-starters, or sharing items for activities you might invent. For example, see the section "Reducing the glut of information" (pp. 107-112), which suggests activities readers might take to diminish information overload.

❑ Assign groups of participants the task of writing articles for the congregational newsletter that will enlighten the congregation about the most important discoveries from the retreat.

❑ If it might help clear the air or otherwise embolden leaders, begin the retreat with one or two additional activities that help participants talk about their fatigue or disillusionment from "trying too hard." (See chapter 2, "Trying Too Hard," for possible topics or activities.)

(Not) planning too hard

In case you want to engage in some activities that approach planning, you might choose some of the following actions:

❑ Try some asset-based planning together, focusing on a fairly significant task, event, or program in which most participants have some interest.

❑ Look at possible "entrepreneurial tests" (pp. 247-248 in chapter 8, the section "The entrepreneurial spirit"). Plan how you can increase that spirit among congregational members.

❑ Talk about the possibility of using more "whole-group planning" methods in your congregation.

❑ Institute a process by which congregational leaders take "sabbaticals" from their leadership duties.

❑ Spend some time together with your pastor. Listen to her or his feelings about Sisyphean ministries becoming nearly unbearable. Plan now what you'll do together to relieve your pastor of overexertive role expectations.

❑ Plan a large social event for the congregation, whose purpose it will be to thank each other for all the work that gets done in this congregation.

❑ Complete the "meeting revision" work you did during the retreat, taking it to the point of agreements and assignments for change.

Recreation and other renewing activities

Sometimes the most enjoyable features of a retreat are the off-task activities in which participants share. Consider some of the following examples for the "group experience" segment of the retreat:

❑ Construct together some lasting artifact of the retreat—for example, a small mural, a piece of a stained-glass window, painted touchstones, clay communion ware for shut-in visits—that might symbolize the spark of hope that was lit during this retreat.

❑ Work together on a small "service project" that could be completed in one or two hours. For example, assemble activity or health kits for use by overseas relief and development organizations, disaster-relief agencies, or groups that provide assistance to homeless people.

❑ Invite a Tai Chi instructor to take participants through some beginning low-aerobic exercises.

❑ Provide a time for cooperative writing in journals. Participants can begin or continue personal journals and invite a retreat-partner's reflections on what they have written.

❑ For an evening activity, view a video of a recent film that depicts some deeply moving spiritual theme, such as forgiveness, simple living, generosity, or life-redeeming love.

❑ Take participants on an "adventure walk" at the retreat facility. There might be surprising or inspiring vistas—for example, sunrise or sunset in a spectacular location—or small delights, such as a little waterfall or shady spot. Participants might be challenged to find and photograph some evidence of "change" or "trying too hard" in nature. The walk might be conducted in total silence, or take place after dark. The value of the activity: participants are joined in a memorable physical activity whose special character they experience together as "fresh" or "new."

Devotions and other spiritual matters

You might increase the spiritual depth of the retreat with activities such as the following:

❑ Imagine and write your own epitaph, a short phrase that characterizes the legacy of your life. Pray together about the gift of your life thus far, and your hopes about what you will leave for following generations.

❑ As a continuing thematic emphasis during the retreat, read together and talk about portions of Ecclesiastes. Contrast the seeming cynicism and the hopeful tone of "the Preacher," and how they compare with your own feelings about being a Christian in today's world.

❑ Take as a basis for devotions the spiritual plea and prayer, "Take away our fears, dear Lord." Prepare times of confession, forgiveness, and reflection about God's power to displace brain-numbing fear with love, hope, and willingness to minister.

❑ Ask individual participants to serve as "life storytellers" during the retreat. Give each storyteller a general focus for reflection or storytelling that is derived from themes in this book. For example, they could talk about their experiences with God-blessed and surprising changes, diminished fear, the sudden lifting of leadership burdens, moments of delightful insight, or joys that come from small steps well taken.

❑ Sing together familiar hymns or songs, after you have carefully examined together the words and phrases that worshipers might have previously overlooked.

❑ Conduct devotions outdoors, setting up "stations" along a path, or finding a special place whose character inspires quiet, joy, or peace.

❑ Use a single Bible story throughout the devotional time, explaining its meaning or connection to the themes of the book. Some possibilities: the dishonest manager (Luke 16); the life of Joseph (Gen. 37; 39–50); or parables about "the kingdom of heaven" (see Matt. 13; 20; 22; and 25).

Ideas " so crazy they might work"

This design wouldn't be complete without a few ideas whose capacity to bounce off walls might match your own wildly creative spirit. Think how some of these ideas might work with the participants you invite:

❑ During the retreat, do something together that is just a bit "childish," like riding bumper cars together, going miniature golfing, skipping rope, or playing hide-and-seek. (What might "childish play" release inside your brains?)

❑ Start and end each workshop with "holy hilarity" and devotions together. See how laughter and prayer work together.

❑ Together write a letter to a former pastor, church official, or former leaders who have moved away, characterizing what you've been doing at this retreat.

❑ Have an "awards ceremony," in which leaders are given strange-but-true "prizes" for exemplary effort in hitherto-unknown categories.

❑ Before the retreat, ask one or two individuals to assist you in furtive practical jokes that will be played on the group during the entire retreat. Rehearse all the possible effects of these pranks, so that no one is harmed or safety otherwise compromised.

❑ If you stay overnight at a retreat facility, schedule an optional experience for those who want to greet the dawn. Include quiet prayer as a primary ingredient, as well as quiet blessings for the coming day.

❑ During the retreat, insist that no one sit next to or participate in a small group with the same person more than once. This will help ensure diversity of opinions, and keep group dynamics from lapsing into their usual patterns.

❑ Invite to the retreat an individual whose sole responsibility will be to record the event on film, on tape, or in writing. This person can "interview" participants during quiet times and meals, invisibly circulate among work groups, or take notes that later get translated into a permanent record of this event.

❑ Invite as full participants especially wise youth, and prospective leaders.

❑ Conduct the retreat at an unusual place—a beach house, outdoors, a stable or barn, a schoolroom, or a bus that stops at various leaders' homes during the two days.

Next steps

You might want to keep the insights and energy of the retreat growing and moving into other areas of your life together. Try some of these follow-up steps to make that happen:

❑ Over the next six months, try any of the activities or questions at the end of each chapter as beginning-of-meeting activities.

❑ Stay in touch with the pre-event e-mail group.

❑ Schedule a "dinner conversation event" about six months after the retreat.

❑ Two weeks after the retreat, check personally with each participant to see what's still lingering from the retreat, what's still unanswered, what's still joyful.

**Dr. Billy Poobah thanks you for your patience
with his make-believedness during the book.
He encourages you to remember
Christ's believable presence among you,
and the power of the Holy Spirit
to bless all your work.**

BIBLIOGRAPHY

Congratulations on being one of the few people who read books from their hesitant starting words to their confident-but-weary last words. Since you probably read the side notes, too, I'm assuming you want a "bibliography" that does a little more than list books. Let's see if I can honor the special curiosity that sends you into the dark corners of everything you encounter.

In the following pages I've listed the books I read in preparation for the writing of this work, but in a way slightly different from what you might expect:

❑ I've added notes about the books, to tempt you to find and read these works for yourself.

❑ I've categorized the books several ways, so that you can decide more easily which of these references you might work through on your own.

Let me guess: You don't stop watching a film until all the credits have scrolled past your eyes You read the preface and acknowledgments in this book. And you have this strange curiosity about labels on most products you use. How did I know? I do the same, just in case there's a surprise waiting.

Books I would read again

Some of these books took me a long time to read; others I had to rush through to capture their insights quickly—we writers work on deadlines! Still others I am not sure I completely understood, especially in their implications for congregational dynamics.

Dozier, Rush W., Jr. *Fear Itself: The Origin and Nature of the Powerful Emotion That Shapes Our Lives and Our World.* New York: St. Martin's Press, 1998. I'd read this book more slowly the second time, and take notes about the people, institutions, and situations I've encountered in the church that match his descriptions of fearful living.

Gladwell, Malcolm. *The Tipping Point: How Little Things Can Make a Big Difference.* Boston: Little, Brown, 2000. An easily read volume, but filled with practical insight that zings with hope. The book comforted and inspired me about complex or chaotic change.

Gleick, James. *Faster: The Acceleration of Just About Everything.* New York: Pantheon, 2000. Gleick calls them as he sees them, and what he sees is a world moving too fast for its own good. I'd love to take his examples and find their analogues in congregational life!

Hagberg, Janet O. *Real Power: Stages of Personal Power in Organizations*, rev. ed. Salem, Wis.: Sheffield Publishing, 1994. This book changed my life, and I still rely on Hagberg's insights in my conversations with faithful leaders who don't see their own power.

Newberg, Andrew, Eugene d'Aquili, and Vince Rause. *Why God Won't Go Away.* New York: Ballantine Books, 2001. If "neurotheology" is going to take off as a field of human inquiry, this volume will be a foundational must-read. During my second look I'd write questions and comments in the margins, then talk about the book with another person who saw the significance of brain science to theology.

Ratey, John J., M.D. *A User's Guide to the Brain: Perception, Attention, and the Four Theaters of the Brain.* New York: Pantheon, 2001. At the time of this book's publication, Ratey's guide is the best compendium of up-to-date brain science. He uses clear language to astound readers gently about the applications of brain science to life's workings.

Whitehead, James D., and Evelyn Eaton Whitehead. *Seasons of Strength: New Visions of Adult Christian Maturing.* Garden City, N.Y.: Doubleday, 1984. Twenty years ago, the Whiteheads saw and named what many of us had wondered about—whether "faith maturity" could be described in a new way. Their descriptions still ring true for me today.

Books written by "prophets"

Granted, I chose as the basis for this book a variety of authors who were playing at society's sharp edges. Some surf the front of the waves of change, others reinterpret what we thought we already knew, and still others look back at history and see what we might have missed.

Block, Peter. *Flawless Consulting: A Guide to Getting Your Expertise Used*, 2nd ed. San Francisco: Jossey-Bass Pfeiffer, 2000. In my mind, Block's "consultant" could easily become the metaphor for "pastor" or "congregational leader."

Davenport, Thomas H., and John C. Beck. *The Attention Economy: Understanding the New Currency of Business.* Boston: Harvard Business School Press, 2001.

The authors look squarely at contemporary society and conclude that "attention" can no longer be taken for granted. On that basic premise, these two scholars and consultants build a case for leaders to take seriously the importance of this new commodity in the business world. Connections to the church milieu would prompt compelling explorations.

O'Hear, Anthony. *After Progress: Finding the Old Way Forward.* New York: Bloomsbury Publishing, 1999. O'Hear's philosophical position of inspired me: "Hold it just one darned minute!" And with that he brings to a screeching halt notions of "progress" and even the notions of "postmodern thought."

Pascale, Richard T., Mark Millemann, and Linda Gioja. *Surfing the Edge of Chaos: The Laws of Nature and the New Laws of Business.* New York: Crown Business, 2000. Good case studies and good writing explain how chaos/complexity science affects businesses.

Putnam, Robert. *Bowling Alone: The Collapse and Revival of American Community.* New York: Simon & Schuster, 2000. Strangely, Putnam's "prophetic voice" gives comfort, because he names a pervasive cultural phenomenon that we church leaders had previously thought applied only to us.

Schwarz, Christian A. *Natural Church Development: A Guide to Eight Essential Qualities of Healthy Churches.* St. Charles, Ill.: ChurchSmart Resources, 2000. Schwarz is out ahead of most folk in applying biological principles to human enterprise.

Shenk, David. *Data Smog: Surviving the Information Glut.* San Francisco: HarperEdge, 1997. Shenk counterbalances the influences of contemporary hype about the "information age" with sensible arguments about information overload.

———. *The End of Patience: Cautionary Notes on the Information Revolution.* Bloomington: Indiana University Press, 1999. Shenk collects the best of his musings on National Public Radio and other venues of careful discourse about the "information revolution."

Strauss, William, and Neil Howe. *The Fourth Turning: An American Prophecy.* New York: Broadway Books, 1998. Because they've distilled American history in a unique way, Strauss and Howe get my vote for creating a "prophetic work." I'm a little frightened that the deeply chaotic time they name as "fourth turning" is only a few years away.

Sylwester, Robert. *A Biological Brain in a Cultural Classroom: Applying Biological Research to Classroom Management.* Thousand Oaks, Calif.: Corwin Press, 2000.

Sylwester was a prophet before he ever wrote a book. Here he tantalizes educators to consider another direct application of brain science: how to manage classrooms. The jump to "congregational dynamics" would be a short hop for this particular prophet.

Tenner, Edward. *Why Things Bite Back: Technology and the Revenge of Unintended Consequences.* New York: Knopf, 1996. Tenner does for "technology" what Shenk does for "information": look at what's behind the curtain. Good examples pepper Tenner's incisive criticism of the presumed worth of technologies.

Books for leaders

Every book I've listed in this bibliography could be a good source of insight about being a leader, but some have special usefulness.

Block, Peter, ed. *Flawless Consulting Fieldbook & Companion: A Guide to Understanding Your Experienc*e. San Francisco: Jossey-Bass, 2000. Block pulls together a delightful collection of consultants whose writing proves his designation "flawless."

———. *Stewardship: Choosing Service Over Self-Interest.* San Francisco: Berrett-Koehler, 1996. In this work and in *The Empowered Manager*, Block raises the bar for all leaders, insisting on philosophical high ground as the essential quality for effective leaders.

———. *The Empowered Manager: Positive Political Skills at Work.* San Francisco: Jossey-Bass, 1987. One of Block's first takes at an elusive matter: how leaders can find a better way to manage their work and their workers in a way that adds to a new kind of "bottom line."

Brown, John Seely, and Paul Duguid. *The Social Life of Information.* Boston: Harvard Business School Press, 2000. This is one of the works that confirmed my feelings about the vaunted "information revolution." Here two practitioners of the digitized arts of information technology slow down the stampede and ask us to look at what's happening.

Cooperrider, David L. *Appreciative Management and Leadership: The Power of Positive Thought and Action in Organization.* San Francisco: Jossey-Bass, 1990. A quiet trendsetter, this book also heralds a philosophy and practice of fund-raising called "appreciative inquiry."

Covey, Stephen R. *The Seven Habits of Highly Effective People.* New York: Simon & Schuster, 1989. It took me two readings and a three-day workshop to understand finally what this book could mean to my leadership style. It started a renaissance in my soul that continues to this moment.

Covey, Stephen R., A. Roger Merrill, and Rebecca R. Merrill. *First Things First: To Live, to Love, to Learn, to Leave a Legacy.* New York: Simon & Schuster, 1994. Covey's summary of "time management" is still the best abiding work in the field.

Goleman, Daniel. *Working with Emotional Intelligence.* New York: Bantam Doubleday Dell, 2000. Goleman's deft examples tell a bigger story: "emotional intelligence" separates effective managers from those who chase after the wrong goals in the wrong ways. If his original work (*Emotional Intelligence*) was good for those who work with children and youth, this volume takes the concept into the daily lives of adult workers.

Hagberg, Janet O., and Robert A. Guelich. *The Critical Journey: Stages in the Life of Faith*. Dallas: Word Publishing, 1989. Although written for a general audience, this work is especially useful for pastors and other leaders because it gently calls for spiritual maturity as an essential quality of leadership.

Holman, Peggy, and Tom Devane, eds. *The Change Handbook: Group Methods for Shaping the Future*. San Francisco: Berrett-Koehler, 1999. At the time of this book's publication, *The Change Handbook* is the best compendium I've found of large-group change methodology.

Klaas, Alan C., and Cheryl D. Klaas. *Quiet Conversations: Concrete Help for Weary Ministry Leaders*. Kansas City, Mo.: Mission Growth Publications, 2000. The Klaases have the eyes and hearts of people who dearly love pastors. The story they tell is rich in detail, as was the original study that spawned its creation.

Lewin, Roger, and Birute Regine. *The Soul at Work: Listen . . . respond . . . let go: Embracing Complexity Science for Business Success*. New York: Simon & Schuster, 2000. This is a good take on the application of chaos science to business management, with a hint of spirituality mixed in.

Mitroff, Ian, and Elizabeth Denton. *A Spiritual Audit of Corporate America: A Hard Look at Spirituality, Religion, and Values in the Workplace*. San Francisco: Jossey-Bass, 1999. A little social science and a lot of helpful anecdotes help establish the notion that leadership in corporate America is increasingly spiritual. The book raises the question "How do corporate leaders' churches equip them for spiritual leadership in their businesses?"

Morgan, Gareth. *Imaginization: New Mindsets for Seeing, Organizing and Managing*. Thousand Oaks, Calif.: Sage Publications, 1997. Unpretentious and easily read. A delightful trip into "thinking differently."

Scott-Morgan, Peter, Erik Hoving, Henk Smit, and Arnoud van de Slot. *The End of Change: How Your Company Can Sustain Growth and Innovation While Avoiding Change Fatigue*. New York: McGraw-Hill, 2001. The authors detail a shapes-and-icons-based theory of organizational development. Their basic thesis is that "stability" is as important to organizations as "change." A metaphor-laced work.

Wheatley, Margaret J. *Leadership and the New Science: Discovering Order in a Chaotic World*, 2nd ed. San Francisco: Berrett-Koehler, 1999. This forthright description of leadership and chaos science respects the viewpoint of each, and offers Wheatley another chance to show how life is spiritual at its core.

Books with the brain in mind

Because the field of brain science is growing rapidly, especially in its applications to varieties of human endeavor, I had to stop trying to keep up with everything that is happening. The following books are a good place for you to start your own reading about this exciting area of learning.

Crick, Francis. *The Astonishing Hypothesis: The Scientific Search for the Soul*. London: Touchstone Books, 1995. The man who codiscovered the complex realities of DNA delivers on the metaphorical promise of the title. Hard reading, with mountains of fascinating detail to swim through.

Csikszentmihalyi, Mihalyi. *Flow: The Psychology of Optimal Experience.* New York: Harper & Row, 1990. If I had written this book with only brain-based insights about "trying too hard," I'd have spent a chapter on the phenomenon Csikszentmihalyi describes so well. In a way, "flow" describes what I most hope for your experience with congregational leadership.

Damasio, Antonio R. *Descartes' Error: Emotion, Reason and the Human Brain.* New York: Avon Books, 1995. Reading this book persuaded me to ratchet up my quest for brain science that applied to everyday life.

Goleman, Daniel. *Emotional Intelligence. New York: Bantam Books*, 1995. *Time* and other journals spotlighted Goleman's original work because it names what so many of us hope for ourselves and those we love: an underlying "intelligence" that yields quality of life. This first look at the subject is aimed especially at educators.

Ratey, John J., M.D. *A User's Guide to the Brain: Perception, Attention, and the Four Theaters of the Brain.* New York: Pantheon Books, 2001. (See earlier description.)

Books with the soul in sight

No matter how hard I tried, I couldn't overlook some exciting inside-the-church works whose insight connected with the subjects of this book.

Banks, Robert. *God the Worker: Journeys into the Mind, Heart, and Imagination of God.* Sutherland, Australia: Albatross Books, 1992. This book sips the Scriptures and finds new ways to characterize God's nature: as a "worker." The opening chapter is a good theological basis for "ministry in daily life" as a metaphor for the church's mission.

Beaudoin, Tom. *Virtual Faith: The Irreverent Spiritual Quest of Generation X.* San Francisco: Jossey-Bass, 1998. Beaudoin is both an irreverent wit and a wide-ranging scholar. Both sides of his persona surface in this first work. Whether "GenX" remains a focus for cultural studies or not, Beaudoin taps a nerve: How do we really know what the people in the pews think or believe unless we're out among them?

Herzog, Willliam II. *Parables as Subversive Speech: Jesus as Pedagogue of the Oppressed.* Louisville: Westminster John Knox, 1994. The book's theses about Jesus' attention to justice are intense. My application of Herzog's thought to congregations is mild by comparison: Compared to religious leaders in Jesus' time, how does today's overexertive church miss its mark and get off-message?

Lebacqz, Karen. *Word, Worship, World and Wonder: Reflections on Christian Living.* Nashville: Abingdon, 1997. This book quieted me down into a worshipful mood and kept me from my own version of "trying too hard."

Nelson, Richard D. *Raising Up a Faithful Priest: Community and Priesthood in Biblical Theology.* Louisville: Westminster John Knox, 1993. Careful, detailed examination of the phenomenon of "priest" through both Old and New Testaments. Includes some hard questions about the concept of "the priesthood of all believers."

Oberman, Heiko Augustinus. *Luther, Man Between God and the Devil.* Garden City, N.Y.:

Image Books, 1992. A good example of how new ideas are formed when cultural context is taken into full account. A definitive biography of Luther.

Oswald, Roy. *Clergy Self-Care: Finding a Balance for Effective Ministry*, Washington: Alban Institute, 1991. Many of the seeds of my writing are found in Oswald's early ruminations about congregational leadership.

Pierce, Gregory F. A. *Spirituality@work: 10 ways to balance your life on-the-job*. Chicago: Loyola Press, 2000. One of the most pleasant and heartfelt collections of faith sharings by lay folk, with incisive insistence about the shape of congregations lurking behind their testimony.

Reumann, John. *Stewardship and the Economy of God*. Grand Rapids: Eerdmans, 1992. This is the best linguistic examination of "steward" ever written. Ironically, the book is out of print.

Shaw, Russell. *To Hunt, To Shoot, To Entertain: Clericalism and the Catholic Laity*. San Francisco: Ignatius Press, 1993. Simply the best description of clericalism and anticlericalism I have read. Shaw gradually exposes the false propositions upon which clericalism is based. This book should be required reading for all of us who respect pastors who exhibit inner strength.

Stark, Rodney. *The Rise of Christianity: How the Obscure, Marginal Jesus Movement Became the Dominant Religious Force in the Western World in a Few Centuries*. San Francisco: HarperSanFrancisco, 1996.) The sociology is good and the implications vast: The lifestyle of the early Christians was perhaps more compelling (at first) than their message. A fascinating work, filled with new information.

Stevens, R. Paul, and Phil Collins. *The Equipping Pastor: A Systems Approach to Congregational Leadership*. Bethesda: Alban Institute, 1993. The metaphor still holds, and Stevens and Collins's book still opens the idea for easy understanding.

Wilkes, Paul. *Excellent Catholic Parishes: The Guide to Best Places and Practices*. Mawah, N.J.: Paulist Press, 2001. Funded and promoted by the Indianapolis-based Lilly Endowment, this study attempts the classic task of identifying and portraying what's useful and possible. Extensive detail and good case studies.

———. *Effective Protestant Congregations: The Guide to Best Places and Practices*. Louisville: Westminster John Knox, 2001. (See previous entry.)

Other Books

Some of what I read still is bouncing around inside me, trying to stick to some neuronal cluster that might nurture the theses of the writer. While I'm waiting for that to happen, I can recommend these books for their intriguing ideas.

Davis, Stanley, and Christopher Meyer. Blur: *The Speed of Change in the Connected Economy.* New York: Little, Brown,1998. When I first read the book, it made good sense. Now I'm not sure that "blurring" isn't the same as "running too fast for our legs." Still, the idea of "new commodities" was compelling, as well as the idea of "the offer."

Lynch, Aaron. *Thought Contagion: How Belief Spreads Through Society.* New York: Basic Books, 1996. When "social biology" first splashed onto headlines, I didn't pay attention, and so had trouble thinking how this book's theses might apply to congregations. Still, there's something compelling here, something mysteriously simple-yet-profound. I couldn't stop thinking that this author understands churches more than he reveals.

Nahser, F. Byron. *Learning to Read the Signs: Reclaiming Pragmatism in Business.* Boston: Butterworth-Heinemann, 1997. This book packs in case studies, trend predictions, new metaphors and ways of thinking, and straightforward analysis of leadership. I couldn't quite connect it with congregational systems, but still think the attention to "sign-seeing" and "pragmatism" makes it a book worth chewing on.

Rath, Sara. *The Complete Pig.* Stillwater, Minn.: Voyageur Press, 2000. How could I put a book about pigs in any other section? Sometimes it's in the most unlikely places that metaphors arise. Besides, this book delights my memories of childhood.

Trout, Jack, with Steve Rivkin. *The Power of Simplicity: A Management Guide to Cutting Through the Nonsense and Doing Things Right.* New York: McGraw-Hill, 1999. Books that claim "simplicity" always attract me, especially ones whose authors are adept at straight-talking. One thought won't go away, though: If Trout's right, then some of the things I hold dear are closer to "nonsense" than I'd like to admit.

Wurman, Richard Saul. *Information Anxiety 2.* Indianapolis: Que, 2001. Wurman's second take on information overload (the first was in *Information Anxiety*) adds new information, better graphics, and more inspiration to ask hard questions. The nicest thing about the book: You can read it backward, forward, or inside-out. Wurman writes conversationally, as though he were chatting with you in your family room.